Other books by the author

Rush to Judgment
A Citizen's Dissent
Chicago Eyewitness
Arcadia

CONVERSATIONS WITH AMERICANS
by Mark Lane

SIMON AND SCHUSTER : NEW YORK

FIRST PRINTING

SBN 671-20768-7
LIBRARY OF CONGRESS CATALOG CARD NUMBER: 79-129190
DESIGNED BY IRVING PERKINS
MANUFACTURED IN THE UNITED STATES OF AMERICA

CONTENTS

BOOK TWO   Those Who Returned

INTRODUCTION

The treatment of Algerians by the French police, not on the battle-field in Algeria but in Paris during the war, was the subject of a book, *The Gangrene*, published in France on June 16, 1959. The book was confiscated by the government four days later, and one week after publication the police destroyed the plates that had been prepared for a second edition. The slim volume contained the complaints of six young Algerians who said they had been brutally tortured by the police. There are several differences between *The Gangrene* and this volume. In the French work the uncorroborated but thoroughly convincing allegations were made by the victims. Denied by the police, they were never susceptible of proof. Here the victims do not make allegations. Here those who performed the acts of brutality and their friends come forward to place those acts before us. It is for us to place those acts in context. In a country where one cannot imagine the police smashing the printer's plates or confiscating this book, there is yet time for analysis, evaluation and action.

A reader of this book may maintain that there are atrocities in all wars, that war is an atrocity and that both sides generally engage in such conduct. For a sensitive citizen these shibboleths offer no comfort.

First, as Americans we have been educated to believe that while

9

the enemy quite regularly violates the codes governing the waging of war, we do not. If we are now to surrender that concept of ourselves to explain our conduct in Vietnam in relation to the acts of the enemy, we must surrender as well the rhetoric which in the past we have employed to distinguish our cause from theirs.

Moreover, in certain wars both sides do not, cannot, engage equally in widespread atrocities. The obliteration of a village may be in the interest of one side only. Nowhere is that more obvious than in Vietnam. The concept of guerrilla warfare requires that the insurgent forces become one with the population upon whom they rely for support, food, intelligence and cover. Mao wrote it, and in Vietnam the National Liberation Front (NLF) and the North Vietnamese Army (NVA) perfected it. The United States Armed Forces understand the concept well, as Mao on guerrilla warfare is required reading at the Pentagon and is the bible of the Green Berets. No doubt selective executions for the purpose of eliminating opponents, particularly influential ones in the villages, are part of the theoretical and practical operations of the NLF and the NVA. But since these organizations can prevail, indeed exist, only with the support of the people of the country, mass terror practiced against the villagers would be self-defeating. If they were to decimate a village or participate in the widespread elimination of villagers their crime would not be murder; it would be suicide.

The American forces in Vietnam and their allies hunt the enemy in a war that has no front lines. Conventional military objectives, confronting and overpowering the enemy army, capturing strategic areas are barely realizable. Thus the development of new standards of success: the number of villages that have succumbed to "search and destroy missions" and an index that is perhaps unprecedented in the history of warfare, the body count.

No doubt many of the villages that have been destroyed sheltered the enemy and their families. Of course in every instance where a village was burned to the ground non-hostile civilians resided there as well. No doubt when the water buffalo and chickens are slaughtered, the rice despoiled and the fruit-bearing trees withered by deadly defoliants, the food supply of the enemy is reduced. So also is the food supply of any neutral civilians. This program, together with saturation bombing, more massive than all of the bombing engaged in by both sides during World War II, has made large areas of the countryside virtually uninhabitable for the enemy. It is uninhabitable for all civilians of that country as well. One result of this policy is that approximately one million Vietnamese are now forced to live in refugee camps.

The war in Vietnam is in many respects unprecedented in the extent to which its over-all strategy encourages brutality. Counterinsurgency warfare requires too hasty a judgment. A pajama-clad civilian cannot be distinguished from a similarly clad insurgent in the time it takes the round to leave the barrel and strike its target.

Within days after his arrival in Vietnam the American soldier's orientation lectures begin. He is warned that women and even small children may carry weapons or charges, that all young men are to be regarded as suspects, that the trees and tall grass may hide booby traps. Before the week is concluded the enemy has been identified— he is everywhere, he is everyone.

The tactics of the war are dictated by the basic strategy of the war. Children may indeed carry weapons, and booby traps do abound, and much of the atmosphere *is* hostile. The lectures, however odious, are neither irrelevant nor entirely inaccurate within the confines of the war's objectives. It is the war and its objectives, not the lectures that explain them, that constitute the evil.

Against the backdrop of a military victory so real in the minds of the military that they can almost touch it, yet in reality more illusory than a dream, the young American enters his nation's service. Last week, somewhere in the Midwest, he took his girl for a walk and bought her a soda at the local emporium. In six months he may be murdering unarmed women and children in Vietnam. How does the military accomplish this transformation?

We begin with the training. The evidence compels the conclusion that basic training in the Marine Corps is brutal and dehumanizing. Its goal is to reduce individual thought to an absolute minimum and turn young men into efficient cogs in a killing machine. That the Corps is so effective so often reflects poorly upon our civilization. It should be said that basic training in the other services is not designed to accomplish the same ends, or at the very least is less extreme and, although demanding, far less brutal. The evidence shows that techniques of torture are taught by the military but only to

11

those select few who are trained as prisoner-of-war interrogators and not even to all of them. Those who are specifically instructed in torture tactics represent but a small minority of those who constitute the American military presence in Vietnam. It is also true that the SS represented but a small minority of the German military.

That some recruits respond to their new and total environment so absolutely should not be too difficult for us to understand. No doubt most Americans shuddered when they first heard Walter Cronkite deliver the body count on network television. Now, years later, we accept that nightly statistic as we do the ball scores and the projected temperature for the next day. And we, unlike the servicemen, remain in our old familiar atmosphere. We may hold on to our standards and traditions if we care to.

Yet we are not unique among the world's population. In Algeria the French employed methods that rival those that we utilize in Vietnam. The Germans efficiently mass-produced torture and murder and through quantity changed the quality of their crime to one without precedent. The French police and military interrogators mixed water and electrical torture with racial insults. They repeatedly told their victims that they were of an inferior race and not entitled to consideration as fellow human beings. Hitler's Germany stripped Jews of their citizenship, made them non-persons, publicized their inferiority and only then began physically to isolate and exterminate them. Surely it is easier to take a life when you are convinced that the person you kill is not really human. You begin to dehumanize the enemy in your own mind by retroactively denying him a tradition and a culture. He is not Vietnamese. He is a "gook." In various units in the Marine Corps the use of the word "Vietnamese" when referring to the enemy is an offense punished by the mandatory imposition of one hundred push-ups.

At the end of March 1970 First Lieutenant James B. Duffy was convicted of premeditated murder in Vietnam. He had been charged with ordering the murder of an unarmed Vietnamese farmer. After the verdict was read the lawyer for the defense informed the court that the mandatory sentence was life imprisonment. The court thereupon reconsidered, found Duffy guilty of involuntary manslaughter and sentenced him to a $1,500 fine and six months' imprisonment. *The New York Times* reported that several military lawyers attended the court-martial as spectators. One of the officers was quoted in the *Times* as saying, "To a lot of us it looks like another example of the 'M.G.R.—the mere gook rule'—being applied." He explained that the term was used by some Army legal officers because Vietnamese were regarded as less than first-class human beings.

The following week counsel for Duffy reported that "the court imposed the lighter punishment because it agreed with my defense that Lieutenant Duffy had only been doing what the Army expected him to do and did not commit any crime." Yet Duffy had admitted during the trial that he permitted a sergeant under his orders to shoot Do Van Man, a twenty-five-year-old farmer who was bound and unable to move.

In Vietnam several American infantry officers commented upon the Duffy case. One said, "Maybe you think it inhuman to kill a child, but in this war the enemy uses children to carry satchel charges on bicycles." A captain said that he would not shoot prisoners but that he considered them to be "so many pieces of baggage." And Lieutenant Duffy himself said, "Some people might have thought that it was wrong to judge a unit just by the number of kills they get. I think it is the only way a unit should be judged. That is really the only mission we have in the field, to kill the enemy."

If you convince your soldiers that the enemy is less than human, comparable to baggage at best, a child assassin at worst, and then inform them that their mission is to score high in the body-count exercise, you cannot feign surprise when you discover what the war has become.

If Americans know less than all there is to know about the terrible cost the war is imposing upon the civilian population of South Vietnam, they know next to nothing of the real cost America is paying for its adventure. The real price is in the sacrifice of an entire generation.

Some of the untold stories may be gathered in the hospitals in Japan and the United States. Major Thomas Engelsing, now chief of the in-patient service in psychiatry at the Army's 97th General Hospital in Frankfurt, told me that as a result of immediate medical contact with the wounded in Vietnam, "Lives are saved in this war. Lives of men who in any other war would have died. Men with multiple amputations, blinded, very serious brain injuries." As a result, "the Army facilities are now overfilled with men who are not rehabilitatable."

He said that he had received "a directive not to evacuate wounded to the United States because they are just filled up in the States; there is no more room."

Major Engelsing said that the facilities in Germany are so overcrowded that he has had to ignore the directive. A colonel who had just returned to Germany from the United States had told him that conditions in Army hospitals and Veterans Administration hospitals in the U. S. are so deplorable and the facilities so overcrowded that a substantial number of doctors and nurses, unable to stand the depressing scene any longer, have asked to be transferred to Germany or even to Vietnam. Conditions in Army and Navy hospitals in Japan are similar—perhaps slightly worse.

The Administration nevertheless has found a new method for reducing casualty figures. A man with both arms and legs blown off and suffering incurable brain damage is listed by the Pentagon merely as "wounded." When he dies in an Army hospital in the United States or in Japan or Okinawa he becomes a domestic military death—not charged to the war, not added to the total. In this fashion U.S. losses in Vietnam are kept at an "acceptable level," to borrow a Pentagon term. But for each man who dies on the battlefield in this war, doctors and medics have told me, another probably dies elsewhere. And for each who has died, perhaps one or two others will be unable to function ever again. The official figure for American deaths in Vietnam is over 45,000. But a figure several times that would more accurately reflect the number of young men lost forever. Yet even that figure would fail to comprehend the permanent damage done to so many who have fought in Vietnam who have not been physically wounded.

Civilian experiences do not prepare men for the incredible stresses of war, and some men have returned home shell-shocked no doubt ever since shells were first fired. Yet sometimes perfectly normal men may make a rational decision to risk their lives for a cause they believe in. Before being sent to Vietnam the troops are told that their mission is to protect the Vietnamese from devil communism. Before long they are burning villages and killing suspects who they cannot be certain are the enemy. Somewhere along the line it occurs

14

to a soldier to think about why he is there. Often the thought process is provoked by a wound, the death of a close friend or a close call with the enemy, often in an ambush encounter. The Army's rhetoric—"you are here to protect these people"—is no longer an acceptable explanation in view of the Army's conduct. While the young man is still required to kill and to chance being killed he knows that he does not know why. He has no cause, and the decision to remain and fight is not his. He becomes ill-equipped to face, much less to overcome, the strain of warfare.

Even this circumstance has been utilized by the State Department. On occasion figures are released to prove that the deserters in Sweden are malcontents, troublemakers and criminals. These figures are almost always false and have been effectively refuted by the appropriate agencies in the Swedish government. Nevertheless it is true that some of the young men who have been to Vietnam are disturbed and carry around with them excessive feelings of suspicion and hostility. Before dismissing them as misfits one must determine whether they can be considered unreliable because they defected from a system which institutionalizes brutality. Their words make up Book One of this work.

I had met and interviewed them in Sweden, France and West Germany. When I returned from Europe it was with a manuscript comprised primarily of the words of those who had served their country in Vietnam and then deserted. "Why did you desert?" I asked one young man. He answered, "For the same reason that I joined the Army and volunteered for Vietnam—to serve my country."

Scott Meredith, my literary agent, submitted copies of that manuscript to more than twenty publishers within a few days. Representatives of a number of publishers expressed interest in the manuscript but most also expressed concern bordering on alarm. They wondered whether such a book could be published and what adverse effect its publication might have upon the publisher. The most responsible reply came from Simon and Schuster. The editors there were also horrified by the material but were committed to its publication if it could be verified and documented. Several editors at Simon and Schuster and I spent a good part of a day listening to recorded interviews I had conducted in Paris and Stockholm.

Toward the end of January 1970 the publisher made an offer to publish *Conversations with Americans*, which then consisted of Book One, the interviews with deserters, provided I secure additional interviews with people on active duty or those who had received honorable discharges. Another basic request was that I secure from the interviewees documentary support for the statements made in the interviews. I faced the challenge with guarded optimism. The deserters were immune from prosecution so long as they remained outside the United States and so long as they did not confess to any extraditable crime. Certainly servicemen would have more reason to be wary since they were subject to the punitive provisions of the Uniform Code of Military Justice. Even those who had been honorably discharged might conceivably find themselves vulnerable to efforts to punish them for speaking out. Who, I wondered, was about to remove documents from a Marine Corps barracks or smuggle photographs out of Vietnam?

Almost immediately after this I was called as a defense witness in the Chicago conspiracy trial. While in that city I interviewed a former sergeant and squad leader who had in fact smuggled a number of relevant pictures out of the war zone. Later, in the witness room, I talked with Peter Martinsen, who had been a prisoner-of-war interrogator in Vietnam. Before a month had passed I had conducted interviews with thirty-seven active-duty servicemen or honorably discharged veterans, including other prisoner-of-war interrogators, helicopter gunners, squad leaders, medics and men assigned to intelligence units in Vietnam. These interviews were conducted in Georgia, South Carolina, Texas, New York, New Jersey, Illinois, California and Washington. Altogether the men earned well over one hundred medals, ribbons and citations for heroism.

A Marine secured a copy of the Marine Prayer from a barracks wall, I had it photocopied, and he returned it, hopefully before its absence was recorded.

Each person who made a statement was aware of the risk. Each gave me written permission to publish his words. Sometimes the words were in the form of an accusation. Often they took the form of a confession. A number of interviews conducted during the past month are not published here at all, but those that appear in the following pages are typical of the entire body of interviews and have

16

been selected both for that reason and because they also offer some unique fact or insight.

Many of the men I interviewed expressed remorse for the acts they had participated in. Some viewed their disclosures as personally hazardous and, partially for that reason, redemptive as well. Nevertheless in a number of cases I have decided to substitute a fictitious name for the real name of the veteran. In each such case an asterisk follows the name. In addition the names of some of the persons referred to in the interviews have been altered. While I believe that each man is responsible for his own actions I do not wish to be part of the process that concentrates the anger of an outraged society upon a few transgressors whose actions, however malevolent, were the result of a strategy that was approved by the society as a whole.

I have shown my editors at Simon and Schuster all of the original statements containing the name of each interviewee, including those for whom fictitious names have been used. Some of the tape recordings have been heard by the editors as well. The transcripts in which each person is identified have been delivered to a prominent New York attorney who was formerly counsel for the United States Department of Justice.

Should the responsible agencies of government wish to investigate the charges contained in the following statements, the relevant information is accessible to them.

M. L.

Once there was a way to get back homeward
Once there was a way to get back home
Sleep, pretty darling
Do not cry
And I will sing
A lullaby
Boy, you're gonna carry that weight
Carry that weight a long time
Boy, you're gonna carry that weight
Carry that weight a long time.
> *—From "Carry That Weight," by*
> PAUL MCCARTNEY AND
> JOHN LENNON

CONVERSATIONS WITH AMERICANS

BOOK ONE

Those Who Did Not Return

THE TRAINING

- Chuck Onan

Q: What is your name?
A: Chuck Onan.
Q: How old are you?
A: Twenty.
Q: When did you enter the Marine Corps?
A: April 1967.
Q: Did you enlist?
A: Yes, I did.
Q: Where were you born?
A: In Germany.
Q: Is your family German?
A: No. My family is one quarter African, one quarter Cherokee Indian, one quarter Irish and one quarter French.
Q: Did you go to high school?
A: Yes. In Boys Town in Nebraska.
Q: Did you go directly in the Marine Corps from Boys Town?
A: Practically. After a couple of months I enlisted in Oakland, California.
Q: Where did you take your basic training?

A: San Diego, California.

Q: How long were you there?

A: For four months.

Q: Where did you go from there?

A: I was sent to Camp Pendleton for advanced combat training.

Q: Were you prepared specifically for combat in Vietnam?

A: Yes.

Q: How?

A: Lectures, demonstrations, exercises and field work. Also in the mountains. You know, the whole works.

Q: How long did you remain at Pendleton?

A: Between four and five months.

Q: Where did you go next?

A: To Memphis, Tennessee. At the naval air base there. I was in jump school there.

Q: How many times did you parachute?

A: Seven.

Q: How long were you at the air base?

A: More than three months.

Q: And from there, where?

A: To Beaufort, South Carolina, to the Marine air base there. I remained there about one month.

Q: What training were you given there?

A: I went to Scuba school.

Q: Underwater?

A: Yes.

Q: Why were you given such specialized and intensive courses?

A: I was in the Marine Corps Special Forces. It's an elite group, like the Green Berets. They call it Force and Reconnaissance in the Marines.

Q: Were you ever given training in interrogation of enemy prisoners?

A: Yes.

Q: Where?

A: At all of the bases. But during the last month, when I was being prepared for imminent shipment to Vietnam, we got a lot of it. It was Scuba school with jungle-survival courses. We were told there how to torture prisoners.

Q: Who gave you those instructions?

A: Mostly the sergeants. But some officers also participated. Lieutenants and sometimes the captain.

Q: What were you told to do?

A: To torture prisoners.

Q: How?

A: It was very extensive. Many methods were described and advocated.

Q: Such as?

A: Removing a person's shoes and beating him or her on the soles of the feet. That was pretty mild alongside of some of the others.

Q: What other methods were taught? Can you try to remember?

A: I've been trying to forget for the past year.

Q: What other methods were taught? Can you give me one more example?

A: We were told to make use of electrical radio equipment. We were told to attach the electrodes to the genitals.

Q: Did they demonstrate that technique or just talk about it?

A: They had drawings on the board showing exactly how to clamp the electrodes onto the testicles of a man or the body of a woman.

Q: Where were the drawings?

A: On the blackboard.

Q: Did one of the non-coms draw it on the blackboard?

A: No. They were printed documents tacked to the blackboard.

Q: Showing how to attach the electrodes for purpose of torture?

A: Yes.

Q: What else were you taught?

A: How to pull out fingernails.

Q: What's the prescribed instrument for that?

A: Radio pliers.

Q: Who explained that method?

A: A sergeant.

Q: What other methods were taught?

A: Various things you can do with bamboo.

Q: Like what?

A: Stick them under the fingernails and into ears.

Q: Did they ever demonstrate, as opposed to lecture, any of these techniques?

A: Yes. One time they hit a guy on the bottom of the feet; ordered him to lie down and hit him with a rifle.

Q: What outfit were you in during the training?

A: Second Marine. Second Recon.

Q: How many Marines were in the group at these torture-technique lectures?

A: Never more than twenty.

Q: Did you ever receive special instructions on how to interrogate women?

A: Yes.

Q: What did they suggest?

A: They're pretty sadistic. I don't like to talk about it. What good does it do to talk about it? I'm trying to forget, to get it out of my head.

Q: I'm going to try to report just what you tell me as widely as I can. You heard Nixon just say that Song My was an isolated instance, that the American soldiers are generous and kind. If Marines are trained to torture in Vietnam, don't you think that it should be known?

A: Of course, we're trained to torture, but people don't want to know it or believe it. If there is any chance that it can help, though, I'll tell you.

Q: How were you trained to torture women prisoners?

A: To strip them, spread them open and drive pointed sticks or bayonets into their vagina. We were also told we could rape the girls all we wanted.

Q: What else?

A: We were shown how we could open phosphorous bombs without detonating them and then place the phosphorous any place where it would really hurt.

Q: What did they recommend?

A: The eyes—also the vagina.

Q: Was it suggested that any other chemical might be used?

A: Yes. C.S.

Q: How do you use that? Is it a powder?

A: It's a powder until it's detonated. We were shown how to

open the container and use C.S. as a poison. To make them eat it.

Q: Were you ever given lectures about the use of helicopters?

A: Yes. We were told you could take several prisoners up in one, push one out—and the rest would talk. They also make a joke about how one time in Vietnam they took a prisoner and tied his arms and legs to two different helicopters. Then they took off and tore him apart.

Q: Who told you about that?

A: One of my instructors. He was a sergeant.

Q: Did he say he actually witnessed that?

A: He said that he did it.

Q: Were you given extensive training regarding the use of helicopters?

A: We were trained by a lot of experts with helicopters. In fact we were trained in several methods of torture with helicopters. There was one way that on a helicopter there is a rope that goes down the outside—it is an automatic rope that goes up and down for pulling people out of water and such things. That is what is intended. We were shown how if you have a prisoner you can hang him from this rope, and also you can attach to his neck another small rope that's for an emergency. You lower him so he sees the rope around his neck tightening and when it gets tight enough it is going to kill him. That is one way of using a helicopter for torture. You can tie prisoners to the bottom of the helicopter rails, let them dangle there, and go along the top of the trees and that cuts him up pretty badly.

Q: Was that part of your training in the Marine Corps?

A: Yes. These techniques, and also other techniques in which a helicopter could be used. We were also told that the most simple way—the way they use the most in Vietnam—is to take a few prisoners up, those who won't talk. Then you throw the first one or two out to make the others talk. There are special ways to do it—you know, with precautions—so that you don't fall out yourself. We were shown how.

Q: How much torture-interrogation training did you get?

A: It began in my second duty station and went all the way through to the end. At least, on the average, five hours a week for more than six months.

29

Q: That's even greater concentration than you would have had in half a year in your major subject had you been going to college. The law school I went to offered only two credits in criminal law, my major, which meant just two hours a week for five months.

A: Yeah, we were thoroughly prepared to torture all right. And that's just the formal part. It really went on and on. Our instructors, the sergeants, lived with us. We all ate together and slept in the same area and they were always talking about their experiences in Vietnam.

Q: What did they talk about?

A: Killing prisoners, torturing them, raping girls. And they all had photographs of the most gruesome things they had done.

Q: How did the Marine recruits react to this training?

A: Positively. They liked the idea. The Marines are made up of volunteers. They were looking forward to going to Vietnam to use all these new skills. Many volunteered to go to Vietnam. The sergeants made it seem attractive—in a sick way, you know—you'll get a chance to kill and all this.

Q: Did the sergeants ever discuss the treatment of women prisoners as an inducement to encourage Marines to volunteer for Vietnam?

A: Yes, they said that they had raped girls and that any Marine could, that he wouldn't have to worry about being punished.

Q: When did you leave the Marine Corps?

A: February 1968.

Q: Why did you split?

A: I received orders for Vietnam.

Q: How did you feel about the Marine Corps during the training?

A: I was pretty gung-ho until the last phase of the training. Then it all began to seem so sick. They just went too far.

Q: What are you doing in Stockholm now?

A: Going to school. Studying French. Next year I'll begin music school and play guitar and compose. I've already finished Swedish language school.

▪ Terry Whitmore

Q: What is your name?
A: Terry Whitmore.
Q: How old are you now?
A: I'm twenty-two.
Q: Born where?
A: Memphis, Tennessee.
Q: You enlisted?

A: Yup. But it was after I received a letter to take my physical when I was about to be drafted. When I was sixteen I had a serious operation when my lung collapsed and I figured that I would never pass the physical anyway. I figured the man would say, "We don't want you, you're sick, kid." So I went down to take my physical. They said I was in top shape. I didn't want to go in the Army. I thought that the Navy was cool, though—plus all the broads fall for that little beanie on your head. So I went to join the Navy and the man says, "We got this waiting list," and he pulls out a long list. I don't know if it was a fake or real list, but this Navy recruiter shows me a long list and says the Navy does not want me.

Q: Did it occur to you that the recruiter did not want you because you were black?

A: Yeah. Well, I thought about that at the time, but I don't know. Then a recruiting guy comes to see me from the Marine Corps. He's wearing his blues and looking very sharp. He told me about all of the benefits in the Marine Corps. Then the guy tells me, "Look, if you want to be at home for Christmas"—and I groove over Christmas at home, it's my favorite time of the year— he says, "the Army will draft you right away. But if you sign up with the Marine Corps now you won't have to go for three or four months." This was in October 1966. The guy keeps provoking me with "The Army's going to get you, and I'm giving you this chance right now." Next thing I knew I was riding downtown with the cat

31

going to take the final physical and get sworn in. Then I was on that big bird heading for Parris Island, South Carolina.

Boot camp was—there ain't no words in the dictionary yet for boot camp. It's hell two or three times over. The DIs [drill instructors] have you so choked up that you have to ask permission to breathe. You're only allowed to go to the bathroom three times a day, and you don't go when *you* want to, you go when they tell you to. All you heard every day was the word "kill." That word, "kill, kill, kill," was pounded into you. They never called you Marines in boot camp. The DIs call you girls, pussy, shit, anything, but they never call you a Marine. My senior DI was black. I thought that was groovy. When I first went into boot camp I was away from home for the first time, and I see this DI kicking guys, smashing guys' heads, and I wonder "God damm, what have I got into?" Then this black DI comes in, and I say, "Damn, I've got it made! I've got me black DI!" He's a staff sergeant—he's a senior DI. He walks over and grabs a black guy who's standing in front of me. He grabs him and gives him an upper-cut. Punches him on the jaw and then in the stomach. The guy goes down. I'm about to have a fit right then. I'd say to myself, "This guy is black, he's supposed to be on our side, but he's punching the blacks out."

All DIs are gung-ho—kill, kill, kill! Every night before you go to bed "kill" was your motto. You've got to recite a prayer with "kill, kill, kill" in it out loud before you go to bed. And you have to pray for war. There was a printed prayer for war right on the wall, and everyone had to recite it out loud. "Kill"—the word was part of your daily living. "Marines are killers"—that's what the DIs kept saying. Together we have to chant, "We kill." And of course they kept on talking about the differences between the Army and the Marines. We had a course in Marine Corps history. They would analyze different battles. "Remember this battle when the Marines had to go in and get the damn Army out of trouble." Every day, man. "Marines were on Pork Chop Hill." "Marines set up the flag of Iwo Jima." "If it wasn't for Marines there would be no America."

The DIs believed it all, I think, and even if they didn't, they make you believe it anyway. They pump it into your head day after day and by the end of boot camp it's fixed there.

When I came out of boot camp then I was a Marine. And every civilian, every Army soldier, they looked like shit to me. If you weren't in the Marines, baby, you weren't anything. I spent three months in boot camp. Now I think they rush guys through in much shorter time. They used to tell us, "Machine guns can't hurt Marines." But a lot of Marines got killed in Vietnam, and the Marines are hurting now. So they are rushing guys through boot camp now. We had bayonet training in boot camp every day. We had to scream "kill" when we stuck the bayonet into the dummy. Then we had to beat the dummy up, hit it with a rifle butt and stick the bayonet into it. And we had to call them dummies a dirty motherfucking gook, or slant-eye. You believe that? Here we was standing there yelling at a dummy. It seems pretty crazy now, but at the time it did seem normal. We called them VC, Charlie, gook, slant-eye or slope-head. The one thing we could not call them was Vietnamese. Most of our DIs were veterans. They'd been to Vietnam, and most of the guys on the rifle range were vets. And they would talk about how they tortured prisoners. "You remember the time we were over there, and we drew shit out of that Charlie?" Well, another time a sergeant talked about when he shot an old lady. "I really blew her fucking head off." A sergeant would run up at an old buddy. "Hey, I was in 101, weren't you?" "Yeah, I was in Bravo. Yeah, I was there." "You remember that operation when I shot that old guy in the ass, and I blew that young kid's head off?" These were just reminiscences which we heard a lot of. After boot camp I went to Camp Lejeune in North Carolina. For ITA training.

I left Lejeune, I had orders for special assignment, sea duty, then I really had it made. Sea duty is a two-year term. You're just there with the squids, you know, the Navy. You go right on their ships, just guarding their ships, for two years. Man, I had it made, I had skipped Nam. I went home on leave after about a month at Lejeune. I was real big time when I went home in my boots and uniform. I was a Marine—you know what that means? Means I can beat your ass, man. I was really indoctrinated, fucked up in the head.

About three days before I was due to leave home for Norfolk for sea duty I got this telegram. It was orders to report back to Lejeune. I called another guy who had gone with me through boot camp. We had met at the air terminal in Memphis on our way to the Marine Corps, and we were in boot camp and Lejeune together. And he was one of the few guys who had got sea duty also. His name was White, and since everything runs in alphabetical order we were right next to each other the whole time. He's a white guy. He got this telegram too. First thing I did was I jumped on the telephone and called him. "Check your mailbox lately?" He says, "Yeah, man, I was about to call you and ask you the same thing."

I knew what it meant. I had a strong hunch I was on my way to Nam. But I couldn't tell my mother that. "Mama, I'm going back there, probably I need a little more training. Probably I'll have to learn to say 'kill' a few more times, and then everything will be all right." She said, "Son, you're going to Vietnam." I said, "No, no, just going back for more training."

When we got back to Lejeune the guys laid it on us. They said, "I guess you know you're going to Hot Nam." I was for the war then. I was scared but I didn't want to show it, and I said, "O.K., let me go over there and kill a couple of gooks." I remember what my DI told me in boot camp. "You are going to fight a war, you are going to fight that dirty, stinking, slant-eyed mother-fucker over there in Vietnam. The reason that you are fighting them is that how would you like this dirty little red, stinking mother-fucker to be over here in the United States raping your sister, fucking your mothers, and destroying the country—how would you like that?" We were supposed to growl very loud. I mean, we didn't like that idea, we almost blew the roof off the building. We growled real loud and almost lifted the top off the building. But the DI said something like "Girls, I think you'd like the mother-fucker over here. I don't think I heard you loud enough." So we were supposed to growl and yell "kill." We were Marines. We were dirty and hard.

34

THE MARINE PRAYER

Though I Walk Thru the Valley
In the Shadow of DEATH
I fear No EVIL
For I Am the Biggest
Baddest Mother-Fucker
In the Valley

Now I Lay Me Down to Sleep
I Pray the LORD the WAR to Keep
So MARINES can come and Save the Day
And I Can Earn My God Damn PAY

God Bless the United States
God Bless the Drill Instructors
God Bless the Marine Corps

THE PRAYERS WILL BE MEMORIZED

▪ Mark Worrell

Q: Your Name?

A: Mark Worrell.

Q: Where are you from?

A: I grew up in California and went to a university in Oregon for a couple of years, from 1964 to 1967. Then I ran out of money and enlisted. The talk out there was: "Let's beat the Vietcong in Vietnam before we have to fight them in California." You ought to see the size of the Vietcong navy. So I joined the Marine Corps in May 1967 at the age of nineteen and a half.

Q: Where were you trained in the Corps?

A: Boot camp at San Diego for eight weeks. Then two weeks specialized infantry training at Camp Pendleton, in California too. The training was all about killing. We had to scream out, "Kill, kill, kill" a lot. We had some ideological training also. They told us that the Army was shit, that the only service of any value was the Marines. It was a real effort to develop the feeling that we were elite killers. And throughout the entire training they emphasized the animalness of the Vietnamese. They were subhuman, we were told. We could do anything we wanted to them when we got there. They told us you could kill this gook and then cut him apart. He wasn't human. I went through a staging battalion just before I was sent to Vietnam. There it was really intensive. Every effort was made to glorify the extermination and torture of these lowly Vietnamese. The sergeants always called them gooks or slope-heads. They never called them Vietnamese. One recruit called them Vietnamese once and the sergeant told him he was a "goddamned gook lover."

▪ Ed Treratola*

Q: Your name is Ed Treratola?

A: Yes.

Q: Where are you from, Ed?

A: Huntington, Long Island.

Q: What does your family do?

A: My mother works for Blue Cross and my father has a taxi-cab cooperative with some associates.

Q: Did you enlist or were you drafted?

A: I enlisted in the Marine Corps to go to school, aviation school.

Q: What had your education been until then?

A: High school.

Q: Which one?

A: Huntington High School.

Q: And just when you graduated you enlisted?

A: Yes.

Q: For three years?

A: Four years.

Q: Did you make any arrangement for any special education before you went in?

A: I arranged for an aviation contract. I was going to go to school to be a jet mechanic, but in the final stages of the school I was color blind, so they transferred me to the infantry.

Q: Where did you take boot camp?

A: Parris Island.

Q: When was that?

A: In May of '67.

Q: You enlisted when?

A: In May.

Q: And then you started right away?

A: Yes.

Q: How long was your training?

A: I spent eight weeks at Parris Island and then they moved me to Camp Lejeune, where I spent another four weeks ITR—that is, infantry training. It's a specialty school: mortar men, rifle men and machine guns.

Q: After Camp Lejeune where did you go?

A: I went to Memphis Tennessee. I went to aviation school there and I was there for two weeks. When I went for my physical I was color blind, so they put me in a holding company for another two weeks and then they moved me to Camp Pendleton in California, where I went through another eight weeks of training.

Q: During all your training were you prepared for service in Vietnam?

A: That was the main point of all my training right from boot camp—to go to Vietnam.

Q: What was the training like?

A: In Parris Island we were not allowed to be alone. We had to stay in our billets the whole day unless we were accompanied by an NCO, and it was like a living hell. We could not open mail until nine o'clock, and that had to be opened in front of an NCO, and we were continually harassed and were made to run around singing about killing gooks and Cong, and when we had to go and eat we went to the mess hall and we had to yell "kill" at the top of our lungs three times before we were allowed to eat. If we didn't say it loud enough they would make us do exercises and say, "This is for the dirty bastards in Vietnam" and things like that. Push-ups and all sorts of calisthenics.

Q: What was the song you had to sing?

A: It was like an airborne song, but we used to run around saying, "VC, VC, kill, kill, kill. Gotta kill, gotta kill, 'cause it's fun, 'cause it's fun."

Q: " 'Cause it's fun"?

A: Yes, that's what we had to say.

Q: Did you have to say any other things like that?

A: We had a prayer on the wall. All the Marine barracks in Parris Island have this prayer. It's a prayer for war. Every night before we went to bed at nine o'clock we had to pray that there'd be a war, so that the Marine Corps could be always on the move, because that was their job, to fight.

38

Q: What kind of actual training did you have in terms of use of a bayonet, or a rifle, or other weapons?

A: In boot camp I had two weeks of bayonet training, two weeks of knife fighting, two weeks of hand-to-hand combat and then it was mostly lectures on what we were to expect in Vietnam, most of the time.

Q: Did you ever have any training either at boot camp or later on in advance training where you were told how to interrogate prisoners?

A: No. I never had that because I was a grunt. It's mostly the reconnaissance and special intelligence squad that gets that, but we were told that if we ever did catch a prisoner we probably would not bring him in, anyway.

Q: Who told you that?

A: Well, we had one NCO down there. I forget his name. He was the first Marine to burn a village in Vietnam. He had a picture in *Life* magazine, I think, and he had a Zippo lighter and he was torching up the huts. He almost got a discharge from the Marine Corps for that, but instead he was placed as an instructor at boot camp and everyone sort of looked up to him because he used to come and tell us how many Cong he killed and tell us about the villages he burned and how much fun it was, and how we were going to enjoy it when we got there.

Q: Did he ever talk about the interrogation of prisoners?

A: No. When he went out it was mostly on search-and-destroy missions, because that is what the Marines do. We go through a village and we completely destroy it and then the Army comes through with tractors and levels it. We never take prisoners.

Q: Was there anything else about the training which you think is significant?

A: I think it was when we were having our winter-survival course. There was an NCO up there and he had a little white rabbit in his hand, and he was petting it. Everybody was looking, wondering what the hell was going on. Then he says, "Well, you men have to learn how to make boots if you are going to stay alive out in the cold." I don't know what good winter training is. And he took the rabbit and snapped its neck off and then skinned it in front of everyone. We were continually exposed to this sort of brutality.

Like when we were on the rifle range, if we didn't hold our rifle a certain way they would make us pull back the bolt on an M-14. It never happened to me, but I saw it happen to a friend. He had to stick his tongue in it and let the bolt fly home on his tongue, and that would just cut it open and you would get a big bruise. And we had to stand at attention while NCOs beat us if they felt like hitting us. And we were put in shower rooms, twelve-man shower rooms, thirty men. They put rubber ponchos over us and squeezed us in there and turned on the hot water and threw ammonia in the shower and told us to start fighting each other. If we didn't fight each other we had to stay in there longer, so most of the time we just beat each other senseless.

Q: Was there a lot of talk about going to Vietnam?

A: Everyone was looking forward to it, because it was like we would go out on a bayonet course and the instructor would say, "Slash," and we would slash the bayonets into the target. Then he would say, "Kill the gook," and we would jab it in. After a while you really want to kill someone, because they make it seem like it's really interesting and will be a lot of fun. After a while you just don't care any more, you give up.

THE EXHORTATION

To the troops in Vietnam

Come home with the coonskin on the wall.
> —LYNDON B. JOHNSON
> President of the United States

I do like to see the arms and legs fly.
> —COLONEL GEORGE S. PATTON III
> Commander, Eleventh Armored
> Cavalry Regiment

THE STATISTICS

▪ Alan Cohen

Q: What is your name?

A: Alan Cohen.

Q: Where are you from?

A: Newton, Massachusetts.

Q: What had you done before entering the Army?

A: I had graduated from high school and attended Boston University for one year. I dropped out and was about to be drafted, so I decided to enlist in the Army Security Agency, which is a branch of Army Intelligence. I was trained in the United States for over a year. First I went through regular basic training in New Jersey, at Fort Dix. Then I went to the Defense Language Institute in California, where I took a thirty-seven-week course in Swahili. Then, after some leave, I went back to the East Coast and took a classified intelligence course in radio traffic analysis. Then I was shipped to Kagnew Station in Asmara in northern Ethiopia. It's the northern provincial capital.

Q: What did you do there?

A: I originally was intended to use my Swahili training in intercepting East African radio intelligence networks and interpreting them and forwarding relevant intelligence information to Washington. We were all given Top Secret clearance. All of our work was covert. The cover mission for the Kagnew Station was rapid relay of communications between Africa, the Middle East and the rest of the world. We were also supposedly trying to communicate with Telstar and other satellites. This work was going on but primarily as a cover mission. Our real mission was in the area of the transmission of radio intelligence regarding troop deployment in Africa and the Middle East. We had a staff of hundreds who worked only on the Middle East question. The responsibility was to siphon out gross intelligence and classify it and send important relevant information to the National Security Agency at Fort Meade, Maryland, where the armed forces intelligence was correlated and deciphered.

Q: Was this operation pure Army intelligence or were other agencies also involved?

A: Present also were the Central Intelligence Agency, the National Security Agency, Army, Naval and Air Force Intelligence.

Q: How long were you stationed there?

A: For eight months.

Q: Did the station operate to relay other intelligence back to the United States?

A: Yes. In addition to transmitting data about the war in the Middle East, we had access to daily and weekly reports from Vietnam. We served as one of the distribution centers for daily reports. One became quite aware of the gap between raw intelligence information and that which was released to the news media back in the States. The difference between the facts and what the newspapers were given to publish was startling. The American people were led to believe one thing through the only sources available to them, while we knew that the facts were very different. This had a very disillusioning effect upon a number of us. We read the reports of casualties, as an example, for a week or a day and then compared them to stories in *The New York Times* or the Boston *Globe* and the Boston *Herald*.

Q: How did the news reports differ from the raw intelligence data?

A: The American casualties were cut down for press consumption and the enemy's casualties would be greatly exaggerated.

This was common procedure. We saw this all the time.

Q: Were the figures substantially altered?

A: Oh, yes. If a platoon of Americans was wiped out, thirty men killed in one short action, and this happened, the report to the press would read, "two killed, six wounded." This was in 1968 when there was quite a bit of combat going on. Everybody knew it. Everybody was quite aware of it. Many were disillusioned. They saw through their role as important intelligence operators.

Q: How did you gain access to this raw data?

A: The information came to Kagnew. We were to relay it to Washington. Only Top Priority Stations received this information, and Kagnew was such a station. They operated on a need-to-know basis. You only saw, theoretically, what you needed to see. While the Ethiopian station had no direct interest in the figures from Vietnam, we still got them because we were on a top-priority mission. Our mission was top secret since we were acting there in violation of our agreement with the host nation.

Q: How was the American agreement with Ethiopia violated?

A: We were invited by the Ethiopian government to sit on their land, which the American government paid for. The intelligence base was so secret that nobody in government circles in Ethiopia knew its real purpose. Whenever there was a tour Haile Selassie would come to Asmara himself. He got a tour of the base. He'd be taken into completely unclassified areas—the mess hall, the administration buildings—but they would never let him see anything that was really going on. There was a signed agreement that any American intelligence operation cannot conduct intelligence operations on its host country. We violated that constantly by doing detailed intelligence reports upon the liberation movement—they called themselves ELF, the Ethiopian Liberation Front—in northern Ethiopia, which at that time was quite strong.

Q: The enlisted men involved in this work were obviously at least somewhat gifted intellectually. Many no doubt had been to college. How did they react to this duplicity?

A: We never had any sizable meeting, but a few of us would sit around and talk about the situation. We were dismayed by the false figures, the violation of international agreements, and for some of us it opened our eyes as to what the Army was up to, was all about.

45

■ Steve Woods

Q: Your name?

A: Steve Woods.

Q: Where are you from, Steve?

A: From North Weymouth, Massachusetts.

Q: How long were you in the service?

A: I was in the Navy for two years. I enlisted.

Q: Why?

A: I didn't have enough money to continue school. I was attending school for structural design. I knew I'd be drafted and I thought I would prefer the Navy to the Army. I was eighteen then.

Q: You were in the waters of Vietnam?

A: Yes, on the aircraft carrier *Oriskany*. We were in Vietnam for nine months.

Q: What was your assignment?

A: I was a jet mechanic, AJV. We gave pre-flight inspections and post-flight checkups and repairs to the planes.

Q: How many jet planes were operated from your carrier?

A: Three hundred.

Q: How many went out on a mission?

A: It depended upon the attack, the code. Perhaps one hundred. It varied.

Q: What kind of planes were there?

A: A-4s and F-8s.

Q: In the months you were on the carrier how many jets were lost?

A: Some came back so damaged that even though we had spare parts we couldn't repair them. They were tossed overboard. They weren't exactly shot down by the enemy—they made it back—but they could never have made it up again. Including those as lost, we lost all three hundred planes. The ship went back to the States empty. No serviceable planes. Not one. The few we had on board we threw off, too badly damaged. We had better luck with the

46

pilots; they have, I would guess, a fifty-fifty chance. They bail out and we had an escort service just to pick them up.

Q: What do you think of the military statistics about American planes lost?

A: What can I think? They are lies. I don't want to say anything political, but those figures are all lies. We lost more planes from our ship alone than the government says was lost during that time. Of course, not even the other side knows the real figure of planes lost.

Q: Why not?

A: Well, if the plane is hit but makes it back to the carrier and we dump it off later, how would they know that they shot it down? Also, some are lost as a result of our own men.

Q: How?

A: I don't even know if I should mention this, but some of the pilots are wise guys, real nasty. We get up early to service the planes and give them a last-minute check-out. Then the pilots take off. We wait up on the deck until they get back and then our work really begins, you know, trying to repair them and check them out. Sometimes a pilot is a real wise guy and one of us will tape a screw driver in the intake. Then the plane is catapulted off, and then when he races his engine the whole thing explodes in the air.

Q: Have you seen that done?

A: Yes, three or four times.

Q: Why?

A: The pilot was too vicious.

Q: Do you mean in terms of bombing or strafing civilians?

A: No. He might speak in a nasty way to the mechanic.

THE WAR

■ Richard Dow*

Q: What is your name?
A: Richard Dow.
Q: How long were you in Vietnam?
A: Thirty-three months.
Q: How long were you in the Army?
A: Seven years, five months, eighteen days.
Q: What was your rank when you were in Vietnam?
A: Sergeant E-5.
Q: What was your assignment there?
A: Squad leader of a six-man pony team, which is an alert and reconnaissance. We were to seek the enemy out, come back, divulge the information we got, have a larger force go in and destroy.
Q: What terminated your activity in Vietnam?
A: I was wounded on a patrol where we engaged the enemy. Tried to break contact. I was wounded quite seriously.
Q: Where were you wounded?
A: Two wounds in the leg, in the hip, stomach, shoulder and chest.

49

Q: Where were you sent after being wounded?

A: I spent two weeks in the 97 Air Vac Hospital in Vietnam. From there to the 106 General Hospital in Japan and then from there to the General Hospital in Presidio, San Francisco.

Q: How long did you remain in hospital from the time you were wounded until you were discharged back to duty?

A: Eighteen months.

Q: Did you receive any honors or citations for your conduct in Vietnam?

A: Yes, I did.

Q: What were they?

A: Bronze Star, Army Commendation ribbon, Distinguished Service Medal for Gallantry from the Vietnamese government, the Presidential Citation, which was awarded to my team, several Vietnamese ribbons, plus the campaign ribbons and some Purple Hearts.

Q: How many Purple Hearts?

A: Five.

Q: How did you feel about the war?

A: At the time I was there I didn't really know what was going on. I was told to fight, and that's what I did. Now that I know what's happening through my own experience I'm against this war due to the fact that we kill innocent people. We are just as bad as the Nazis during the Second World War when they executed Jews. We kill innocent people—maybe not even Vietcong, but somebody says Vietcong—destroy them. We destroy them.

Q: Could you describe an operation that you saw in which innocent people were killed?

A: Yes, I can. A village north of our position. We got a report —Vietcong in the area, go and interrogate the village and find out. We went up, interrogated the village chief. The village chief was a Cong sympathizer—told us to leave. We left. Came back with a larger force and completely tore the village apart.

Q: How?

A: Napalm, mortar attacks, heavy artillery, land assaults, armored vehicles—a full-scale attack upon a small village.

Q: How many people lived there before the attack?

A: About four hundred.

Q: How many survived the attack?

A: One.

Q: Who was killed, then?

A: Everybody. Women, children, water buffaloes, chickens, goats, everything.

Q: Who gave the order to destroy the village?

A: It came down from our Battalion S-2.

Q: S-2 is battalion intelligence?

A: Right. Which came down from division intelligence through the chain down to our platoon leaders. Our platoon leader gave it out to the squad leaders and in turn the squad leaders gave it out to the squads.

Q: Was this an unusual action?

A: No. We've had other actions like this where we were told to completely burn a village down but not to kill everything. I know of other cases where we have killed people.

Q: What village was this?

A: Bau-Tri.

Q: Where is that—where was that?

A: About a hundred and fifty miles northeast of Saigon.

Q: What has been the policy of the U.S. Army—so far as you know it—regarding prisoners?

A: Well, sometimes they take prisoners and sometimes they don't. It depends on the situation—on how bad the unit is being hit. If they want to find out where the main group is. Or find out who's helping them—who's transporting weapons in to them. Things like this.

Q: Have you ever been given an order that you were to take no prisoners?

A: Yes, I have.

Q: By whom?

A: The lieutenant. The platoon leader.

Q: On more than one occasion?

A: Yes.

Q: And what happened then?

A: We didn't take any prisoners.

Q: What does that mean?

A: We killed everybody we caught.

Q: Wounded?

51

A: Wounded too.

Q: Were killed?

A: Yes.

Q: How were they killed?

A: Forty-fives, M-16, machine guns, stabbed them with bayonets.

Q: Wounded lying on the ground?

A: Yes—unable to defend themselves. They were out of action. They couldn't have done any more.

Q: Did you see this yourself?

A: I participated.

Q: Why?

A: After a while you just become like an animal—you just do it out of instinct, you just don't realize any more.

Q: How many prisoners or wounded did you kill? Can you make an estimate?

A: Of my own personal kills?

Q: Yes.

A: I'd say maybe two hundred and fifty.

Q: You personally?

A: Yes.

Q: And how many did you witness, do you think?

A: Maybe two, three thousand.

Q: Of wounded being killed?

A: Oh, yes, wounded, and civilians being killed without reason. Men, women, children, everything.

Q: Do you know what the American military attitude is toward the interrogation of prisoners?

A: The interrogation is generally done by a Vietnamese national who is in the military of Vietnam and who is attached to an American unit.

Q: What size unit is assigned a Vietnamese interrogator?

A: A company. They'd have one man who would work right with the S-2 of the company.

Q: Have you witnessed any interrogations?

A: Yes, several with prisoners I've caught and brought back in. I've witnessed maybe twenty-five or thirty-five interrogations.

Q: Could you describe some?

A: Well, I caught a boy—maybe seventeen years old. I shot him in the leg. He went down. He was armed. I disarmed him, applied first aid to him, called a medivac helicopter in and went with him back to our company CP. He was given medical aid and then we interrogated him.

Q: Did you see the interrogation?

A: Yes, I did. I witnessed it. The Vietnamese national, the CIDG, started. The boy was wounded in the thigh. He had been sewed up and given plasma. During the interrogation I saw the CIDG reach down, take the bandage off his leg and hit it with the stock of the rifle to make it bleed again. The kid's losing a lot of blood. Tell him they'll bandage him up if he'll talk. The kid wouldn't talk. So the CIDG pulled a bayonet out and split the leg wider than what the bullet hole had made. That wasn't bad enough; they went ahead and killed him.

Q: How did they kill him?

A: Through torture.

Q: How did they torture him?

A: Chopping fingers off—one joint at a time. Sticking a knife just enough to make him bleed.

Q: Where?

A: In his face, his stomach, his hands, his legs, his arms, making him bleed.

Q: How long did that go on?

A: About three hours. Finally the kid went out. They couldn't get him back to regain consciousness. The CIDG pulled his pistol out and shot him in the head. After he was dead they cut off his scrotum area—they castrated him—and sewed it up in his mouth. Then they stuck him out in the middle of this village where they had a sign on him—anybody touch him and they'll get the same treatment. Nobody touched him. They do women just about the same way.

Q: Did you ever witness that?

A: Yes. We were on a beer run to Saigon. One of the guys was upstairs above a bar with a prostitute. We heard him scream. He had been assaulted with a razor blade by the girl. We got an MP to take him to the hospital. We took her to the closest military installation from where we were. They got her, tied her down and split her

53

from her vagina clean to her throat. They killed her immediately.

Q: You saw that?

A: Yes, I did.

Q: Did you see any other mistreatment of women?

A: Yes, I seen—but they're not nice to talk about and I'd rather not. I couldn't discuss these things with women present.

Q: Would you two mind leaving us alone for just a few minutes? What did you see?

A: I saw one young girl caught. They said she was a Vietcong sympathizer. She was caught by the ROK—the Royal Army of Korea. During interrogation she wouldn't talk. They stripped all her clothes, then they tied her down. Then every man in the battalion had intercourse with her. Finally she said she couldn't take any more, that she'd talk. Then they sewed up her vagina with common wire. They run a brass rod through her head and hung her up. Then the commander of the group, a lieutenant, severed her body from her head with a long saber. And I seen one get burned with a hot bayonet stuck dead into the vagina.

Q: Who did that?

A: We did.

Q: American soldiers?

A: Yes.

Q: How many American soldiers participated in that.

A: Seven.

Q: Who was the girl?

A: Daughter of a Vietnamese chief—he was a Cong sympathizer. We stripped her, tied her down and heated a bayonet up with a fire. Run it across her breasts—and into her vaginal area.

Q: Did she die?

A: Not right away. We had a man with us. Took a leather shoelace from his boot. Wet it down. Tied it around her throat. Left her hanging in the sun. Rawhide shrinks after it gets dry. It just slowly strangled her to death.

Q: Where were you born?

A: Rupert, Idaho.

Q: Where did you go to school?

A: In a little place called Bend, Oregon. Elementary school and high school. I went for almost five months to New York University.

Then I joined the Army.

Q: Before you joined the Army would you have believed that American soldiers could possibly do the things that you later saw them do?

A: No. I couldn't honestly believe that a man, especially an American—I don't think that Americans—I didn't think at that time that an American was capable, was capable of malicious, sadistic torture.

A new guy who just arrived there got sick to his stomach when he saw these things. After you're there a while it doesn't bother you. Some of them actually enjoyed it. You come perverted after a while.

Q: You killed over a couple of hundred people in your thirty-three months in Vietnam?

A: Yes.

Q: Do you now know why you were there?

A: I can't honestly say. I was told we were going to save the Vietnamese from the Communists. We didn't save anyone. We just killed. Why were we sent there? I can't honestly say.

▪ Jimmy Roberson

Q: What's your name?
A: Jimmy Roberson.
Q: And you are from where?
A: Washington, D.C.
Q: How old were you when you entered the Army?
A: I was nineteen when I enlisted.
Q: Did you attend high school?
A: Yes. I didn't finish it, though. I quit. And then I went to night school when I went into the Army. I'd almost finished enough credits for my last year. Then when I came into the Army I took

some tests that they said if you pass them you get your diploma. So they said I'd passed them. I took these five G-3 tests, and I came out with good scores.

Q: When did you enlist?

A: It was the first of April, '66.

Q: And where did you take your basic?

A: I went to do basic at Fort Gordon, Georgia.

Q: And where did you get AIT?

A: In Fort Jackson.

Q: South Carolina?

A: Yes. I was sent to a unit that was preparing to leave for Vietnam. It was building up a battalion. And I was there a couple of months, and then we all moved down on a boat with a couple of other battalions.

Q: A boat for Vietnam? You went by boat?

A: Yeah. Twenty-one days.

Q: And where did you arrive in Vietnam?

A: Oh, we arrived in Vung Tao. It's on the coast. And we got in at night. We couldn't get off, so we had to dock out till morning before we boarded these things to land on the shore. You know, landing craft.

Q: How long were you in Vietnam?

A: For a year.

Q: Did you see combat?

A: Well, not all the time. You see, I was on a kind of unit of support to the First Infantry. My unit was the 36th Signal Combat Support Unit. We went over there, and they told us that we would be in the field half the year, with communications, and there was a lot of drivers in the company, a lot of truck drivers, and that we'd be doing things that we were not necessarily trained in. We'd have to do things, you know, other jobs, you know, whether we wanted to or not.

Q: When did you see action?

A: Oh, right at the beginning. It was just mortar attacks and things like this. A few mortar attacks.

Q: On your unit?

A: On the compound I was in. And there were not many attacks, maybe once in a while a few cats would get killed, but not that many. And then, like after a month we were attached to the First Infantry, and they moved us to a place by Dzi Anh where they'd got a big infantry base. And we came there, we came under their jurisdiction, so they told us that we'd be doing what they said, and that just because we were in a signal unit, that didn't mean anything. We'd have to pull patrols and things like that.

I mean, you can't fight the Army, not one man. About this type of thing, you know. We were going out on day patrols with, you know, infantry cats that had been doing it for a long time and they were teaching us several things. And then we had to pull night patrols—I mean, the day patrols weren't bad—and then we had to pull night patrols and to pull guard on ammunition dumps and things like this. It was after a couple of months that, you know, things started getting hot like. We had to go out on a big operation, and it was a big operation called Cedar Falls. And this was about forty miles north of Saigon. They got a big woods up there called Hoan Son Wood where there was a big enemy concentration. And like we pulled the operation—first I was just pulling convoys and we get hit a few times, and then like I was getting into a little trouble because I was getting involved in things. Smoking.

Q: What percentage of the guys would you say smoke?

A: I'd say at least seventy-five percent. Then I was told that I had to pull back and pull guard. And then like everything got kind of mixed up with me because I was getting involved, I was really hitting things heavy, and I was getting my mind really—it was really getting on my nerves, the whole thing. I wanted to just drop out of everything. And I told them I was sick of it, you know, pulling these convoys, and I wanted—I mean, I didn't even know why the hell I was there. And like—but I did, I went ahead and pulled my guard and things, but I stayed pretty stoned, well, like after pulling guard —a little while—then I was thrown in with these infantry cats and like we had—it was like the end of the operation—they were making a big sweep and we had to go—I had to go out with them on search and destroy. I didn't want to go, but like I had to go anyway and like we were all pretty, pretty high. I mean, I'd say, like I said seventy-five percent of the cats on the whole operation were just gone completely.

Q: What were they smoking?

57

A: Mostly grass. A few opium. But we were making a big sweep and, like, everything is a little hazy. Certain things you get yourself pretty messed up. I don't know, we were coming to—I don't even know the name of the place, just a little, little place. But anyway we got into some—we got ambushed and a few people got killed.

Q: GIs?

A: A few GIs got killed and a few people from the village, you know, accidentally got into the way of things, of the fire, then they got killed. A few women. And old men. And like there was a big squabble, you know, and like the next thing I know they told me, some cat told me, that we best go out and smoke, because we might have to be doing something. And, I don't know, I didn't understand quite what was happening. And like the next thing I know we got the word down from the sergeant that we had to, like there was about fifteen or twenty people, I'd say, at the most.

Q: In the village?

A: Yeah, that were left. But there wasn't too many to begin with. Some were already evacuated. They weren't supposed to be there. They were told, I mean, there were VC in the area, and they'd been warned, I mean, they weren't supposed to be there. The officers on our base were pretty pissed off because some cats got killed that wouldn't have gotten killed if they'd been warned by the people in the village. So, I don't know, next thing I know a sergeant he just said, "We're going to get them, we've got to finish all of them." And like, I don't know, I didn't really understand what he meant. I mean, I don't think he was right or anything. But I didn't, I don't know, I was pretty stoned. The next thing I know it was a few people, there was about a platoon of us with them M-16s, and I don't know who started it off, somebody started firing, so I started firing, and . . .

Q: How many people were killed?

A: All of them. Around about fifteen or twenty.

Q: Who were they?

A: It was like—mostly it was all what we would say old people. And a few women.

Q: Any children?

A: I think there was a couple. Maybe. They were pretty big. But like we were told to be hush up about it. We were told nothing would be said about it afterwards. And, like, nobody even knew where we were at. And we didn't know the name of the place we were at. Some of the cats cracked up afterwards. *I* even cracked up afterwards, like . . .

Q: What do you mean—they cracked up?

A: Mostly cats were stoned. Like, you know, as far as myself, you know, I happened to look into somebody's eyes, a woman's eyes, and she—I don't know, I looked, I mean, just before we started firing, I mean. You know, I didn't want to. I wanted to turn around and walk away. It was something telling me not to do it. Something told me not, you know, just turn around and not be part of it, but when everybody else started firing, I started firing, and then they came in, some other cats after we left, and they came in with bulldozers. Just destroyed the whole village. Half of it was destroyed anyway, and it was like it was never there. I mean, there was a big hole dug and all these bodies were thrown in it and then, pst, we moved on.

Q: All was covered up?

A: Yeah. Like nobody knew the name of the place, and when the people asked questions, you know, we asked questions, we were told that if we said anything, we'd be severely punished.

Q: Who said that?

A: The sergeant. He told me he was just taking orders, though. So like having nothing said about it, but like afterwards, the operation ended, then we came back to base camp. Some of the cats were really cracking up. They were getting some guys to a hospital.

Q: How many guys went to the hospital?

A: I don't know. Just a few cats cracked up. Some of them liked it. Like this guy Mitchell. He was a big guy, over six foot. He was known in the First Division for being a good soldier. He never talked back and he did everything they told him. His specialty was long-range reconnaissance patrol. This is a special thing they make up of guys to be specially trained. And they drop them out of helicopters in a certain area, and each one has a certain job. And they are supposed to take prisoners and then bring them back. And then they radio in for a helicopter. And then they come and pick them up. And this guy was completely gone. He used to carry a hatchet, and he had it sharpened like a razor, and he'd sneak up on people that were coming up the bushes, and instead of taking them alive he'd just cut their heads off, he'd put the heads in a bag and bring them back. It was in the First Division, and if you killed a certain number of the enemy you got a three-day pass, but you had to bring back their ears. He would bring back their heads. They would send you to a place where there wasn't too much fighting, like on the beach where you just would get mortar attacks. It's a recreational center there. They kept on giving him medals.

Q: Did you actually see him with a bag full of heads?

A: I was in my tent, at the base camp. He'd come back in. He was always laughing strangely. And he would say things like "I got me another one. I got me another little slant-eye." The whole war was crazy, but having him around was too much. I was sitting in my tent, like this, just thinking, and he came in, back from one of his patrols, he had a burlap bag. He sat beside me on my bed. Next thing I know, he opens up the bag and three or four heads fall out on the bed—they were cut off at the neck. When he did that I just started screaming. He was laughing while he was pulling the heads out on the bed. I wondered why they didn't send him to a hospital. But the Army liked this guy. He did what they told him. And he enjoyed it, he actually enjoyed it.

Q: Did you ever hear of torture of prisoners?

A: I've seen a few beat up. One time the Tiger Division of the South Korean Army—they don't play around, they are trained to kill—they took this prisoner and they hung him up to a tree, and the guy comes up with a knife and says, "I'm going to slice on you." And he cut him up, and then the man started to talk.

Q: Did you ever hear about prisoners thrown out of helicopters?

A: I never saw it, because I wasn't in a helicopter, but I heard about it. They said that when they get prisoners they take them up in a helicopter and "You talk or we'll push you out." If you've got five prisoners, you push the first one out, and the second one is going to get the message.

Q: Did you ever see a village burned down besides the one you made reference to?

A: Yes. Sometimes the sergeants would say, especially if some of the guys had been wounded or killed, "We don't care what you do, do what you want, we don't care. You can rape the women or whatever you want."

60

Q: Were the women in the villages raped?

A: Sometimes when we were out on patrol in the field for a long time without women. Some of the cats would get real horny, and when we came to a village where they had some young girls, we'd say, "We want to see some chicks. We're going to be nice, but we can be mean if we have to." One village chief said no. And we kicked a few people and knocked over a few things. Then he said, "O.K., you can have any girl you want." Then we took a few girls. The girls would be in the huts, and we would have guards posted outside, and then a few guys would go in and take the girls. Maybe a squad or two. Maybe fifteen guys. The girls were fifteen, sixteen, seventeen or eighteen, around there. If we saw some girl who looked young, we'd just say, "You! Now! Or else!"

Q: Were the girls ever killed?

A: There was one village which we were told was off limits. But one guy went down there anyway because he got horny. He never came back. Some guys found him later with his throat cut. So some guys took it on their own to pay this place a visit. They found this chick who they thought did it. They killed her. Another time they took a flare gun and stuck it up into a girl and fired it. It blew her apart. There are so many crazy things that were done. Sometimes some of the chicks who were fighting for North Vietnam were captured. I heard they cut their fingers off. Some guys caught a girl who they said had given VD to one of the guys. To teach her a lesson, they poured turpentine into her vagina. These are the guys that are completely gone, they are not even humans any more. In some of the outfits there are a lot of guys like that. Like in the First Division, the First Cavalry, the Fourth Infantry, the 173rd Airborne. Sometimes they get drunk or they get stoned and they brag about the things that they've done. There was one time I split. I stole a two-and-a-half-ton truck.

I was getting bugged, I was having nightmares, and I kept seeing the face of this lady who looked at me at this village. That was some hell of a look. It was like she was trying to say something to me. And I felt that everything was closing in on me. And so I went to see my girl friend in Saigon. I wanted to get away but I didn't know how. And every time I went to her place the MPs would pick me up because they would know I was there. I was talking to my girl in Saigon and she told me she had a sister who lived in a village about forty miles away. And she told me it was a little village and I could split there. She said I would be treated all right. I went to the village with the two-and-a-half-ton truck. And when I got there I realized that I'd been there before, on an operation.

They didn't even know I was gone the first couple of days. I had brought a lot of stuff to the village, C-rations. I went to the cat who was the head of the village. He spoke a little English, not much. And I could understand a little Vietnamese. And he told me I was welcome there. At first I felt so funny being there. It was like it wasn't really happening, it was like it was a dream. I always got along good with the Vietnamese people when I first got there. First couple of days in the village I just did what everybody else did. I helped out in the rice paddies. The people were always pointing at me and saying, "He's Number-one GI." I was trying to teach some of the people to speak English the best way I could. I was getting really involved in this village, and I was forgetting about everything else. And I kept thinking that I was getting content, I wasn't a soldier any more, I was part of the village. I was wearing Vietnamese clothes. I felt as if I was doing something different, I was serving a purpose there, not like the purpose I was sent to Vietnam for. I was really getting to know these people. In the village we got up pretty early. We ate some rice. There was some water buffaloes about the village. We would head out into the rice paddies, and the women would do their little chores. I wasn't used to doing this, but I really felt that I belonged. I had got into a wholly different thing and I didn't want to be part of the war any longer. The people in the village were so friendly to me. I'd get the truck—I didn't have a hell of a lot of gas, but a lot of the kids would get on the truck, hot-rod around the village. There was a girl there, I was devoting a lot of time to teaching her English. She became sort of infatuated with me, always hanging around, and looking at me really funny and all. But she was just like a little kid.

I'd seen helicopters fly over before, and I had ducked. I'd run into a hut or something. But this one time, after I'd been in the village about two weeks, I was out in the fields with some guys, and a helicopter was flying over—it was flying low and I didn't have a chance to hide. I had this Vietnamese outfit on that I wore, with a big hat that they wear, a Vietnamese hat. And I crouched down a little when the helicopter came. But they were flying too low. They circled back around, and then they landed a little bit from where we were at. I thought of running, but it was too late to do anything about it. So a couple of guys came out, one was an officer, they just laughed when they looked at me. They had a picture of me, and they looked at the picture and they looked at me. And they just started laughing and laughing and they said, "What in the hell are you supposed to be? Are you a papa-san or something? You know you're not at home." Then the officer said, "Have you had fun, playing your little games with the gooks?" He said, "You really love the gooks, don't you? It seemed like you spend more time with the gooks than with the Americans." I didn't know what to do. I was standing there, and I said to the officer, "Look, man, you cats may enjoy this goddam war, but I think it sucks, and I don't want no part of it. Why don't you just let me stay here till my time is up?" They looked at me as if I was crazy, and I said, "I'm happy here, O.K.?" But they said, "You're real runny, but you got to go back. They want you in your company. You are neglecting a few duties." So I had to go back. When they took me back all the Vietnamese people in the village got really upset. They were hollering up at the officer, "Number-ten GI, Number-ten GI," which means you are really bad. That means you can't get any lower. Number ten is the lowest. And they were hollering, "Number-ten GI, don't take Number-one GI away." And this little girl there she started crying. I wanted to run over there and give her a little kiss on her cheek, but the officer wouldn't let me. I had to go into one of the huts and get my uniform, which was all rolled up in a corner, and then they took me back in the helicopter.

In the helicopter on the way back they kept on calling me a gook lover. And I kept saying, "Look, man, they're people and they showed me more feelings than you ever have." I said, "I would rather be with them than be with you. You don't act like my people, not like the people I grew up with in the States. Something has happened to you." In a way I knew it couldn't go on forever. I was the only American and I knew they would find me. I had my rifle there and I kept wondering what would happen if the village got raided.

Q: What would you have done if American soldiers came into the village firing? What would you have done if an American outfit had moved in and started shooting up the village?

A: I don't really know. That's something I thought about a lot. I don't know what I would have done. Maybe put the rifle to my head and blown my head off. I was always worried about that. That was in my mind the whole time I was there.

Q: When you got back to the States did you tell anyone about your experiences in Vietnam?

A: I didn't feel much like talking when I first came back. But in a couple of weeks I told a few friends about it. They acted like they didn't want to hear about it. So I got the message and I didn't say anything more. The whole thing makes me feel bad when I think about it. I was having a hard time sleeping. I kept on having nightmares. I had these dreams of seeing the same people.

Q: What people?

A: The people from the village.

Q: The village you lived in?

A: No, the village where we killed the people. Sometimes I see the same person—there will be twenty of them, but it will be the same person looking at me with these eyes. And I'll wake up screaming.

Q: Was the person a man or a woman?

A: It was a woman. And I had only seen her for a few seconds, but I looked into her eyes, and she was looking dead at me. It was like she was saying, "Why? What have we done?" And I'll never forget that woman's look. And I have never forgotten how I felt about that woman.

Q: Was your attitude toward the Vietnamese typical of a sizable number of GIs?

A: No. I got into a little trouble in Vietnam. They said I was too nice to the Vietnamese people. They said I wanted to be around them too much. Even one time they started to call me a gook, and they said, if you like the gooks so much, why don't you fight for them? When they brought me back from the village they thought I was crazy, and I had to go and see my commanding officer. He said I was making a lot of problems. They sent me to the medical ward in a hospital in Saigon. There are different parts of the hospital but they have one block blocked off, where they keep the real severe cases. They threw me in there. They said I was completely gone. I talked to the so-called Army psychiatrist they had there. I told him I wasn't able to go back to the war. So they kept me there for a while. Some of the guys are really crazy there. Some guys woke up in the middle of the night and started screaming. Another guy kept on making noises like a mortar shell. One guy kept singing "I am a tin soldier." One guy kept on calling me Bill. I kept on trying to tell him my name was Jim. Then he kept on saying, "I'm sorry I killed you, Jim." I was really going crazy then.

They let me have a little freedom, so I split and went to see this Vietnamese girl I knew in Saigon. But the MPs came and took me.

After my tour was over in Vietnam, they sent me to Germany, to Mannheim. I know a lot of guys who were nice guys back in the States, but Vietnam changed them. Some of them were really shy cats in the States, but after two or three months in Vietnam they were just killers. They didn't even know who they were. They were completely different people.

• Alan Camden

Q: What is your name?
A: Alan Camden.
Q: Where are you from?
A: Gary, Indiana.
Q: How old were you when you entered the Army?
A: Just eighteen.
Q: When did you leave Vietnam?
A: April 1969. I got malaria and was sent to a hospital in Japan in October.

Q: Were you against the war before you entered the Army?

A: Yes. But after I saw Vietnam and what was going on there I was much more strongly against it.

Q: What did you see?

A: For one thing I saw officers and sergeants order men to mutilate the bodies of the dead enemy. We were told to chop them up.

Q: Did you see that often?

A: It happened just about every time it was possible.

Q: How were the bodies mutilated?

A: A lot of guys had Vietnamese ears. They also cut off other parts of bodies and threw them around. Also poked eyeballs out. I saw American soldiers torture a Vietnamese to death. They beat him, kicked him and then poked out his eyes. He died as they were taking his eyes out.

Q: How old was he?

A: I would say about sixteen.

Q: Where was this?

A: Just north of Quang Tri.

Q: When was it?

A: In May of '69.

Q: Who were the people who tortured him?

A: They were members of my platoon. Mostly just enlisted men. But a lieutenant was also in on it. He was the one who started it.

Q: What is his name?

A: Willig.

Q: Did he order the men to torture the boy?

A: No. He just said, "How would you guys like to take care of this gook?" He put it in a way to encourage them without giving a direct order. It wasn't an order. It was a challenge.

Q: What outfit were you with?

A: A Fifth Infantry Division, mechanized.

Q: What company?

A: I was with B Company of the First of the 66th and then I went to A Company, Seventh Engineers.

Q: What were you with when they tortured the young man to death?

A: The First of the 66th.

Q: Where were you stationed?

A: When I was in the Fifth Infantry Division we were about twelve miles south of the DMZ. I was a medic and with the infantry unit. Originally, when I first came to Vietnam I was assigned to a rear unit as a pharmacist in the dispensary, but we lost several medics out in the field, and I was told I was supposed to go out in the field and replace them, the medics that were killed. It would be for a short time and then I would be back in my pharmacy, but as it turned out I stayed out in the field. I was a conscientious objector. I did not have a weapon. I would not carry a weapon. In my unit it was kind of the in thing to do to have the enemies' ears in your jar. They would go up to the dead enemy with a knife. The people in our unit would come with knives and cut off the ears of the dead enemy and put them in alcohol jars and keep them in their hootches, and the guy that had most ears was the guy that was looked up on the most. In my hootch there were twenty guys and of that twenty guys fifteen had ear jars. It was a pretty popular thing. Another thing, the fingers are pretty popular too, cutting off fingers and putting those in alcohol jars. They would keep the ear jars on a shelf—just over their beds. Over there the best soldiers are the ones with the most ears. I think the reason for this is that the training—it is responsible. It started when I came into the Army I did not have a C.O. status then, and I was sent to Fort Campbell, Kentucky, and I went through about three weeks of training there, and then I got my C.O. status and they sent me to Fort Sam Houston to finish my basic training. But during those three weeks at Fort Campbell, I was constantly drilled to kill and I just couldn't take that. A lot of these guys, you know, that is what they join the Army for, to go to Vietnam and kill the gooks, but I had no goals to kill anybody, but this was drilled anyway. You know, when we entered the mess hall you had to say, "Kill, kill, kill!" and your serial number when you ran in. Well, I think that all of this drilling into you, you got to kill, you got to kill, and it just builds up a certain amount of hate. And to kill is not enough, and so you take it out some other way by taking the ears or fingers—by mutilating human bodies—except by then you don't consider them to be human any more.

A: So we were going to Hot Nam. We were in for two weeks more training. We were shipped to Pendleton in California; we got no leave. I arrived in Vietnam July 1967. We got a commercial flight from Japan to Vietnam. As our plane landed there were helicopters firing right near the airport; they were firing tracer bullets. Well, we landed in Da Nang and we knew that we were in war. I was scared. All we could see was this red line coming through the sky. We couldn't see the helicopters, it was too dark. And you think, man, that mother-fucker is right out there, and I'm here two hundred yards away, and you think this shit is for real, they are not playing now.

I was shipped to a unit south of Da Nang, I was sent to First Marine Division, First Battalion, Bravo Company. Bill White was sent to A Company. About a month later he stepped on a booby trap and got a medical discharge. His arm was blown off or something.

I'm not ashamed to say it, a couple of days later when I got shipped to my unit I was scared, real scared. Everywhere you looked you saw a Huey, and you'd see flares—pop-ups lighting up the sky. And you'd hear mortars and rifles and machine guns. And you'd know he's out there. But you can't see him. You hear the artillery rounds being fired. I got so scared I sat down one night and started crying, "O Lord, O Lord, take me out of this place." I'd only been there a week, and I hadn't even been out on patrol yet. A few days later it happened—it was the first time I was out in the bush. We had to set up an LP [listening post]. We went out that night and we walked for a long time. I saw my first guy get blown to fucking bits. He was a squad leader. He stepped on a box mine. He was told not to go out on the LP that night. He was short—he was going home in two weeks. The sergeant said to him, "You are kind of short, no sense your going out." He said, "Yes, I'm going. It'll be my last LP." He went. I walked over that mine, and then I heard this gigantic explosion. This guy had a pop-up flare in his jungle trousers, and the mine set that off. It lit him all up. It lit all of us up. It blew him away from the waist on down. That's what I saw when I looked up. Half a man flying up the air, all lit up in this fantastic white light with this deafening sound and blood flying all over. Then the flare burns out, and it's dark and quiet. No one says anything. Then one guy says, "He's got it. He's dead." Then a guy starts to yell, "You dirty mother-fucker slant-eyes, we're going to get you. We are going to carve our initials in your head." And soon we were all yelling— just screaming out into the dark jungle.

The platoon spent the night there. But one squad—my squad— was sent out on an ambush post. We broke up into twos. And I spent the night all alone in the jungle, just with one other guy. That was a long night. The next night *we* got ambushed. We were walking around on the sand dunes where there are no hiding places. There was a grassy hill with some trees on it. All of a sudden there was gunfire from the hill. It was the first time I'd been fired at in my life. In boot camp I've heard the slogan "Machine guns can't kill Marines." At this point I thought machine guns and any other thing could kill Marines. You learn it ain't like boot camp. That dummy you'd been beating on now is shooting back. In boot camp the dummy used to just swing around; this one here, he fights back. I heard a lieutenant—he was a boot lieutenant—I think he had less experience than I had. He starts yelling, "Let's get some fire on that hill." We were firing laws—that's a kind of rocket—up on that hill. We were just firing at the mountain. After we quit firing it was quiet. And somebody yells out, "Anybody got it?" And somebody says, "Who got it?" And George yells out, "Me!" Old George had a bullet hole in his leg. He just sat there in the grass just laughing. He's laughing and he's yelling, "Goddam, I'm hit." I crawled over to him. His leg was all bleeding. He said to me, "You know what this means?" He had been wounded twice before, and the rule is three and you're out. That's why he was laughing. He said, "Look at that, man, look at that wound, I'm hit, I'm getting out of this shit!" He's pointing to his leg and he's laughing. "This is my way out of this shit! Out. Out." Andy was the next most experienced guy in our squad. He takes the squad leader's position. Andy was a groovy guy, he's a white guy from Milwaukee. I get to learn the names of the guys, and I get to learn a little bit about the guys. Their names, where they come from. Then I met this guy named Kaminski, he's Polish. This guy is really crazy. If it hadn't been for Kam I would have probably cracked in Nam. He kept my morale going. He was so nutty. We could be in the middle of a fire fight with guys getting killed. And Kam would be down there laughing. I tried to get into his crazy moods with him. It helped me along. That was the first night me and Kam were together. We were sitting around a little deserted hamlet. Me and Kam had dug a little hole. And we were sitting in it. Then a Marine got shot that night by a Marine. This was a shock to me, too, but I was still learning. We were sitting out there. About ten feet in front of us there was this little bush. We were sitting in front of it, as a matter of fact, you know, we were rather low. Kam says, "You take the first watch." I say, "O.K., man." So Kam sleeps. I think he starts to dream or something. But anyway he wakes up, and I'm sitting there and I'm still watching that bush and maybe I saw something that night and maybe I didn't, I don't know, but I heard something in those bushes, and I said, "God damn!" And Kam woke up and, man, he jumped. He says, "Hey, man, there's something out there?" I say, "Yeah, I think so." So we both set up our weapons real slow, and we aimed at this bush. So all of a sudden Kam just starts firing, you know, at the bush, man. I didn't see nothing. He said he saw something. Then I started firing too, you know, at the bush, man. I started squeezing off. Then he throws a grenade out there. So then the word came down the line, "What the fuck is that, man, what the fuck is that? You shoot anybody?" "Don't know, man. I ain't going out there. If you want to look, you better look yourself." And me and Kam were sitting there, and we stayed awake the whole night, you know, 'cause, man, suppose a mother-fucker was out there and we didn't shoot him. So we sat there all night looking at that fucking bush. We were scared shitless all night.

This Kam guy through just about every battle we were in kept my morale. Then he stole so much. He was a real go-getter, man. He kept our squad loaded with stuff. Once in a while he'd get a ride into Da Nang, and he would buy something for the whole squad, he would always buy everything for the squad. He went to Da Nang and bought the whole squad these ambush hats, you know, the shit that the Australians wear. And Kam went back and bought this tape recorder, and he spent a whole bunch of money taping, you know, just playing the jukebox, records and stuff. Then he would bring it back and our squad heard the latest hits. He would go inside the battalion area and he'd get cards and things. This guy was a real gangbuster, man, I mean, he kept the morale for the whole squad, you know. He was point man. You know, like a scout. In fact, he was so nutty that not only our squad liked him but the whole platoon liked him. And then he got caught one night, man, they could have shot him for that shit. They call it sandbagging.

One night when we were in not the battalion area but we had our own little camp set up in the bush. And Kam had an LP that night. We knew that the man was out there, because they'd been hitting us all day, firing at us. Kam had a fire team—that's supposed to be four men—so he had four men and then he had this LP. So we sat and talked, and Kam says, "Man, look, we ain't going out there. Them mother-fuckers will catch us out there, man. Listen, here's what we are going to do." So the four men they'd get the radio and take it inside this little hootch that we'd built. And the radio man he'd get inside the hootch and all four men with him. And we'd wait in that hootch all night, smoke, talk, do anything we wanted. But about every hour or so the radio man would say, "Ssshh." He'd call in to the battalion headquarters about, say, fifty feet from us. When you've got that radio, you can sit right beside them. They don't know where you are. They just tell you to go here, go there, they set up a map for you.

Q: Where did they think you were?

A: Hundreds of yards out, man. In the bush, near the Cong. The guy, he says, "Sshh . . . This is LP-One. We don't see anything . . . contact you later . . . over now." Click. "Now, what was that, man, what were we talking about—oh, yeah . . . about the block man." You know we did this a lot, man. I did it too when I got to be lance corporal, when I had a fire team. Kam's fire team got caught that particular night. I don't know how it happened or how he got caught, but something happened. They didn't give it away. Somebody walked by, a sergeant who was checking or something. Then the boot lieutenant, he kind of dug Kam because sometimes Kam stole shit and took it to him. He didn't do anything but warn him, you know. Gave him an official warning, smiled at him, you know

—"Poor Kam, don't do that no more"—give him a pat on the back, you know. He could have got shot for that. He was endangering the lives of everybody. Good old lieutenant. He was boot. He was sand-bagging too. We get an order to go across some fucking waters. Charlie's shooting at us from the other side. Guy says, "Look, go overside there, we got the order." We were sitting and looking at the bullets coming over across the river, and we got the order to go across that. "I ain't going across that river," the lieutenant said. He radioed back that we were over there. But when the risk is deep, man, then fuck it.

I saw Kam do something once. I saw him shoot an old lady. Kill her. I didn't dig that too much.

Q: Why did he kill her?

A: This was the first part of this massacre that we were in.

Q: What was the town?

A: I don't know. Just hamlets. Near Quang Tri, not far below the DMZ.

Q: When was it?

A: This was November 1967, right after Operation Medina. We were in these fucking mountains, and we're waiting. It was daytime. Kam was walking point. I'm walking cover man for him. Me and Kam and this guy named Jessup, we were tight, we were running buddies. All of us were experienced by now. We had been in numbers of battles and we were still alive. So Kam was sitting down on the ground, and I was sitting there, I was tired. Jessup was in the back somewhere. Kam was watching the ground. I didn't pay any attention to what he was looking at or anything, but about five minutes later he called me, he says, "Come here, man, look at this shit, come here." I walked across his open, and I saw the funniest thing I've ever seen. You know, those giant red ants, huge, and two of them were fighting, and Kam and I was sitting there watching them. Kam says, "I got this one—you got that one." So we heard a guy say, "We're moving out pretty soon." "Look, man," I say, "I can't cover you with a seventy-nine." You need an automatic weapon for covering. So he called Jessup up there. "Jessup. Need a cover, man!" Here comes Jessup. As Jessup got to the open that I was just sitting by, a hail of fucking bullets came right across his head. Automatic fire. Pa-a-ang. God damn. And I started squeezing off that seventy-nine. Boom-boom. To cover him. And Kam started to fire off an automatic. So they sent out some radio signals to close in on that side, and we were going to close in on this side. So I don't know if I killed these people or not, it's hard to say. But I saw some people —there were no children, some women, just some people, running across, to a hootch. Kam says, "Hey, man, there goes Charlie— knock that mother-fucker out quick." So I just turned around, and I took good aim, and I fired on the hootch which I annihilated that mother-fucker with that grenade launcher, and the mother-fucker fell in 'cause I put about four rounds to it, and all of them were dead-eye hits. So if they stopped in that hootch, they were dead. But we didn't search the hootch. When we got to the hootch there was a bunker, a ground bunker. We were like on an assault line— walking to it. Kam stopped and he looked into this bunker. "Look at this shit, man, look at this shit." And I walked over to the bunker, and there was this old lady, she was really an aged lady, maybe eighty years. She was coming out of this thing. So as I turned around, that split second, Kam unloaded half of his magazine into that lady. On automatic, you know, and it scared me, you know, because I didn't think he was going to fire. And I jumped. I just looked at Kam, for a minute or so I just stared at him. "God damn, man, you shoot that old lady?" So then I was scared to look into the bunker. The lady had to have been really messed up. And Jessup ran over to the bunker, and he looked in, you know, and he started, "God damn, Kam, look at the shit, man, look what the fuck you did." So Kam, he pulls out a grenade, throws the grenade in the bunker. Blows that old lady's body to a million pieces. To damn near threads.

Q: Why did Kaminski do it?

A: Oh, he says he just wanted to do something.

Q: Why did he kill her, though?

A: He didn't give any explanation.

Q: What do you think—I mean, you know the guy?

A: I don't know. Kam just stood there looking at what was left of the body. And he was frowning. He had this weird look on his face. I started walking away. Then we started to burn down all the hootches with matches and lighters. There were people in them. When they tried to come out we shot them. We stayed around that place for a long time and we smelled burned-up bodies. That's a goddam horrible smell. Kam took a rag and tied it around his nose 'cause he couldn't stand the smell of the bodies burning. Guys were shooting up the livestock. Killing water buffaloes. My platoon was doing the cut-off for people who were trying to run from the burning hootches. Also people were running from the platoon at the other side of the hamlets. That platoon was doing the assault. They were killing them, massacring the whole village. Our job was to cut off the escape area. To kill any that came our way. We got them. We had them all blocked off between the two platoons. I got up on this little mount and there was about eight, nine or ten cows. And I fired my seventy-nine right in the middle of them—stampeded them. And they ran right into a machine-gun team that had been set up. Zap-zap-zap, they were all killed. Cut to pieces. It was a big kick. We were looking at these cows get slaughtered.

Then we were walking down this track—still moving. And we saw a fairly good-sized, nice little Vietnamese house. Andy says, "Whit, take your team up and take care of that house." I say, "O.K., man. Jessup, Skip"—he's carrying laws—so we cross this little creek into this house. I fired into the house before I went up there. Fired a seventy-nine in. It was a brick house. Jessup goes up on one side, Skip goes up on the other side. They went wild. They went inside the house and started tearing things off the wall—wrecking everything. Then I went in the house. Me and Jessup started looking for money. A lot of them have money hid. Then we burned down the house and burned down everything around there. We started moving down the track.

Q: How many people do you think were killed in that massacre?

A: It would be hard to say—to know the exact amount. We wiped out those hamlets completely. But I don't know for sure how many had been there. You get these little hamlets—maybe thirty people live there, and you get these hamlets maybe every fifty or one hundred yards. We just went through that mother-fucker and left nothing that I saw.

Q: How many hamlets did you go through in that sweep?

A: Thirteen hamlets. It was in a little valley.

Later that night I heard an officer give the order to kill the children. I was standing right next to him.

Some guy had stepped on a booby trap and they were calling for evacuation—for a helicopter to take him. So we had to set up a ring —for the helicopter to land—to guard the helicopter. I just happened to be standing alongside the officer when the radio man said, "Look, sir, we got children rounded up. What do you want us to do with them?" The guy says, "Goddam it, Marine, you know what to do with them. Kill the bastards. If you ain't got the goddam balls to kill them, Marine, I'll come down there and kill the mother-fuckers myself." The Marine said, "Yes, sir," and hung up the phone. About two or three minutes later I heard a lot of automatic fire—and a lot of children's screaming. I heard babies crying. I heard children screaming their fucking lungs out. I heard 'em. And that got next to me. I heard a machine gun go off. You know a machine gun when you hear it. There were a lot of children. It lasted only twenty or thirty seconds. We didn't, they didn't get all the children, though. 'Cause the next day we went into some other hamlets. And I saw a little girl. It really bugged me—I knew her parents had been killed. She had her little brother with her. It had to be her little brother. She was carrying him. She was just standing there—like "What is going on?" She saw us tear the hamlet apart. They had two water buffaloes inside a big hole—I guess that's how they keep them at night. We walked up on this place. And five or six feet away is this big tree. And the little girl is standing at the tree, holding her baby brother. We're standing around this hole and Jessup says, "Look at this shit. We're going to have some fun." So these two water buffaloes, they can't run, they can't go anywhere. So Jessup takes two grenades, takes the pins out, and throws them into the hole and gets back. We heard this big explosion go off. The ground trembles. And we hear the buffaloes—they're moaning. We walk over to the hole, look down at the hole. The buffaloes are all torn up. There was a big hole—as big as a person's head—in the side of the buffalo. You could see everything—his guts hanging out, everything, but he wasn't dead. He's just lying there and moaning. Jessup is flipping over this. Laughing. Then he says, "I'm going to put that mother-fucker out of his misery." And he unloads most of a magazine into the animal's head. This little girl is standing there looking at us. She don't know what to say. As we walk by she's just looking at us. Her little brother is crying, but she's just looking at us, sort of puzzled.

Sort of in a daze. She was about five or six years old. The baby was less than a year old.

We left her under the tree. I don't know—I'm scared to say—but I think they killed that kid. I left. I didn't want to see it. I knew some guy was going to come along and shoot her while I was standing there—and I couldn't stand to see that. So I left. I'm sure some guy killed her.

It was one of my plans to adopt one of those kids. They were so groovy to me. I really dug those kids. In fact, at home I have a whole big album of pictures that I took, one of those little Swinger cameras; and in all of those pictures there are kids. I'd get as many kids as I could hold, in my arms, on my neck, all over, and have my pictures taken.

That was the only huge massacre I was in. But civilians got killed almost every day if we were around them. You'd be in a hamlet and a guy would say, "Hey, man, shoot that sonofabitch over there." The guy would turn around and fire an M-16 in his chest. Wiped out. It was a farmer—didn't have no gun. That's common—knock off a civilian for the hell of it.

Q: How were prisoners treated?

A: Prisoners? We didn't take too many prisoners. We caught one guy. Kam had caught this young guy—a little guy. We had this big black platoon sergeant. He walks over, grabs this little guy. The platoon sergeant stands about six feet five inches and weighs about two hundred pounds. He holds him by the collar and drives his knee into his stomach and groin. I thought he'd break the guy in two. Just looking at that shit hurt. We'd say, "Do it again, beat the shit out of him."

We were out on Monday the fifteenth, 1967. On that morning we moved out. We were way north. Right on the DMZ. Spotter planes had spotted a big movement. So we were sent out—Bravo Company was—to ambush them. We got to the Zone before daylight set in. I had my fire team all ready. I had my telephone. Each fire team had one. My team was spread out. I was reading jive magazines. All of a sudden I hear them call to the CP that they spotted two enemy, ten yards in front of them. So Kam calls in, "Lieutenant, we spotted two of these mother-fuckers about ten yards in front. Should we open up?" The lieutenant says, "No, hold it a minute." I throw my magazine down and load up.

About a minute later or so they open up. I heard those bullets go off. I don't know who started it, but everybody's firing. The lieutenant is on the phone. "Whit, keep your eyes on the rear." "Yes, sir." This lieutenant comes down the hill like God, talking loud. "Get on the fucking line." He's standing there like an idiot, yelling, giving orders. "We're going to charge this way." He's a boot. I think he's been in about two months. He's a fool. He's screaming. I move my team over. I'm the senior seventy-nine man in the platoon. I hear the lieutenant—"Whit up." I report to him. "I want you to lay a couple of rounds into that bush over there." "Yes, sir." I fire off three rounds.

Then the fool says, "We're going to move up. We're going to charge. We assault."

It was wide open. No place to hide. The lieutenant keeps on yelling orders—you just don't do that out there in a fire fight.

We walk out and five seconds later all hell breaks loose. That whole line in front of us opens up. We could see nothing but gunfire. And the first one to get hit is that lieutenant. He was standing three feet from me. And the impact of the bullet knocked him back and off his feet. Like a damn airplane taking off and crashing. The first thing I did was hit the ground. I was lying there in the open. Then I got up and turned around and ran. One other guy got up and ran with me. We were the only two in the platoon not killed, wounded or trapped. I got up behind this barn, me and this other guy. The lieutenant is about ten feet from me. And he is calling. Who is he calling? Me. He's crying, "Whit, I'm hit. Whit, I'm hit." I turned around and screamed to the other guy, "Cover me. Damn it, cover me." And I did a John Wayne. I went back to get the man 'cause he was calling my name.

Charlie did not shoot. He could have shot me easily. Like a damn sitting duck. But they let me go up there. There was no place to hide. They spared me. I know this. When I picked up the lieutenant, he was shot again—in the leg. But no one shot me. Why? 'Cause I'm black? I don't know.

I dragged the man behind the barn. He had a hole in his chest.

His lung was punctured. He was gasping for air.

There was our radio man, Sully. He was calling in smoke rounds for protection. The smoke came in and it was possible to move. Sully and I pulled the lieutenant back. Then we called a couple of other Marines, "Hey, we need some help." Then I hear Jessup's voice screaming for medical aid. He's screaming "*Corpsman*" over and over. This hurts me 'cause I think he's hit. He and Kam were my closest buddies. Three other Marines try to help. And a round of automatic fire cut all three of them down. They were white.

One was killed. Two badly wounded, arms and legs. Then we saw a corpsman. It was his first time out. He was scared. I screamed at him, "That way, you mother-fucker—that way." And I was pointing towards Jessup. He had a roll-up stretcher on his back. I told him to throw it over to me. We put the lieutenant on the stretcher. We took two steps and Sully got hit. Sully was white. He looked just like Clark Gable. He had a mustache just like Gable. He used to trim it all the time in a foxhole. He couldn't believe he was shot. "They shot me. Can you believe it? They shot me." He was shot in the ass.

Now the smoke rounds are coming in. They sound like mortars. One landed just four or five feet from me. I dragged the lieutenant back. Then I see a black Marine and a white Marine—and they help me pull the lieutenant out.

Then I go back to see about Sully and Jessup. I take off my seventy-nine jacket with all the grenades and put my seventy-nine down, grab my forty-five and go back to the bushes. I start to call, "Sully, where are you?" The black Marine came back with me. We both grab Sully—he couldn't crawl, he couldn't move his legs. His bullshit had ceased then 'cause the pain had hit him. We dragged him out of there. We set the wounded in this bomb crater. A lot of the guys were standing in there for protection. I say, "Look, I want someone to go back with me. I need one volunteer." I never seen nothing like it before. Nobody said anything.

So I took off alone to get Jessup—through the mud and bullets. I started to scream, "Jessup." After I called him three or four times he heard me and answered, "Over here."

The black Marines were behind me. They said, "Go ahead, we got you covered." I got up and ran five or six yards. Jessup, the corpsman and another guy was there. Jessup had not been shot. He was trying to bandage another guy—he was hit bad. The guy was going mad trying to run. There was another guy there with his head blown off. Jessup looks at me like he knew I wanted to ask who it was but was scared to—it might be Kam. I said, "Who is it?" He says, "It's Moe." He was one of my buddies also. I had late watch with him that morning. He was from a small town in Connecticut. That morning he was telling me about what he was going to do when he got back home. What he had waiting on him.

Andy was there too, near the side of a rock. And I said to him, "Where's the rest?" He said, "Up front. They're pinned down." I started crawling out, up front. I looked at Moe and started crawling up. Jessup threw smoke grenades in front of me. I crawled five or six feet to a bunker. There was a big rock there and two Marines in the bunker. They were frozen—they couldn't do anything. Another guy was there but he had been hit five times. He couldn't move. There was a machine gun in the bunker.

A guy came from behind me, jumped in the bunker and started firing the machine gun. I asked a seventy-nine man there to throw me his seventy-nine and some rounds. And I started firing from near that rock. The other guys there dragged the wounded guy back the same way we had just come.

So the machine gunner and I are there all alone.

Then the jets came. They started dropping red smoke right on us. Red smoke means "enemy position." And then I knew we were really in trouble.

Charlie knows what red smoke means. They knew the jets were going to come right in on them with explosives and napalm. So they had to get out. But instead of leaving we waited until Charlie jumped out of these holes—right in front of our position—and tried to run away. We had a good time. We started picking them mother-fuckers off. We popped them off. They had to run even when we were shooting, 'cause they had no chance if the jets came. We got a lot of them. There were five or six M-16s there, the machine gun, the seventy-nine. I was having a good time picking up one weapon, firing it, and then another.

Then we heard enemy mortars coming in on us. So we started to get out of there.

79

One of our tanks, in back of us, was picking up the wounded and the dead.

A mortar round landed a few feet behind me as I was crawling out. I caught shrapnel in my back and legs and arms. The concussion picked me up and threw me down on the earth. I couldn't see. I saw in waves and I screamed, "I'm hit." I couldn't feel my legs. I thought they had been blown off. I was afraid to look. The other guy was hit too. I said to him, "How bad am I hit?" and he says, "Not too bad." Then I looked down at my legs. My jungle trousers had all been blown off, my legs were all blood. The guy says, "Let's get out. Let's go now." But I couldn't move. I was getting ready to die. I said, "Lord, let me die now." The jets were ready to bomb the area. Charlie was running by. I thought it was all over.

Then this guy takes my hand and starts to drag me. But my canteens on my cartridge belt slowed me down. Then he takes off my belt and pulls me.

Then the jets came in with high explosives. If it was napalm it would have killed us.

We just laid there while the bombs were exploding around us.

Then something happened that I will never forget. This tank came near us. We started yelling. This other Marine screamed at the top of his lungs, "We're hit. Come help us." The tank was only twenty yards away.

I know goddam well they heard us. They heard us. Then the tank backs away. The mother-fucker turned around and left us—and we were down.

When the battle was just about over a platoon came in to count the dead—and they found us lying out there. They were surprised that anything lived through that bombing.

I went to a field hospital first. One of my DIs from Parris Island was there in the hospital. He had been in Nam two weeks. He got shot in that same battle I was hit in. He had been shot five times.

I saw the doctors look at me. They sort of shook their heads, wrote something down and then they gave me a shot and I was out. I woke up on an operating table at Phu By. The doctors gave me some more shots and I was out again.

I woke up in bed. I looked like a mummy. I was wrapped in bandages from my head to my foot. Next to me was my buddy Skip.

He was in the next bed. He was real bad, shot in the stomach. I don't know whether he made it or not. Right across the way was Sully. He was on his stomach 'cause he had been shot in the ass. Our outfit really took a beating in that battle.

They strapped me on a stretcher—put me on a plane back to Da Nang, where I stayed at an Air Force hospital for a couple of days. Then I was flown into Cam Rahn Bay. I thought I was home when I landed there. Giant concrete air strip all lit up. Paved streets. Sidewalks. Nurses walking on the plane. I said, I'm out of that shit, I'm home. I had just woken up and I thought I was in America. Then I saw a jeep pull up with a sixty machine gun mounted on it, and I said, Oh, no, I'm still here.

They rolled me out of the plane onto a bus and shipped me to the hospital. It was real close to Christmas.

I was in an Army hospital there and I was telling those soldiers that I've been in the bush. That they had it easy while the Marines were fighting the war.

I was lying there in the bed and those guys come into the hospital, waxing the floors, scrubbing walls, moving beds out so it don't look so crowded. I knew that morning something was coming through, but I didn't know what. They never did that before. They said, "The man is coming." I said, "Who?" and a guy says, "LBJ."

Then a thousand newsmen with cameras and lights all come in. Then come some officers and President Johnson with Marshal Ky, and Westmoreland was there too. Johnson stops and talks to the wounded. The press is writing it all down and taking a million pictures. Then he comes over to my bed. Some officer says to him, "Lance Corporal Whitmore, wounded in action," etc., etc.

The President walks over with a Hawaiian shirt with a million colors in it and brown slacks. He grabs my hand and he says, "How are you doing?" I'm practically dying, but I say, "Fine, sir, just fine." He looks at me and says, "This job that you've done for your country, we appreciate that." Then he introduces Ky, a tiny little mother-fucker. He shakes my hand too. Then Westmoreland is there too.

Johnson sees I'm all bandaged and there's no place to pin a medal on me. So he pins it on my pillow. He says he knows I'm anxious to get back and finish the job. Yeah, very fucking anxious.

81

Later they sent me to Japan. I had a long operation—they were taking shrapnel out every day. I couldn't walk. The doctor says to me, "You will never go back to Vietnam." I tried to learn to walk again. It took a long time. From a wheelchair to crutches. I was on physical therapy—everything. I knew I was never going back to Vietnam. I tried to walk, but it was damn hard. It was like being a baby all over again.

Finally I learned to walk, with a bad limp, but I could move.

The hospital was crowded. Jesus, it was so crowded. They tried to get people out of there as fast as they could, as soon as they could move. They told me I was up for a Bronze Star or Silver Star.

On my twenty-first birthday I got my orders back to Nam. That was on March 6.

I had been walking for only two weeks. I could barely walk. I had a bad limp. They needed guys there in Nam and there was no room in the hospital.

I knew I wasn't going back to that hot hell of a jungle with fucking bullets. Not after I had had a taste of civilized life in Japan.

The black scene of Vietnam hit me again.

I had a Japanese girl friend. She was real cool. I never gave deserting any thought. My girl friend was strongly anti-war. Most Japanese are. And she used to ask me, "Why are you fighting in Vietnam?" And, goddam it—after all I had been through—I couldn't fucking tell her. I didn't know. After getting all shot up—"Why are you fighting in Vietnam?" and I had no answer.

I didn't know.

I kept thinking about the bombs, the killing, the tank that took off and left me.

Soon after that I deserted.

Now I drive a fork lift for a furniture firm here in Stockholm. I got a great apartment. I'm O.K. The life here is fine.

Sometimes these peace people or left people they ask me, "Don't you regret what you did in Vietnam?" Look, man, I don't regret it that I had to knock off a few people because all them people I knocked off were trying to knock off me. I regret that I had to go to that mother-fucking country—but I don't regret killing them people, man. They were trying to kill me first. I was just a faster man —I beat him to the draw.

82

The way I feel about Vietnam—I don't give a fuck about North Vietnam or South Vietnam. Them mother-fuckers can fight forever. I don't care as long as they don't fuck with me, man.

▪ Joseph Arthur Doucette, Jr.

My name is Joseph Arthur Doucette, Jr. I was born in Philadelphia, Pennsylvania. In November of 1945 my family moved to New Hampshire and my father started a ski school, which he still owns and operates.

Q: When did you enter the Army?

A: July 17, 1961. I was then eighteen. I had graduated from high school and I quit college, the University of Wisconsin, in disgust. I expected an intellectual challenge—it was strictly mush. I put in one semester playing the game, but then I quit. I knew there was no way I could avoid the draft anyway, so I enlisted to just get it over with. I wasn't doing anything important then. I thought I might as well go in now instead of waiting around until I was doing something I really wanted to do and have it interrupted.

Q: Where did you go?

A: I took basic training at Fort Dix, New Jersey. Then I was trained for nine weeks as a cryptographer at Fort Gordon, Georgia. From there to Korea, the 51st Battalion. I stayed in Korea for three years and I enjoyed it very much. The country really fascinated me. I learned to speak Korean fluently. The culture was completely different from what I had been used to and it was really a challenge to me to try to get inside of it. The people in the company gave me a lot of static. They'd say, "You're just like a Korean. You ought to be in the ROK Army."

I had security clearance. I had to have it to go through crypto school. When I got to Korea they put me in for Top Secret clearance. They needed secret operators. I got that with no trouble. In January 1964 I was sent to Fort Lee, Virginia. I couldn't stand that. I had a lot of black friends there. I was in Detachment Five of the Strategic Communications Command. It was impossible to go off post with them for a social evening. I really don't care too much for the South.

My enlistment was over and I didn't feel like going out and looking for a job. I was a sergeant by then.

Q: You re-enlisted?

A: Yes. I was given a re-enlistment option and I chose to go back to Korea. Stayed there thirteen months. I was assigned to Fort Monroe, Virginia, but then the assignment was changed and I was put on a special assignment to Washington, D.C., to the Defense Intelligence Agency. I had to be reinvestigated. Top Secret clearance wasn't enough. I required certain intelligence clearance. Then I was assigned as a courier in DIA for six months. I finally went to Vietnam in July of '66. I stayed there for a year. I was the noncommissioned officer in charge of the First Infantry Division distribution authority. We performed the maintenance on all the cryptographic equipment in the division.

Q: Where were you stationed?

A: About ten miles by air northeast of Saigon at Dzi Anh Base Camp. It was division headquarters. One time we were coming back from Phu Loi and we picked up three Koreans and their prisoner. Their truck had broken down. The prisoner was a young girl and they really abused her very badly. One of them took an M-2 carbine, put it on automatic and took off the safety. Then he stuck it in her stomach and ordered her to take off her pants. He made her strip entirely and stand up at the edge of the truck, completely naked, as we drove through villages. He was screaming to the Vietnamese, "Here's your VC. They're all prostitutes." This was horrible, just sickening. But it was mild compared to many of the other occurrences.

Q: Such as?

A: They took prisoners up in helicopters.

Q: Who did?

A: The Americans. And interrogate them. If they didn't answer they pushed them out the door. That happened often. They would take three or four and start questioning the highest-ranking one. If he didn't answer he was thrown out. The infantry guards who participated told me that generally one of them would talk before they were all thrown out.

Q: Did you receive any training in interrogation techniques?

A: I arrived in Vietnam in the First Infantry Division in July of 1966, and August of 1966 I attended patrol-training. I was in a class for non-commissioned officers and we received a block of instruction covering approximately a day and a half of instructions in which we were taught techniques in interrogating prisoners. The class we were in received training in long-range reconnaissance patrols because we were almost all sergeants and would lead those patrols. They gave us training in methods of interrogating prisoners and what to do if the prisoner would not talk, how to make them talk, torture them, stick their heads in the water until they almost drowned and then pull them out, take their shoes off, tie their feet together and beat them over their soles with rifle barrels, stick bamboo slivers into their ears to puncture their eardrums, take a field telephone, the TP 3-12, and put the connecting wire to it, then take the other end of the wire and attach it to a person's testicles and crank it—this causes a high-voltage shock, there is no amperage behind it, just voltage, but it is extremely painful. We were told to use these methods to make people talk. And I remember a particular instance in the class, there was a very young corporal there. We never saw him again after that. He said, "What happens, what are you supposed to do if you cannot do this? I think this is sort of wrong." And the sergeant who was instructing the class said, "NCOs follow orders." In other words you do what you are told, and if you want a verification of this, I am sure that the training records are still available. . . . And there should be lesson plans for these things.

One of the purposes of long-range patrols is to capture prisoners. We were shown how to torture them in the field in case bringing them back might be too difficult. Torture them, get the information, then kill them, if it is too difficult to bring them back.

Q: Did you ever participate in a search-and-destroy mission?

A: In December of 1966 that First Infantry Division participated in Operation Cedar Falls, which was a large search-and-destroy operation involving three infantry divisions—the First, 25th and Ninth Infantry Divisions and two light-infantry brigades—the 196 and 199 Light Cavalry Brigades—11th Army Cavalry Regiment and the 173 Airborne Brigade. This was in the Iron Triangle. The first day of the operation, the First and Second Battalions, 28th Infantry, the First Infantry Division was air-assaulted on the village of Ben Suc on the Saigon River, which is on the base of the Iron Triangle. There was intelligence that Ben Suc was used by the NFL as a staging place for the raids on Tan Son Nhut—that had occurred in October and November of 1966. The village was sealed off in about five minutes, meaning that nobody could get in and get out of it, and the people in the village—there were no men there, it definitely wasn't, couldn't have been an enemy village. There were no military-aged men, able-bodied men, just old people, women and children. They were given fifteen minutes at gun point to collect whatever of their belongings they could carry with them by hand. They were loaded on an LCU [utility landing craft] on the Saigon River and taken downstream to Phan Quang; from Phan Quang they were transported by truck to the vicinity of Phan Voi and put into what was termed as a resettlement camp. I saw that resettlement camp, and it looked to me very similar to a Nazi concentration camp. Double barbed-wire fences, machine-gun towers. You could not get in or get out. These people were existing on, they were given just enough rice to keep alive; they were given Army blankets that the American Army was getting ready to destroy because they were worn out; they were living in tents that were damaged, almost useless, and there were American Military Police guarding this concentration camp initially, and then the South Vietnamese Army took over. And they started shooting without warning anybody that was within a certain area of the fence. These people under the terms of the Geneva Convention were non-combatants; there were no arms on them, they were carrying no sort of weapons, they were wearing no uniforms, and the village itself was burned. What was left after the burning was dynamited, it was plowed into the ground, and the ground was salted. I went to Ben Suc about a week after this had happened in a convoy, and there was nothing there except bare burned earth. That was what was left of Ben Suc, and it had been done by the Americans. I never saw the Vietcong do anything like that.

Q: Did you favor our participation in the war before you arrived in Vietnam?

A: Yes. I went there thinking that basically the American presence was correct. When I left there I knew that we didn't belong there. I saw our brutality and lack of concern for the people. Some unthinking, callous people might say that there are excesses in all wars. That may be true, but our presence there is for the purpose of defeating, not defending, democracy.

Q: What makes you reach that conclusion?

A: I was in Vietnam when they held the elections for President and membership in the National Assembly. The American observers sent over said it was a fair election. I was in the village of Dzi Anh on the day of the elections. I had to go out on an assignment and I had to go through all kinds of red tape to get off the base camp. The military didn't want us to see the democratic elections, I presume. But I went by the polling booth of Dzi Anh. They had Saigon troops there. They were stationed so that they could see how each person voted. How can you vote democratically when someone with a weapon is looking over your shoulder, and he can see who you're voting for? There were no neutralist candidates allowed. The one who came closest to being one was thrown in jail by Saigon. How many Americans have died, and how many more Vietnamese, mostly innocent civilians, so that that fraudulent election could take place? And how many more will have to?

▪ Ed Treratola* (*continued*)

Q: When did you ship out to Vietnam?

A: In February of '68.

Q: Where did you land?

A: First I landed in Japan and we stayed there for twenty-four hours for a briefing on what to expect when we got there. The way they explained it, it was like all hell was going to break loose. When we got off at Da Nang it was, you know, hamburger stands and Vietnamese women in miniskirts. It looked like a regular base in the States. Then they took us to a plane and they shipped me out to a place called Phu Bai. Then they gave me my helmet and my gun and fatigues and boots and they stuck us on a plane, a C-143, and told us we were going to a place called Khe Sanh. Well, we didn't know what it was and we got on the plane and we were circling around and we heard loud noises like thunder. The back of the tail section of the plane got three big holes in it. And they told us to sit still because we were going to have an emergency landing, and we went in and we got shelled by the VC because they had the airport surrounded, and they stuck me on a machine gun and the rest of the guys—I wasn't in too much contact with them—we all got split up all over the area.

Q: How long were you in Khe Sanh?

A: From the beginning of the siege to the end.

Q: Which was how long?

A: Three months—till April 10th, I think the last day of the siege was.

Q: What were the casualties at Khe Sanh?

A: Oh, we never heard any figures, but we were always short of men, and like the grave, the place where they kept the bodies was always filled and it got so bad up there that the bodies started rotting because they didn't have time to bury them all.

Q: How did you leave Khe Sanh?

A: The first time I left Khe Sanh was during the middle of the siege. I lost my eyeglasses and I took a plane back down to Phu Bai, to the rear. It was a Huey, a copter, with some bodies on it. And as we were flying down to Phu Bai we were going across like a rice field, and there was a little old farmer down there with his water buffalo, and they were going through the fields, and the pilot was drinking beer at the time, and the one gunner was near the one exit and the other gunner was on the other exit, and they said, "Well, we better go down and have some fun," and they buzzed over him low and scared the shit out of the water buffalo. And then they went down and shot the water buffalo. The old guy got mad and then we went down again and dropped a five-gallon tin of water on the old man. Killed him, I guess. It was just—just for fun.

And then I got down to Phu Bai and I had to go down at Da Nang, so I had to check my gun, and I got down to Da Nang and I went down, the first thing I did was to go to the black-market section in town, and we went down there and the little kids were coming up to us and asking us for money, and I said, "Diddi mow," get out of here. So he says, "Come on, Marine, boom-boom, we go to the skimmy house." So I looked at the MPs up the road, and they gave me the high sign that I could go in and I went in with the buddy and he had his forty-five on and he was really scared because down at Da Nang he'd heard all these things about guys getting stabbed in their back when they were in bed and everything. And he went with this one chick and I went with the other chick, and all of a sudden we heard all sorts of screams, and he pistol-whipped her with the gun because he couldn't shoot her, because I'd taken the ammunition.

Q: Why did he hit her?

A: Because after he was through he didn't want to pay. He said she charged him too much, and the little kids were running through and they were going through his pants pockets trying to take his money. So he beered up, and then they went to complain to the MP and the MPs just looked at the girl and they watched the guy walk away, and they said, "Sorry, we don't understand."

Q: Was she hurt badly?

A: She was . . . ah, yes, pretty bad, because she was bleeding all over the place, her face was a mass of blood, so I guess he must have smacked her pretty good. We laughed about that for the rest of the . . . most of the way. It was like a big joke. Finally, I went down and got my glasses. I came back to Phu Bai again, and right at the same time they had the siege at Khe Sanh, that was where Hue city was going on, and over there it was a fairly modern city, and it was the capital of Vietnam, and some of the guys from One-five were drinking in the pub in Phu Bai, and like these guys had on watches, you know, all the way up their arm. And they had stacks of piastres, and like we asked them "What's going on?" He says, "Oh, wow, we are having a blast down in Hue." He says, "The gooks in there and it's a big city, there are some Americans in there." He says, "We are just blowing the place apart and looting the shit out of it." And so we wanted to go down there, so we were going to steal the jeep to go over to Hue, but they had the premises blocked off, so we couldn't get out. All these guys were coming back, and they had all these diamond rings on and the guys were driving around on the streets—they had motorcycle stores, and just wrecking the motorcycles, and they weren't even looking for the gooks or anything, and then they—there were mostly civilians and things in the town, and they killed all the men and they said they were Vietcong, and they just—they went through every building and they killed everything. And looted everything they could carry, especially jewelry.

Q: In Hue?

A: Yeah.

Q: When was that? You remember the month?

A: Yeah, it was in . . . about May of '68, and they made it up to be that they were all Vietcong in the infiltrated Hue city, but the Marines just got the order to go in there and destroy everything. And one particular buddy of mine, Lance Corporal Howard Key. He comes from Long Island too. Freeport, Long Island. We went through boot camp together and we met over there. And his life was saved by a Vietcong. He was wounded, and they put him inside and a girl patched him up, a North Vietnamese medic, and when they, the girl was going out, Key's two friends called her and killed her.

Q: The girl who helped him?

A: Yeah. This all happened in Hue. They blew her head off with a forty-five. She had just saved his life.

Q: And he told you that story?

A: Yeah.

Q: Why did they kill the girl?

A: Because she was a gook.

Q: How did they kill her, do you know?

A: Shot her, and . . .

Q: These were soldiers who had lots of watches on their arm?

A: Yeah. These were all Marines, because it was a pretty big thing, Hue city, because it was a rich city, and a lot of Americans lived there, and there was a couple of payroll officers in there and everything. It was a pretty modern city. And they went in there, and they killed everything, and then they took the artillery, and they blew up a place called the Citadel, which was a Catholic church, and it was

90

a beautiful place. It was a fantastic city, and I saw pictures of it before it was blown up. And then they called in the B-52s—this was right at the end of the siege of Khe Sanh, after they already got all the Vietcong out of there—and they just B-52'd the whole city, and then they just leveled it to the ground, and there is no more Hue. And this was after the village was all secured.

Q: Did you ever go through any villages?

A: After Khe Sanh, we went up to the Quang Tri area, and we used to throw crates of C-rations at the old ladies on the street. Knocked them down. Probably killed some of them. And we'd just say—if we were questioned, but we never were—that we were just distributing food. And then to the young children we had these blue tablets, and you heat C-rations with them, and they look like candy, but when you light them on fire, there is no fire, it's just a really tremendous heat, and we used to light them and throw them out to the little kids, and then when they pick them up in their hands it just burns right through their hands.

Q: Did a lot of guys do that?

A: Yeah, we all did it, because when we got back from Khe Sanh so many of our friends were killed, and it was just—I couldn't take Vietnamese people any more. It was like I was going out of my way to be nasty. 'Cause if I saw an old man or an old lady in the street on the way I checked them, or hit them with my rifle, or tell them to keep moving, or ask them for their papers, and just as often, if they didn't have their papers, we shoot them.

Q: Did you see that?

A: We did that ourselves.

Q: How many did your squad execute just because they didn't have their papers?

A: It was in Quang Tri, it was an insecure area, and just ourselves, and one day we got four or five people. And we used to go on like shore patrols through the dunes, because it is mostly beasts and things up there. And we'd see the peasants, they'd be walking with their water buffaloes. If they didn't have the papers, we had the right to . . . oh, not really the right, but we could have said they were running, in a way, because they couldn't say anything. And we had so much hate from Khe Sanh that nothing mattered to us any more, and since we didn't really get the chance to have any hand-to-hand combat with the Vietnamese up there, it was mostly hide and seek and no real contact, it's like we were really itching for blood—and it was ridiculous because . . . I don't know . . .

Q: You said you threw C-rations at the people. What does that mean? That's a can, of course?

A: No. We threw the whole case.

Q: The whole case?

A: Yeah.

Q: From the truck?

A: Yeah.

Q: And it would hit somebody and knock them down?

A: Yeah. And, well, I imagine that they were old enough, that we could kill them, but we'd be zipping through the village about thirty or forty miles per hour, and we never stopped to look back, but they'd just be splattered on the road and we'd sit around laughing, because we were allowed to throw C-rations off to the Vietnamese people, because we were there to pacify them, to help them in the village.

Q: Did your officers know about this conduct?

A: Oh, all the officers knew it was going on. In fact, Lieutenant Foster, he told us, he said, "There is no sense in even taking a prisoner. It's ridiculous, because we don't need them and Marines don't take prisoners."

Q: He was in your outfit?

A: He was my lieutenant.

Q: Your platoon leader?

A: Yeah, the platoon leader, that's right. And he got his orders from Colonel Elmer Rogers. Colonel Rogers used to come around and he used to talk with us and he never said *so* much, but he like never said anything when the officers were speaking, he'd just sort of sit back and nod his head.

Q: He was there when Foster said to take no prisoners?

A: Yeah. Every time before we went out on a patrol, Colonel Rogers used to come with the gungy sergeant, and both of them used to come and before we went out past the perimeter he used to shake our hands and they'd tell us, if they wanted a prisoner, you know, bring one or two, but if they're going to slow you down, kill them.

Q: Who said that?

A: The lieutenant. My own job when I was over there was either if we saw the enemy we would make contact with them and destroy them, and if we had any trouble in the villages, any sniper fire, any hostility from the villagers, we were to take them up and line them on one side of the village, all the people, take out all the young men and bring them in for interrogation and they'd never come back home again.

Q: Did you actually do that?

A: We did that in Quang Tri, nine miles south of Quang Tri. There's a place called Hoa Na Beach, and it used to be controlled by the 101st Airborne, and our battalion went down there to take it over from them, because they were getting so much trouble down there. They were getting so many casualties, and we were told that if we had any trouble there we were just to take all the young men in the village and not to arrest them or anything or kill them, just take them and have them send to Da Nang for interrogation.

Q: Was that done?

A: Yeah. We did that to two villages, and then most of the other villages smartened up, except when we started doing that they wouldn't give us any more sniper fire, they put booby traps up for us, so what we'd do was we'd get an old lady and we'd make her walk in the path in front of us in the jungle, and we told her, we said, "You're going to walk the way *we* tell you, and if there are any booby traps, you better tell us now because if you don't we're going to kill you." And the woman usually—this happened one time —it was that she walked up, and then she'd stop, and she wouldn't go any further. So we had an ARVN, he was a lieutenant, he was the interpreter, and he was up with Lieutenant Foster, and he said, you know, "Go," and she wouldn't move, so, you know, we knew the booby trap was there, so we just said, "Go," you know, "or we shoot," and she finally led us right to the booby trap after about five or ten minutes. And then we let her go back to the village, and then there was the word out that we were to go in by cover of night and kill her.

Q: Kill her?

A: Yeah.

Q: Is that what happened?

A: Yeah.

Q: Who did that?

A: It was four volunteers. Lance Corporal Pitcairn and his fire team.

Q: Why wasn't she killed then?

A: Because it would have been like an embarrassment, because we had to be careful in Quang Tri, because we had so much brass and Army generals watching us, so we had to do things sneaky. And the lieutenant wouldn't mind and—because the Marine Corps and the Army don't get along because their ways are so different. And so we had to be devious.

Q: Who sent the team in? Who asked for volunteers?

A: A Corporal Clam. And he told Corporal McMillan—Corporal McMillan was in charge of twelve men. He took Lance Corporal Pitcairn's fire team, because he was a really gone old guy who wanted a promotion, and he volunteered for a lot of things. I don't know how they did it, because there was a complaint that she was found dead, and we blamed it on VC, Vietcong. We marked it off as a Vietcong casualty.

Q: Were you present when any villages were burned down?

A: Most of the things I saw were brutality aimed at individuals, but we never got the opportunity to burn down a village.

Q: You heard about it?

A: Yeah. Well, there is always talk about villages burning down, because things like that happen every day in Vietnam, it's been happening since '66. You hear about it in boot camp, and that was like everybody wanted to at least burn down a hootch where the Vietnamese lived.

Q: Did you ever see any prisoners questioned?

A: No. I never saw any prisoners questioned. I have seen them being transported to Da Nang. No, we didn't have time to question them.

Q: Have you ever seen any prisoners killed?

A: Yeah, that happens all the time. It's—we don't have time to take any wounded, and we can't call in helicopters because they endanger the pilot's life, so they kill them.

Q: Have you seen that often?

A: Yeah. That happened whenever there was a fire fight and there was any wounded Vietcong.

Q: What would happen?

A: If there wasn't an officer, they were killed immediately on the spot.

Q: And you saw this?

A: Yeah.

Q: How was it done?

A: M-16. You take an M-16 and you go around and, you know, look for them, look at the wounded, and you shoot them, and then after a while it used to be, you know, just to get like a game, so we'd shoot them all up with M-16 and then we'd pile the bodies up in a pile and we'd take a law which is portable.

Q: It's like a bazooka?

A: Bazooka, right. And open it up and—pooh!

Q: Fire at the bodies?

A: At the bodies, yeah. They'd mostly they'd—pooh, you know. One or two would disintegrate and go all over the place.

Q: How many wounded would you say you saw killed?

A: I couldn't say exactly because it was, like, you just went along. I think it may be about . . . I guess in the fifties, sixties, maybe. But anything that was lying on the ground we shot.

Q: Did you ever see mistreatment of women?

A: Once in a while if we were out on a long patrol, and we hadn't seen a girl for a long time, maybe four or five of us would go into a village and take a girl and bring her out to the jungle.

Q: Have you seen that?

A: Oh yeah. Often.

Q: What happened?

A: Well, we take the girl, and we usually just placed a hand over her mouth, and two guys drive away and bring her to the bush and hold a rifle to her head and explain to her to lie on the ground and don't scream, otherwise she'll be killed immediately, and however many guys there are—well, they all do what they want. And if the guys are in a good mood they let the girl go. If not, they kill her. It depends on how they feel, or what happened on the patrol that day. If somebody's buddy got killed, he usually kills the girl. Sort of like sanctions.

95

Q: Was that a regular thing or occurrence?

A: Ah, that was like when we were out in the bush for a long period of time, and like we just got the opportunity to go into a village, because we didn't see women that often. It used to happen all the time, because whenever anybody wanted a woman, all they had to do was go and take her. It was just as simple as that. Because you had a rifle and nobody in Vietnam argues. They are just passive.

Q: That was a regular practice?

A: Yeah. Whenever the guys felt like going, sometimes every night. And the villagers complained enough. Sometimes the brass would say, "Well, look, cool it for a little while," you know, "at least let it happen with little more time in between." But we were never discouraged.

Q: Nobody said you can't do it?

A: No.

Q: And no one was afraid of being tried or punished for rape?

A: No. We were just told, "Take it easy. If you want to do something, at least be a little more tactful." Once they gang-raped a French nurse.

Q: Who did? Where and when was that?

A: In Khe Sanh, and that was during the middle of the siege, toward the end. And, well, there were rumors going around about her. In Bravo they just went out on a patrol the day before, and they made contact with the enemy. And it was . . . thirty men were out, and twenty-eight of them got the Bronze Star that day, and the captain got the Silver Star.

Q: What did they do?

A: They ran into the North Vietnamese Army dug in just outside of Khe Sanh, and they fought them hand to hand, and they were fortunate enough to capture a nurse, and she wasn't Vietnamese, she was French. She was bandaging the gooks. They brought her back . . .

Q: To Khe Sanh?

A: Yeah. And the officers had her, you know. They raped her and then they gave her to the sergeants and the sergeants raped her, and then to all the other men and they had theirs, and then

96

they just disposed of her because they didn't need her any more.

Q: How did they kill her, do you know?

A: Yeah. They blew her head off. It was with a forty-five.

Q: You saw her body later?

A: Yeah. We used to go up just after we got through securing our area—we lived in trenches—and we'd go up to right near the air strip and look at the bodies that were brought in that day from the field.

Q: Then she was there?

A: Yeah, they had them . . . there were so many bodies that they had them lying out in long lines like that, on top of each other.

Q: Did you take any pictures of them?

A: Oh, I took pictures.

Q: You don't have them with you?

A: All my pictures were censored, and all the pictures at Khe Sanh were censored and anything of a dead body was censored.

Q: Could you have sent them back to the States?

A: No. Because you had to have your film developed by the military. And then they'd just screen the pictures which they didn't like, and the only way you can get it done was by smuggling it out to the States. But a lot of guys used to bring the cameras with them out in the field and like during the fire fights snap pictures and then take pictures of the bodies. But it was forbidden. And you don't see those pictures.

Q: Were any pictures taken of the interrogation of prisoners, or shooting at prisoners?

A: Whenever the Marines go out they have a special scout. And these guys were the ones that took care of that, and like they take pictures of the terrain and things like that sometimes they take pictures of prisoners, but we never watched them getting interrogated 'cause we were just out in the field. Everything I saw was mostly like, you know, cruelty. One person doing something to another. I never saw mass murders although I heard of them. And I never saw a village being burnt down, just heard of those, and the only village that we did burn down was outside of Khe Sanh, and that was a Montagnard village and they weren't near there, because the rumor had it that the North Vietnamese Army came and killed all the

97

people. But the truth of it was that the American B-52s hit the area, and like the only thing that was standing of these huts was like twigs and then big huge craters.

Q: How long were you in Vietnam?

A: Almost six months.

Q: And you were wounded?

A: Yeah.

Q: How did you get wounded?

A: I was out on a patrol at Khe Sanh, and I got hit in the eye with a piece of shrapnel, so I—I just got my Purple Heart and I said, the hell with it. And then when things started really getting bad, they were going to send us afloat and then we'd have had to hit all the different beachheads in Vietnam. I went and I said to my first sergeant, I said, "Remember the wound I got in my eye?" and he says, "Yeah." I said, "I can't see." So they brought me to the doctor and I told him, I said, "Look, man, I want to get out of here. Can you send me down to Da Nang?" He sent me to Da Nang and I went to an eye doctor down there, and he looked at me and he says, "Well, there is nothing wrong." I said, "Well, I am going to write a letter to my Congressman," and he says, "Well, wait a minute." And then he sent me to Camp Craig, an Army hospital in Japan, and I stayed in an eye ward and I was there for about a month, and I just looked at all the guys in there, and I realized how lucky I was that I bluffed my way out of Vietnam.

Q: Was the hospital crowded?

A: The hospital was the most sickening thing. It was worse than Vietnam. I had a fellow next to me and he used to cry every night to go home to his wife. They had shaved his head, and he had stitches going all through his head, and his whole head was like swollen up, and they did a brain operation on him, and he was blind in both eyes. And they were supposed to send him back to the States, but because he used to cry and refused to eat his food, you know, he used to call for his wife and his kid, they made him stay there longer. And then on a bed across we had another guy with his face removed from below the eyes, his whole nose and his whole jaw, just taken off, and it was like just raw flesh with a gaping tongue hanging out, with a respirator in his throat so he could breathe. And I saw people with no legs and no arms, and just like vegetables, and the nurses, they didn't give a damn—I mean they wouldn't give anybody any attention because it was too sickening because you couldn't look at a guy without almost throwing up. I had to get moved, because the people in there were so sickening and it stank and everything.

Q: Was it crowded?

A: Well, it was packed, it was, over capacity, because they were sending Marines there. And they couldn't get these guys to go out fast enough to the States, because the American hospitals were crowded. And so most of the guys were being held up there and they just wanted to go home. But they wouldn't let you. Anyway, I deserted.

Q: Why did you desert?

A: It was after my first day in Vietnam that I realized that the war wasn't what I was told it was, because the people . . . We were told that we were going to help the people and defend them and protect them from communism and people trying to take away their land, and that the people really liked us, and that they looked up to us because we were, you know, we were like their—saviors. And when we got there, the people sort of, you know, they looked at us funny, and the old women would sort of like keep away, walk away, and the children would run away when we came, and the only time they'd come in contact with us was to sell us something. And then after the longer you stayed there, the more you got to hate them, and the more you got to hate them, the more you'd take advantage of them, and you just start beating up people for no reason, and, say, you'd go through a village and you would shoot a couple of shots, you know, in somebody's living quarters, and like nobody cared. And you became sicker and sicker every day.

I had a friend that had a pet skull. He chopped the head off, and he used to keep it in his tent. He put a hat on it and he used to put on puppet shows for the people at night. There was one village we went through. There was a dead body there, and it was an old lady curled up like with her knees up against her chest like this, and she was just like stiff. And, well, we were going to play a joke on a sergeant, so my friend takes a canteen, and he started to throw water in her face, you know, and the sergeant says, "What are you doing, what are you doing with that woman?" So my friend he took his pistol and he just phew-phew-phew-phew-phew—right into her face. Blew her head off. And he was just playing, joking.

Q: Yes, I see. How does it all seem to you now?

A: I used to get upset about talking about it. It wasn't so bad in . . . I don't know, I get . . . It was sickening when I . . . think about it, it was sickening, but that didn't bother so much as the hospital bothered me. That was the only thing that really definitely made me change my mind about the war, because of the treatment that people had in the hospital. They went over there, and they lost part of their body for their country and they weren't even given proper treatment, and they weren't even given medicine, they weren't even given pain killers. The nurses would sit and drink coffee, and it was so bad that I had to go over and give guys drinks of water in the middle of the night and things like that, because the nurses wouldn't get up. And I was like I shouldn't have been there in the first place, so I was O.K. because, really, I was fooling, but it got sickening and I got so many nightmares and I kept seeing all these guys and just . . . I couldn't go back there, not for that. That was, I think, the thing that really made me just pack up and get out.

Q: What does your family feel about you being in Sweden?

A: My father never wanted me to go to Vietnam in the first place, and he didn't want me to go in the Marine Corps, because he was in Germany during World War II and he was a sergeant, Battle of the Bulge in the Rhine, and he told me, "I just hope you'll never get into combat because it's a horrible thing." That's all he would ever say to me, and I never thought much of my father. I said, he must be really stupid. And then when I finally called him and when I was safe he'd learned that I was in Sweden, he started to cry and he said, "Thank God that you're alive, and you did the right thing."

Q: Your mother feels the same way?

A: Yeah, my mother isn't an American, she just became American. She was English and so she has no great love for the country.

Q: Do you have any brothers or sisters?

A: Yeah, one brother, and he's seven years younger than I am, and he is suffering now for what I did.

Q: In what way?

A: He's persecuted because his brother is a deserter.

Q: How old is he?

A: He's fourteen, he's just in high school, and he had most of the same teachers that I had, and like people give him a rough time because my town was never much involved in the peace movement, such a small place. Like the kids they make fun of him and tease him.

Q: What's his feeling about you being here?

A: He doesn't—he has no political—he's too young. He just wants me to come home so he can see me again.

Q: Ed, you saw a great deal of brutality in Vietnam. You participated in a considerable amount of it yourself. What was it about the hospital scene in Japan that turned you off the war or, to put it more precisely, why didn't the brutality in Vietnam turn you against the war?

A: I don't know. Maybe I didn't have much of a chance to think there. But when I saw those guys in the hospital, it was terrible.

Q: You saw mangled Vietnamese bodies regularly.

A: Yes, but it was different. In Japan—I mean, these were Americans.

▪ Robert Moragne

Q: Your name is?

A: Robert Moragne.

Q: Where are you from?

A: Baker, Oregon, a small town in the eastern portion of the state.

Q: Did you enlist in the Navy?

A: Yes, I did.

Q: What was your education before enlisting?

A: I had graduated from college. I learned I was going to be drafted into the Army, so I joined the Navy. I went to Naval Officers' Candidate School. First I took my basic training in San Diego. I didn't have any orders at that time for OCS. I went for basic training for ten or eleven weeks.

Q: When did you enlist?

A: In September of 1967. I started basic at the end of that month. I remained at San Diego for about three months, on what is called a commission hold. I was doing mainly clerical work. Then I did receive orders of OCS. And I attended OCS at the school at Newport, Long Island, beginning at March 1968 for sixteen weeks. I graduated from that school as an ensign.

Q: Did you have any feeling about the war when you enlisted in the Navy?

A: No, I wasn't actually against the war. From the beginning I didn't think that the U. S. should have been involved in the war, but I never took part in any protest against the war.

Q: What college did you attend?

A: Oregon State.

Q: Was there a movement there against the war?

A: Actually, it is a very conservative school. And at the time I was going there, there wasn't any organization whatsoever against the war. Perhaps just a few small peace marches.

Q: What happened when you finished OCS?

A: I was sent to Amphibious Warfare Training School. Then I took a ship-handling rules-of-the-road course to become more familiar with international regulations and the maneuvering of ships. And from there, after some leave, I was sent to Japan. I was assigned to a ship in Japan, which was a tank landing ship which deployed regularly from Japan to Vietnam.

Q: How long were you in the waters of Vietnam?

A: For five months on two occasions. From the latter part of October 1968 to part of December 1968. And then again in January and February and part of March 1969.

Q: What were your duties in Vietnam?

A: The duties of the ship were primarily logistic. We supported two basic types of operations. One was a marked type operation— we supported swift boats and helicopters. We controlled the coast of Vietnam. The other was to support mobile marine forces. We went into the Mekong Delta through the river system. Here we were supporting the Navy and Army troops. We acted as a home base. We regularly fired at the shore, usually during the nighttime. Just as a matter of course. To make sure that there wasn't anything surviving.

Q: What did you fire at?

A: Just at coordinates. Didn't know what was there.

Q: Could have been a village?

A: Perhaps. We fired three-inch fifty-standard ammunition. They are explosive projectiles. They are three inches in diameter. I should like to add at this point that I will hesitate to discuss certain details about the military. I do not want to do anything treasonous. I am not out to help the other side. So I will just as soon steer clear of detailed discussions of military operations. I will say that regularly whole areas were bombed and shelled without concern for human lives, without concern for human welfare. Entire areas were delineated as Vietcong areas. But the local people in the area were mostly farmers or fishermen. Many were politically unaware. They were primarily trying to make their own livelihood. Many of them were killed because they were at the wrong place at the wrong time. We had prisoners regularly on board for interrogations with an army interpreter on board. We had entire family units with women and small children.

Q: Do you know why they were picked up?

A: No, I don't. It was an Army-Navy joint operation. The Army would pick them up and bring them on board. The Army might go to a village and pick up whoever was there and send them back to a camp or prison.

Q: When did you leave the service?

A: In April 1969.

Q: Where were you then?

A: In Japan, our home port. We'd go there regularly for maintenance.

Q: What was the name of your ship?

A: The *Washtenaw*. It was a tank landing ship.

Q: Did tanks actually land from it?

A: No, this is the primary design function of the ship. It is a shallow-bottom type craft which can approach the beach and land tanks directly on the shore. But we didn't carry tanks. Instead we generally had the tank deck filled with ammunition and mines.

Q: Why did you desert?

A: It was the result of a decision that I made over a period of time when I was in Vietnam. When you are there you can see the contrast. The U. S. is the foreign element in Vietnam. The people taken as prisoners, the people routinely destroyed were part of the land. They were people involved in self-determination. And we were interfering in that. I'm not a Communist or even left of center, but I could not sanction our trying to force our own ideology upon these people. It was for the people to decide for themselves how they wanted to live and what type of government they want. In addition to the reasons which were made due to Vietnam I have another reason, and that is the military environment itself. Which I did not enjoy at all. Even though I was in the position of an officer, I did not have the freedom to express opinions and ideas which I had myself. All opinions to be expressed must be official. Even though I did not have a bad position myself. People on the ship were routinely punished by a primitive naval punitive system, which is not representative at all of due process. The punishment might be captain's mast—three days on bread and water.

Q: That's an ancient concept, isn't it?

A: Yes, sort of rooted on the authority of the Navy. Because basic constitutional rights are removed when you are in the military, such as freedom of speech, freedom of expression, adequate representation at trials and so forth. I believe that the whole military court-martial system is not conducive to basic human civil rights.

Q: I imagine that an officer who is about to desert is in a different position from an enlisted man who is about to desert.

A: Yes, that is true. An officer who deserts is a lonely man. You can't talk to other officers about it, and you can't talk to enlisted men about it. Therefore you can't get into contact with an underground organization which helps other deserters and war resisters. It is very difficult to know whom you can trust, and you find that you are isolated. You have to try to give the appearance of impeccable conduct until you finally leave.

▪ Harry Plimpton*

Q: What is your name?

A: Used to be Sergeant Harry Plimpton.

Q: How long were you in the Army?

A: Eleven years.

Q: How long were you in Vietnam?

A: Nine months and twelve days.

Q: What was your rank there?

A: Sergeant—E-5.

Q: What was your assignment?

A: Squad leader in a Ranger battalion. I was sent on a lot of seek-and-destroy missions. We actually went out and found them—and destroyed them.

Q: How long have you been in France?

A: Almost three weeks.

Q: Could you describe a seek-and-destroy mission that you were on?

A: Well, going through a village one day—this time I had a seven-man squad—coming to this village, the squad in front of me got hit. Three men were killed. Approximately three weapons were used—I believe one was an automatic weapon. We backed off, carrying our dead with us and our wounded, got back approximately two hundred or three hundred yards away from the village, and our company commander—a captain—had our mortar platoon set up and told them to level the village—"blow it off the map."

Q: Did they?

A: They blew it all to pieces. We went through afterwards and you could find pieces of arms lying here, pieces of bodies, crater holes, the village itself was on fire—straw huts on fire. The ones that weren't being burned we burned ourselves.

Q: How many people had lived in the village?

A: I would say approximately five hundred people.

Q: How many survivors?

105

A: We found no survivors. We found pieces of bodies. Napalm had burned some of them up so bad you couldn't tell if they were men or women.

Q: What was used against the village?

A: Napalm, white phosphorous A.G., smoke, flares, small arms, machine-gun fire. Everything that we could throw.

Q: Had you ever seen any other village leveled in a similar fashion?

A: Yes.

Q: On more than one occasion?

A: Yes. If we'd come to a village and think that they were Vietcong sympathizers or maybe hiding Vietcong there we'd pass the word "burn it." And we'd burn the village down.

Q: Who made the decision to burn the village?

A: The highest-ranking man made the decision. I personally had to make one decision myself.

Q: What was your decision?

A: Burn it. We burned everything they owned. Livestock and rice crops. Everything. All the houses too, of course.

Q: Do you know anything about the military treatment of prisoners?

A: Military treatment of prisoners—well, sometimes you're given word "no prisoners." In other words if you find a man lying and you think he'll die from wounds he's got, you leave him. If he won't die from the wounds he's got—by the time you walk off he should be dead.

Q: What does that mean?

A: You shot him.

Q: Did you ever shoot a man under such circumstances?

A: Yes, I did. I had to shoot a man with a 357 Magnum pistol once.

Q: He was wounded and out of action?

A: Yes, he was wounded. He was gut-shot.

Q: Did you see other soldiers participating in the execution of the wounded?

A: Yes, I did.

Q: On how many occasions?

A: You could see this practically every operation.

Q: Did orders come down during operations of take no prisoners?

A: Yes, they did.

Q: Who did they come from?

A: Mine came from my platoon leader. I, in turn, had to give them to my men.

Q: Where did the platoon leader get his orders from?

A: The company commander, who got his from the battalion commander and on up.

Q: Did you ever see prisoners interrogated?

A: Yes, I did.

Q: How did that work?

A: We took five up in a helicopter once, started talking to one, he wouldn't talk, we threw him out of the helicopter.

Q: What was your rank at the time?

A: I was sergeant E-5. I was one of the prisoner guards at the time.

Q: Who made the decision to throw the man out of the helicopter?

A: The S-2 officer. A lieutenant.

Q: Was just one thrown out?

A: No, there was not. We had five prisoners. Four were thrown out of the helicopter.

Q: What happened to the fifth man?

A: The fifth one talked. Then he was sent to a POW compound.

Q: How high was the helicopter when the men were thrown out?

A: Approximately three thousand feet.

Q: Were these five men soldiers?

A: They were Vietcongs.

Q: Were they soldiers?

A: They were partisans.

Q: Did you ever witness any other mistreatment of prisoners?

A: A young girl was tortured by the Vietnamese Rangers. She was tortured very slowly. It took her approximately three days to die.

Q: How was she tortured?

A: They took her clothes off. Then they stuck hooks into her legs near the back of her ankles. They spread her apart, hanging

107

her up in a tree like a pig you're going to butcher. They hung her by these hooks spread open that way. Then they took a piece of bamboo about three feet long and about as thick as your wrist and rammed it down into her—into her vagina. Then they put splinters of bamboo through her breasts and into all the soft spots of the body. Under the armpits, into the stomach. It took her three days to die.

Q: Did you witness this?

A: The Americans were ordered to turn their backs. We were told not to look so that we could say we did not see it. But we actually saw the woman and what was being done to her. But when we walked right past her we were told to turn our heads to the other side.

Q: Did you see any other prisoners interrogated?

A: Yes, saw a man interrogated once. He was beaten very severely.

Q: By whom?

A: American forces. U.S. forces.

Q: What was he beaten with?

A: Fists, rifles.

Q: What happened to him?

A: They took him to a hospital. He died on us. Then there was one case where we captured one that was shot up very badly. He was shot with an M-16 rifle. Through the left knee and the right ankle. It looked like he would lose his right foot and his left leg. He was bleeding very badly. I was sitting beside this man. Sergeant Matthews—he could speak very good Vietnamese—he told the man that if he talked, give us the information, we would save his life. If not, he would cut his throat. The man talked. After he told us the information we wanted we gave him plasma, gave him morphine, carried him for approximately six or seven thousand meters to a clearing. Put him on a helicopter, sent him back to a hospital. What happened to him after that I do not know.

Q: Why did you leave Vietnam?

A: I was wounded in the knee, thigh and hip.

Q: Were you given any citations?

A: Purple Heart, Army Commendation Medal and the Vietnamese medals.

Q: Where were you when you were wounded?

A: In the Iron Triangle.

Q: How old are you now?

A: Twenty-eight.

Q: And you have been in the Army since you were seventeen?

A: Yes.

Q: Where are you from in the States?

A: Texas. Central part of the state.

Q: Do you come from a religious family?

A: My mother is very religious. I'm religious too but not as much as my mother.

Q: You're a Baptist?

A: Right.

Q: How do you reconcile your religious beliefs with your conduct in Vietnam?

A: I believe I will have to answer for what I've done. Especially certain things.

Q: What things?

A: I killed a young girl there. I know, for one thing, of a village where I called napalm on. I believe that I may have to answer for these on the day I die. Did you ever see what napalm does? Even if it doesn't kill you you're disfigured for life. A piece of napalm hits you in the chin it's liable to burn your whole chin off. White phosphorous hits you, you can't put it out.

You see some of your best friends, young men, they shouldn't even be in the Army some of them. You see them die. Young men. You get angry, crazy angry. Later you go into a village, you see an old man with crutches, home-made type crutches, he can't even hardly move and he sees us come into the village and yet he tried to run from us. Children screaming, running from us. They were terrified of us. It makes you very sick. You sit down and say, "What have I done?"

▪ Michael Schneider

Q: What is your name?

A: I was born Dieter von Kronenberger. That is what it says on my birth certificate.

Q: And your present name?

A: Well, legally changed to Schneider by my father, to Michael Raymond Schneider.

Q: When did you enter the Army?

A: I came in the Army early 1965, May.

Q: You enlisted?

A: I enlisted fifteenth of May 1965.

Q: What had you been doing until then?

A: I was working for the California Division of Forestry.

Q: What kind of schooling did you have?

A: I quit college in my first year.

Q: What college?

A: University of California in Los Angeles.

Q: How has your family reacted to the fact that you deserted?

A: My father says I'm a traitor. He says you have an obligation to be loyal to any army you are in. He's a colonel in Vietnam. He recently replaced Colonel George Patton as the commander of the Eleventh Armored Cavalry Regiment. The colonel says I should be loyal just as he has always been. He was a captain in World War II. In the Nazi Army.

Q: Your father is a colonel in Vietnam?

A: Right. Full colonel. Commanding officer in Eleventh Cavalry Regiment now.

Q: And when did he go to Vietnam?

A: This is the second trip. I got there in '66, he got there later. First time he went over was in February 1967, and then he went back a few months ago.

Q: And what was his role during World War II?

110

A: Well, he was a—initially, he was just an armor officer in the German Army. But somebody had seen him and liked him and had connections in the family and all this, Prussian aristocrats, and a friend of somebody in the family knew General Heinz Guderian and General Guderian knew somebody in the family and he ended up with my father as his aide. He was on his general staff.

Q: And what happened to the general?

A: Well, he was cleared of any war crimes by the Nuremberg tribunals and he is just a German citizen now.

Q: Your father was a captain in the German Army?

A: Right.

Q: And then we went to the U. S. When?

A: In 1948.

Q: How did your father happen to come to the United States?

A: It was kind of a haphazard thing. The Army wanted Guderian, because as far as armored and mechanized warfare is concerned Guderian is probably the Number One man. He invented modern mechanized warfare in his own little head, him and a few other people, and he wrote a book on army tactics, the way it should be. He was instrumental in developing Hitler's Blitzkrieg.

The U.S. Army approached Guderian after he was cleared by the Nuremberg and asked him would he like to come to the United States and be an instructor, and Guderian told them "No," flat right out, "I do not want to have anything to do with you."

They searched and searched and searched, and they found a young German officer who had delved quite a bit into armored warfare with Guderian, and they asked him, and he seemed to be interested. That was my father. So in '48 he went across, and they paid the trip for the whole family to the States. We lived in Radcliff, Kentucky—it is right next to Fort Knox and he was a civilian instructor there.

Q: For how long?

A: Just about, well, just till before the Korean War broke out. He had put in for a commission to the United States Army and he was granted it just before the war broke out as a captain in the United States Army.

Q: Got his old rank back?

A: Yes, and then some now.

Q: And then what happened after he became a captain in the Army?

A: He was no longer a teacher or anything but he stayed at Fort Knox at the armored school for, oh, about three months. After the Korean War started, then he became a company commander in Korea with an armored company. Then he stayed in Korea till the war was over and then came back to the States and then to Germany as a company commander. He was a battalion commander in Augsburg, Germany, in the 24th Division, at the time I came in the Army and then promoted again and now he is a full colonel and a regimental commander.

Q: How long has he been in Vietnam? On his second tour.

A: Let me see, I deserted in June and he left in June, so this is November, almost December.

Q: And how long was his first tour?

A: Just short of a year. He was supposed to stay in Washington, but he just went back to Washington briefly. I do not know, he never told me what he was doing there. I figured it was probably something secret. But Colonel Patton, who was the commander of Eleventh Cavalry Division—you know, General Patton's son—came back to the States. He was going to take flight training and they sent my father back as his replacement.

Q: You were in Vietnam for how long?

A: A year and a half.

Q: Where were you?

A: Well, I spent my first year with the First Brigade, 101st Airborne Division, and we were supposed to be based at Phan Rang, but we hardly ever saw the base camp. We were moving all around the country.

Q: You jumped?

A: Right.

Q: How many times?

A: Oh, well, I did not make any combat jumps. I made five jumps for the Vietnamese, down at Bien Hoa, just to get my Vietnamese wings, and then I made two which are called joke blasts just for the fun of it—one was when I was leaving for Phan Rang and one when I came back. I had a friend who worked there and he arranged it.

Q: How many times did you jump altogether?

A: Well, I got forty-seven jumps in the Army and eighteen in civilian life.

Q: What were your duties in Vietnam? What was your rank?

A: I was a sergeant and a squad leader, but at one time while with the 101st I was what we call long-range reconnaissance. We just call it recondor-alert, and I had the highest rank and the most experience, as we had no officers. I had four teams, six men each, and you might say I was a platoon leader, but that is supposed to be a lieutenant's job. But when at 196 I was just a squad leader.

Q: And what did you do as a squad leader or an acting platoon leader?

A: I was just, you know, the man in charge. The word came down to me, and then I passed it on down.

Q: What was the word?

A: Well, you know, whatever they wanted us to do from day to day. Tell me what to do, and then I told everybody else what to do.

Q: Well, let us go into that. What did they tell you to do? And what did they do from day to day?

A: Well, as far as the infantry platoon—a lieutenant tells me, "Well, Schneider, take your squad and move up such and such on the right flank. We will move to such and such point so many meters"—and I will just move out and I will put someone on the point where we go.

Q: Were you ever present when villages were attacked?

A: Yes, I was.

Q: How many times?

A: Hard to say. I did not keep track. Most likely dozens. We made it quite a habit of where we could . . . to put on Zippos to roofs.

Q: Burn down the villages? What about the inhabitants?

A: Well, we told them we were going to do it beforehand, but a lot of times, specially in the highlands, the inhabitants would either be underground or have completely left or, you know, have slipped into the jungle because they were afraid of us or knew what to be expecting. And we would find an empty village, with nobody living there. If we found any livestock, you know, we would go around killing pigs and chickens and burning down the village.

Q: On whose orders were the villages burned down?

A: Usually there is no actual order for it to be burned down or anything unless it comes from higher up. Like we had a village which we thought was a problem to us because of the way it was situated on this road which we needed to supply our companies. The companies were separated from the rest of the battalion. We had to supply it by truck, all the ammunition and everything. There was no road leading out to it at all. We had to get supplies to it with helicopters. The village was right up against the road. They built the road through the village. The engineers had done it, so they decided, well, we are going to tear down the one half of the village on the other side of the road and a hundred meters in on this side of the road. We went around telling the villagers, "Well, you will have to move out." They moved out or they were supposed to move out, and a few families did not move out and we went ahead and burned their hootches anyway. A few people got a little wild here and there and we ended up burning the whole village.

Q: Anybody killed?

A: Not that I know of. I have seen one instance where the people have been killed by the ROK Marines.

Q: Civilians in a village?

A: Right. The road went over this bridge we had to one company—it was Third Company—and it went down further and connected with Highway One. And these ROK Marines were coming in convoy about ten, fifteen trucks back from an operation further south, and they came through this village and they got some sniper fire. They stopped and dismounted and surrounded the village and some few of them went in and started setting hootches on fire. Everybody that ran out they shot, and we were watching it from a hill up in the distance and it kind of made me sick. Some people saying, "Get them! Get them!" Well, I guess—I just didn't like it.

Q: Did you see any American soldiers participate in anything like that? Killing villagers?

A: I saw a couple of villagers that they thought were VC, we had classified as VC suspects, one of them was beaten so badly that he later died from the wounds that we inflicted with the butt of a carbine. I have seen a lot of mutilation of bodies and things, but—

actual murders. I do not know if I should bring this up myself or not, but I killed some prisoners myself one day. Down at a bunker. I was mad and a friend of mine had been killed. They sent me back for psychiatric treatment—they just said it was combat fatigue, and it was the shock of seeing a friend killed, but it happens quite frequently.

Q: How many did you kill?

A: There was three of them.

Q: And you saw other prisoners killed by American soldiers?

A: Oh, always. We had a battalion commander who did not like to take prisoners or Chieu Hois. He would fly around in his helicopter and say, "No prisoners, no Chieu Hois." This was a license to kill right there. The only time they really took any prisoners were when they thought they needed some information or so.

Q: Did you see prisoners interrogated?

A: Well, yes. I have done interrogation myself.

Q: What did you see?

A: There were several different methods. There was a method with the field telephones and the electrical shock method. There was one where you take a leather strap and you put it around the neck while wet and it dries and chokes very slowly around the throat. Or you can just slap people around, beat them. There are several different methods. Whatever somebody feels like doing at the time. Driving sticks into your toes. I have seen quite a few Vietnamese doing this. Small pieces of hardened bamboo slipped underneath the fingernails.

Q: With the field telephone, that is electrical torture? Where are the electrodes attached?

A: Oh, you take the two ends of the electrodes and then attach them to the testicles and then you crank the telephone and the only marks it leaves are occasionally just a small burn, but it is quite painful.

Q: How many people have you seen interrogated in this fashion?

A: I did it once myself on orders.

Q: Who were the orders from?

A: From my platoon leader, one Lieutenant Drew.

Q: And what were the specific orders?

A: He said, "See what you can get out of him and here is the telephone." So that meant you go ahead and hook it up and crank away.

Q: You saw many people tortured this way?

A: Several times before that and several times after. But that was the only time I did it myself.

Q: Who did the torturing?

A: Just anybody they handed the telephone to at the time.

Q: Who was it you said gave the order to take no prisoners?

A: That was a battalion commander, Lieutenant Colonel Walters at the time. Later he left and Lieutenant Colonel Graffis came in and took over the battalion. And he was about the same way.

Q: He gave the order to take no prisoners?

A: Well, not in so many words, but he would say, "I do not think we need any prisoners," or "Don't find any prisoners."

Q: And what would the GIs do if they found the enemy?

A: Well, I saw one instance where a Vietcong came out with a Chieu Hoi pamphlet that the Air Force and Army distributed over there. It's supposed to be a safe-conduct pass for defectors who want to come over to the other side, repatriation they call it. One of them came running out into a clearing waving one in his hands, and one of them said, "Oh, a Chieu Hoi!" and went pam! pam! and down he went.

Q: Killed him?

A: Right.

Q: Why did you leave Vietnam?

A: Well, I was shot in the right femur. I had four weeks left of my tour before I would have left the field and gone home. I was sent to various hospitals from Da Nang to Japan.

Q: Were you given any medals for your actions in Vietnam?

A: Yes. Bronze Star, Purple Heart with oak-leaf cluster, Silver Star, and all the regular campaign and service medals.

Q: Were you ever punished or chastised for murdering the three prisoners?

A: No.

▪ Jerry Dass

Q: What is your name?

A: Jerry Dass.

Q: You were a Green Beret?

A: Yes. I received a great deal of special training in the U. S. and when I was sent to Vietnam I was at the Special Forces Detachment B, S-5.

Q: When did you arrive in Vietnam?

A: We landed in Bien Hoa November 27th, 1967, just a month and a half before the Tet offensive. From Bien Hoa we went down to Saigon, where Special Forces has two detachments. One at 240 and the other is Camp Goodman, where the S-5 is. From there I was sent to Nha Trang to sign in. Nha Trang, by the way, is the headquarters of the Special Forces, First Special Forces in Vietnam. From there we were given orders to go to Bien Hoa to train people. On Highway One there is an A camp and there we were training ARVN troops and CIDG people. By the way, half the force of the Special Forces consists of CIDG, the ARVN people, and they are also stationed in Nha Trang and their job is normally to go first and also to guard drivers and so on, because Special Forces has a lack of people. So in Bien Hoa we were training these individuals and then, unfortunately, that was the time of the Tet offensive, so we had some trouble. We received orders to go down to a pagoda and a cemetery on the highway—Bien Hoa Highway—and down there we were helping people build whatever was destroyed by the so-called VC. In the Special Forces we operated on a twelve-man basis, a team consisting of a captain, a lieutenant, a medic, a demolition specialist, radio operator, intelligence sergeant, a light-weapon man, a heavy-weapon man and an engineer. So here we are after spending a month and a half helping old people and so on. Then all of a sudden we receive some orders stating we were to stand by until the choppers came and picked us up. No matter what the figures are in Vietnam, always the Army kind of exaggerates, because

117

if they think there are only four or five so-called VC you always get a figure stating that there are about three or four hundred, or maybe a battalion or company. My captain, by the way, at that time was Captain Stit—Wilbert Stit, Jr.—and my first lieutenant was Lieutenant Schram, and my company commander in Nha Trang at that time was Colonel Ladd. And I asked my captain what was going to happen to the people whom we just helped, for a month and a half, build their villages and treat them and train them. He says, "Well, as far as we are concerned, they are VCs." The next day you could see the village was completely wiped out. And from there we moved up to our company in 240 and there again during the Tet offensive, I do not know whether you know, the entire village was completely destroyed. Also we had in our S-5 detachment Filipino people and some of them were killed, and so we went out to look for their bodies and, unfortunately, some of them were dead. Also from there we went down to the so-called Cho Lon sector—that is the Chinese sector of Saigon—and down there again the Cobras were at work and the ARVN so-called Tiger Platoon. And the headquarters of the ARVN troops is also with the Special Forces, S-5, that is in Camp Goodman, just behind the Free World headquarters. And in Cho Lon what I saw again was really bad, because men, women and children were just taking their loads away from the houses down there, and carts and carts of dead people lying around there, and at the sides of streets you see just barbed wire all around. And you have so-called VC—actually people cannot distinguish who is a VC and who is not. As far as I am concerned, Vietnamese are still Vietnamese, they all look alike. And here you see people just like cattle, even the wounded, all together surrounded by barbed wire. What happened to them later I really don't know. From there we went to Da Nang, because we operate in the twelve-man basis A-team, and we move around a hell of a lot. So we moved down to Da Nang. Da Nang, by the way, is Company C of the Special Forces. That's where there is the interrogation, and that is where we trained Montagnards and so on. In Da Nang again, that is where I saw some of the interrogation of prisoners, and it was terrible. People were tortured, some to death. My job was as demolition specialist, so I had nothing to do with interrogation, but still I was curious to see how prisoners were treated. Down there again they pulled nails out of individuals, started cutting the fingers and dipping heads in water, and then, later on, killing them. This is the Special Forces interrogation sergeant with a so-called ARVN "translator." Part of the Special Forces people in Vietnam are the ones who do the dirty job of translating, though we can understand the Vietnamese a bit because at Fort Bragg we have language training at JFK Center, prior to going overseas. Down there it is handled by these ARVN people and our so-called interrogation sergeant, and also the brass is always there. The relationship between us in the Special Forces and the brass is different from other forces, because there is nothing like rank and file down there, because the captain's and the officer's life depends on us, because there are only two officers and ten enlisted men. So whatever we do goes. And there are some incidents that occurred when some of my friends got killed, and I know some of my buddies who used to collect nails and also ears of Vietnamese. They don't give a damn. I don't know whether they think they were doing the right thing or not. As far as I am concerned, I felt a bit more, because before I joined the Army I was born in Asia, in Malaysia—that is not too far away from Vietnam. When I went to the States when my parents died, I was adopted by American people. And that is how I joined the Special Forces.

While I was training, all the time they were telling us how to kill. I went to my basic training at Fort Ord and my infantry training at Fort Polk, Louisiana, and then jump school at Fort Benning, Georgia, Special Forces training Fort Bragg, North Carolina. Then I was stationed at the Sixth Special Forces group—that is a local unit at Fort Bragg—before I went to Vietnam. Then after Da Nang we also received final orders, and in the Special Forces you do not know where you are going or what is going to happen. And we got a final briefing last minute and you are kept in isolation and then you take off, to whatever exercise or mission we have, and our next mission was near the DMZ.

I was wounded in that mission and sent to Okinawa and then back to Japan. I then deserted because I thought I had seen too much already.

Q: Did you ever see any prisoners killed?

A: Yes, as I said, the only prisoners I saw killed was in Da Nang. That is, people whom they got enough from, and they tortured them and just finally put a bullet through them and took the bodies away. Because, as I said, Company C is also headquarters for training the CIDG people and behind Company C you have everything. You have a beach down there as well as a rifle range. That is where they get rid of the people whom they don't want.

Q: Why did you volunteer for the Special Forces?

A: For the same reason most of the other guys did—for money. With special jump pay and demolition pay, I was making 780 dollars a month. I am Asian. It would not be easy for me to make that much money at a job in the United States.

- ## Mark Worrell (*continued*)

Q: When did you go to Vietnam?

A: I got there in October of '67. I was around Da Nang the whole time. I was in an artillery unit, Fourth Battalion, Headquarters Company, Eleventh Marine Regiment, First Marine Division. It was twenty miles south of Da Nang near Dien Ban. We had infantry patrols which went out. One day a patrol brought back a prisoner. He was wounded. They just threw him on the ground and the soldiers stood around him. The sergeant yelled, "Hey, anybody want to kill a gook?" The prisoner did not know any English except the words "Geneva Convention." He kept saying that. He was very young. He could have been a VC. They started shooting at him. Near misses at first. And then the bullets starting hitting him in the legs. There were about fifty Marines standing around and cheering every time a bullet hit him. No one wanted to finish him off and end it, but finally someone did. His ears were cut off and the body was taken away and given to the village for the Vietnamese to bury. The guys would carry the ears on strings. In the hootches they had them hanging from the ceiling. In the infantry units the hootches that were quarters for twelve might have ten strings. They were very proud of how many ears they could rack up. Some of the officers would have ear collections also. Some guys were against it. They would fire during fire fights but they would never try to hit anyone. They knew that if they protested about the ear collections that they might get shot in the back the next time they went out on a patrol, so there were no complaints.

Q: What did the artillery fire at?

A: Sometimes a fire mission was called in on a village. They might take five rounds and walk them in on a village. Getting one hundred meters closer with each round. When you're firing a 155 it only takes one round and there's nothing left of the village. The FOs—forward observers—would call in the shots. Officers were always aware of this since they checked out each round to make sure no fire was being directed at friendly troops.

Q: Do you know anything about assaults upon villages made by personnel rather than artillery?

A: Yes, a Marine unit had been on an operation up in the north, around Quang Tri. They found a military hospital underground. They found over fifty Vietnamese who were severely wounded. They shot them in their beds. Killed every one of them. This was during October 1967.

Q: Have you seen prisoners questioned in Vietnam?

A: I've seen wounded Vietnamese tied up and beaten by a sergeant and enlisted men. I've seen prisoners subjected to the water torture where they stuff his mouth with a wet sock, as a gag, and pour water into his nose. I saw a prisoner stripped, his hands tied behind him and a field telephone used on him. It has two wires. One was used to puncture his tongue, the other wire was put into his penis. Then they cranked the field telephone and he screamed and everybody standing around cheered. They asked him another question. He said he didn't know anything and then they cranked it faster and faster. A Marine staff sergeant was also asking questions at this time. It went on and on. His tongue was bleeding, he was screaming, his penis swelled up to twice its size and it was bleeding too. When I protested, they talked about how their buddies had been killed and asked me, "Do you love that gook?"

121

I saw Marines beat a wounded prisoner until he was unconscious. They hit him with rifle butts, kicked him. They picked him up by the feet and lowered him, head first, into the latrine.

In June 1968 I was at the headquarters of our CAP [Combined Action Program] unit, northwest of Da Nang at the Seventh Communications Company, and there was a regular Marine grunt [infantry] unit there. They brought in a ten-year-old boy. A staff sergeant who speaks intelligible but not very good Vietnamese began to question him. He had a knife about two feet long, and only eight inches of it is handle. He began to throw the knife at the boy's feet. The boy was barefoot. He kept getting closer. Finally it stuck into a toe, almost sliced it off. The boy screamed and they took him away.

The way that they torture women and young girls is unbelievable. I don't even like to think about the things that Marines have done to girls. Often it's not even that they suspect them of being VC. Just guys with weird sexual problems abusing little girls. And then they often kill the girls. Some guys collect sexual organs of men and women instead of just ears. That's still considered odd, but maybe it will be the in thing one day.

▪ Julius Bishop*

Q: What is your name?
A: Julius Bishop.
Q: Where are you from?
A: Boston, Massachusetts.
Q: How did you get in the Army?
A: It was easy. I enlisted. I grew up in foster homes, reform schools. I was on my own since I was fourteen really. I had phony identification and I enlisted in the Army when I was sixteen years

old. That was in Denver, Colorado. July 25, 1965. I thought the Army was great. It was the first time I had any security. I was really gung-ho. I went over there and ended up in Da Nang for a few days. I learned how to take apart booby traps, things like that. I got transferred to Pleiku, B Battery support group. I drove a flat-bed twelve-ton truck and picked up parts of busted choppers, helicopters. For salvage. Hueys and other choppers. I was on the road all the time. I was really running a wrecker for helicopters. And there was plenty of them down. All this time the Army thought I was twenty-two years old and they thought I was somebody else. I was with another guy in the truck so we didn't get to know too many other guys well. But there was a lot of brutality, crazy things, that I saw some of.

Q: What do you mean?

A: Guys would have ears hanging from their uniforms. At first—this was 1966—they nailed ears, almost always right ears, to a tree. This was supposed to scare the Cong. Then they started wearing them in strings or hanging them up in hootches on strings. Then they started saving them in jars, with alcohol to preserve them.

One day I was driving a back road and a guy comes over and says he needs some gas; didn't say why. I say O.K. and he starts to siphon some of it off with a hose. They have a girl there, a pretty young girl in a clearing. There are a few guys, all GIs standing around, and a short fat officer, a lieutenant there. The girl is stripped and she's tied to two wooden stakes. I don't know what they had done to her before I got there. They pour the gasoline all over the girl and light it.

Q: Was she Vietnamese?

A: Sure. And they just stand there and watch her burn up. Then all my ideas about kill the enemy, patriotism, gung-ho, that all went down the drain. I always thought that I was fucked up, but those guys, they were real sick. Crazy. I just ran back into my truck and drove as fast as I could out of there. You can just imagine a guy been there a year, eighteen months, and he sees this every day. You think he's going to come back to America as sane as he was?

Q: Julius, suppose I had met you just before you left for Vietnam and I told you some of the stories you just told me. Would you have believed it possible for Americans to have conducted themselves that way?

A: No. I'd say that's something like Hitler pulled. That's sick, that's crazy, that's Nazism shit, not American at all. I would never have expected it. These are clean-cut kids with crew cuts and all. Typical American young boys. Christ no. They have girl friends in the States. I wouldn't have believed it. I never did hear those stories before I went out. You ask me now—I would not have believed it. But then I did see it.

▪ Robert Fossett

Q: What is your name?

A: Robert Fossett.

Q: What was your rank?

A: When I arrived in Vietnam I was a Private E-2. You have my name. My serial number was RA 11549837.

Q: RA? How old were you when you enlisted?

A: Nineteen.

Q: Where were you?

A: I enlisted in Ohio. I was sent to Fort Knox, Kentucky, for basic training. After basic, AIT at Fort Rucker, Alabama. Then thirty days of glorious vacation before being sent to Vietnam.

Q: Why did you enlist?

A: I got my draft notice and people advised me to join so that I could stay out of the infantry in Vietnam. They told me that if I enlisted I could get what I wanted.

Q: Did you get what you wanted?

A: I got what I asked for. It turned out soon that I didn't want it.

Q: Did you graduate from high school before enlisting?

A: Yes.

Q: What happened in Vietnam?

A: I stayed there for about six months and I started smoking marijuana there.

Q: Were you the only one?

A: No. There were 370 men in our company. At least 250 of them smoked. This was the 200th Aviation. We were with the Ninth Division, but when we moved up north we were assigned to the 101st Airborne. My outfit has been consolidated with another one now. Together I think they are now known as the 509th Aviation.

Q: What were your duties in Vietnam?

A: I started out flying as a gunner in a helicopter.

Q: Where were you based?

A: Near Saigon at a place called Bearcat. I was there during Tet of 1967. We didn't have too much trouble there, but enough.

Q: What were your duties?

A: It was a big chopper, a tandem rotor—it had a gunner on the right, a gunner on the left, a crew chief and a pilot and a co-pilot. We fired at huts, houses, sampans, and in free-fire zones we could fire at anything we wanted to.

Q: You fired a machine gun, I assume.

A: Yes. An M-60.

Q: What kind of helicopter was it?

A: A CH-47, a Chinook.

Q: How long were you a gunner on a helicopter?

A: Just about two months. I got sick of it. I couldn't take it any more, so I asked for another job. They assigned me to driving a water truck for the company. Sometimes I drove fuel for the aircraft.

Q: Did you ever carry prisoners in your helicopter?

A: Yes. On several occasions. I remember one time very clearly.

Q: How many prisoners were on the helicopter?

A: Two.

Q: What happened to them?

A: They were pushed off. Both of them were pushed off when we were airborne.

Q: Where was your helicopter supposed to be taking them?

A: To a POW compound.

Q: How was their absence explained?

A: The officer said that they fell or jumped off.

Q: Did this happen regularly?

A: Well, not all the time. But it wasn't a rare event. It happened pretty often. It depended on the feelings of the people in charge of the situation. In our outfit we heard about it happening, say, three times a week. We had seventeen helicopters in our outfit.

BOOK TWO

Those Who Returned

THE TRAINING

■ James Adams

Q: What is your name?
A: James Adams.
Q: Did you enlist?
A: Yes, I enlisted three days before I was due to report for induction.
Q: Why did you enlist in the Marine Corps?
A: Mainly because I needed a 120-day delay and the Marines were the only ones you could join for two years at that time, and nobody else would give me a 120-day delay. Everybody else wanted at least three or four years.
Q: When did you report?
A: I reported for training, I went into training on August 14, 1969, Parris Island, South Carolina.
Q: What was the training like?
A: Well, somebody asked me that when I was home on leave, and I said the only way I can describe the training is that I expected the worst and I got it. It still didn't hit me until I was actually there and it was happening to me myself, no matter what anybody tells

you, or how you try to prepare yourself, you won't really grasp it until it is actually happening to you.

Q: What are the worst aspects of it?

A: The worst aspects of the training would be the complete absolute supervision of you at all times and the brainwashing. I consider it not just getting you used to where you do the job they want done, but getting you to like the job and like the Corps.

Q: Killing, you mean?

A: Killing if you end up in Vietnam, or anything, but just whatever job the Corps has for you you are supposed to do it and like doing it, which I never could see. To me, it doesn't matter whether you like doing something or not, as long as you do it efficiently. The Corps doesn't take this outlook. The Corps takes the outlook that you have to like what you are doing or there is something wrong with you as an individual.

Q: Did you have to use the word "kill" often?

A: Not too often, except when we were in like close combat training or something like this. Then we were told to yell and scream and froth at the mouth or anything else we could do so as to scare the enemy and make him hesitate and give us the edge.

Q: How old are you now?

A: Twenty-one.

Q: What had you done before you went in?

A: I had had two years of college and I was out a year. I went to junior college because I had to pay for myself. I had been working since I was a sophomore in high school. I paid for my first years of college myself and at junior college I could afford to work part time and go there. I was out for a year trying to save money to go to a four-year college and finish my degree. I knew I would probably get drafted, but it was the only thing I could do. I didn't have any money to go on. They got ready to draft me. I tried to enlist in the Navy Reserve the day before I was supposed to get in. They got my draft notice to me. I had ten days' notice and I needed a 120-day delay, so I enlisted in the Marine Corps.

Q: What school did you go to?

A: I went to St. Petersburg Junior College. I graduated from there with a two-year degree in Associate Arts and Science.

Q: Are you from St. Petersburg?

A: Well, not originally. Originally I'm from Evansville, Indiana, but I've lived in St. Pete since June of 1960.

Q: Your family lives there?

A: My parents live there, yes. I came down with them when I was twelve.

Q: Where were you when the facts about the Song My massacre became public?

A: I was at Camp Lejeune in First ITR Infantry Training Regiment undergoing individual combat training and read something about it then. Naturally I caught up on it altogether when I got home on leave around Christmas time.

Q: Were you shocked by what you heard?

A: No. It didn't shock me. It was interesting to see it being brought to light, but it didn't shock me that something like that could happen. Because the way we were trained, I had a course, one of our classes was on assault of an enemy position, or suspected enemy position. The way we were taught in the class was to set up the assault and then you go on what is called a "sweep." A sweep main force stands up and goes forward at a steady pace, a walk, not a run. On an assault, as long as you can keep going yourself, you never stop for anything or anybody. If a buddy gets wounded, you just leave him and keep on going. They say, "There is supposed to be corpsmen there to take care of that job." "You don't bother about it." "You just keep on going." Keep firing at all times. Even if your weapon jams, you're not supposed to stop to fix the weapon, you're supposed to try to fix the weapon as you are marching forward. You're supposed to yell and scream. You fire at anything that's in your line of fire. They assign you sectors of fire; you fire at anything that's in your line of fire, that moves, it doesn't matter what it is. In our instructor's own words, "If a rabbit should jump up in front of you throw a round into it for good measure."

In reference to the wounded enemy, he said that if you were advancing on line, which means that all the troops are abreast of each other, you have a sector of fire to cover, 'cause that way if all troops abreast crisscross fire you will cover everything in the whole emplacement. In reference to enemy wounded, "If you should pass an enemy soldier wounded, lying on the deck, you never leave any wounded that you know about, laying around alive." You would

131

just, like if you had fixed bayonets, reach down, and in the instructor's own words again, "Cut his head off" or "Pump a few rounds into him for good measure." But anyhow, take care of him, but not stop. Not stop to help him or stop to capture anything. Just kill him on the spot and keep on in line and keep firing at everything that moves in your line of fire. That's why My Lai did not surprise me because I could see how if, even if they weren't, didn't intend to kill civilians in the first place, the civilians would be caught in the sector of fire, and if they were instructed the same way we are, to fire at anything that moves within the sector of fire, they would just naturally be shot at.

Q: In boot camp were you given training regarding proper conduct toward Vietnamese civilians?

A: Our drill instructor was telling us that one thing that is really hard in the Marines is to get used to the idea of little kids being killed because, especially when they first get over there, most of them are sympathetic to children. This is the way Americans are brought up, plus the fact that a lot of Marines have their own kids and everything, but they trained us to beware of them, because a lot of them are booby-trapped nowadays by their own people, so that when enough Marines gather around them they release the spoon on a hand grenade or something and just blow themselves up along with the Marines. I had a troop handler in ITR who went one step farther and said that they wouldn't have anything at all to do with kids. If they were in the village that they knew was sympathetic to the Vietcong and where the Vietcong were being harbored, whenever the kids did come around they'd give them cookies, waferlike cookies that they made out of C-3 or C-4, which is a plastic explosive that we use. It is also poisonous. They gave them these cookies, and kids that ate them died. The instructor said something about "This is of course something that isn't talked about, is it, Lieutenant?" And the lieutenant who was there at the time said, "Don't talk to me about it. I did it too."

Q: When was this?

A: This was ITR at Camp Lejeune.

Q: When was that about?

A: Between November 20th and November 30th of 1969.

Q: About two or three months ago?

A: About two or three months ago, right. They were talking about their own experiences while they were over there.

Q: Where are you stationed now?

A: Right now I am stationed at Camp Pendleton, and I'm undergoing my last few days of MOS, basic specialty training in artillery, and I'm due to go to staging next week. That would mean that I am supposed to go someplace overseas. It could be Vietnam.

▪ John Zrebiec

Q: What is your name?

A: John Zrebiec, lance corporal.

Q: Did you enlist in the Marine Corps?

A: Yes, I did.

Q: When was that?

A: October 16, 1968.

Q: How old were you then?

A: Eighteen.

Q: Finished high school?

A: No, I didn't.

Q: Where are you from?

A: Chicago, Illinois.

Q: Where did you go to boot camp?

A: San Diego, California.

Q: What happened there?

A: It was rough from the first day. The first two weeks actually the roughest. Often the guys would be called into the hut pretty regularly.

Q: What was that about?

A: Usually for messing up on a drill field. Caught smoking or something of this nature.

Q: What happened in the hut?

A: The drill instructors would beat them up.

Q: How many DIs would be there?

A: Usually two. Most of the time there were two on duty and maybe another one of them would come in the afternoon. On night duty there is usually two.

Q: Were you beaten?

A: I was knocked out for not climbing a rope. See, there is a limit that you gotta climb this rope in. A limit of seconds. I think it's fifteen seconds. I took about seventeen seconds climbing the rope one day and the drill instructor called me in the duty hut and he asked me why I didn't climb the rope faster. Naturally, what could I say. I was tired. I couldn't climb it. I'm not going to lie about it. I couldn't climb it fast enough. So what he did to me, he —you know a wall locker, you know a steel wall locker?

Q: Yes, I know what a steel wall locker is.

A: I had to jump up on a steel wall locker with my elbows like this. You know what that is, don't you? You've been through that stuff. And I had to stay up there for about fifteen minutes.

Q: Hanging by your elbows?

A: Right, on a wall locker. And he says, "Now can you climb the rope?" And I was even more tired then. And, what could I say? I said, "Yes, sir." So I went outside again and tried to climb the rope and I still didn't make it. So they all started to knock me around. You know, they beat me.

Q: How many times were you in the duty hut?

A: I was in the duty hut twice.

Q: Each time you were beaten?

A: Right. One time I was knocked unconscious.

Q: For how long?

A: I don't really know. They threw a pail of water on me to bring me to after they knocked me out.

Q: Did you suffer any serious injury?

A: Not that time. Once they broke my ankle.

Q: Who did?

A: The drill instructor. Or really a PMI—a preliminary marksmanship instructor.

Q: How did that happen?

134

A: This was on the rifle range and I was in the prone position. There is a certain way you have to have your ankles. One is supposed to be flat on the deck and the other one up. The ankle that was supposed to be flat was up in the air. It was more comfortable for me that way and I could aim better. One day this sergeant, the PMI, came by. He had warned me about the ankle before but it just popped up. This was a week before firing time. He came by and stomped on my ankle. All of a sudden everything went black. I was really in pain. I couldn't walk.

Q: What happened then?

A: I was taken to the Long Beach Naval Hospital. My ankle was broken.

Q: How long did you remain there?

A: About a month and a half.

Q: Did the sergeant have a reputation for being rough?

A: Two days before that he kicked a guy in the ribs with his boot. He broke three ribs.

O: Did you ever report this to an officer?

A: Lieutenant Johnson was a really blue lieutenant. Very gungy. He told me that if I ever told anyone my life would be misery in the Marine Corps. He told me, "Forget your goddam broken ankle."

Q: You are still in the Corps?

A: Yes, I am. I'm stationed at Pendleton.

- James D. Nell

Q: When did you enlist in the Marine Corps?

A: October 1967. For three years. I have just a few more months to go.

Q: Where are you stationed now?

A: Camp Pendleton.

Q: Where did you take basic training?

A: Boot camp was Parris Island.

Q: Was it rough?

A: I was in Nam for nineteen months. In some ways boot camp was worse.

Q: How?

A: In boot camp they try to break you. They are always beating up on the recruits. I saw them break a guy's jaw once.

Q: Who broke his jaw?

A: A drill instructor.

Q: Broke a recruit's jaw?

A: Yes. He smashed him in the face.

Q: What happened to the DI?

A: This kid made a complaint. The instructor was punished. They took away part of his rank, reduced him one rank. Next month, after it was forgot, they gave the DI his rank back.

- Bill Hatton

Q: What is your name?

A: Bill Hatton.

Q: What are you doing here at Camp Pendleton now?

A: I'm working as a tactics instructor. I instruct offensive tactics, defensive tactics, camouflage, you know, the basic art of war. It's my job to make sure these people know their job when they get to Vietnam.

Q: What's your rank now?

A: I'm a corporal.

Q: When did you get in the Marine Corps?

A: I entered the Marine Corps on the second of March 1966.

Q: I understand that you have another assignment at Pendleton in addition to serving as a tactics instructor.

A: Yes, I'm presently on the battalion human-relations board. It's an official Marine Corps project. It's my business to find grievances within our outfit and to basically get assistance and solve these problems. The chain of command simply doesn't work in that respect. Human relations desperately is needed because most people in chain of command simply refuse the redress of rights. They refuse to consider that people have problems. "You're an animal, a Marine," and you're supposed to, in the face of incredible odds, bury yourself as though you had no problems at all. They always tell you, "You haven't got any problems" and "Why don't you act like a man?" and it goes along with other Marine Corps policies. Like "Don't be afraid to ask a question, we'll be glad to make a fool out of you." We feel that if we're able, we're successful in bringing this human-relations program down to the grass-roots level, that we'll have one of the most effective organizations within the military. In other words we will be in the position to guarantee human rights and dignity and constitutional rights. The stuff we've been told we had all along but never have in practice. It's all there in theory, but yet when you try to exercise your right to assemble, your freedom of speech, it's not there. We had a staff sergeant a day ago tell a man that he had no right to disagree with him. This is indicative of pretty medieval outlook in mentality.

Q: Has anyone yet utilized the procedures?

A: Yes, there have been a number of people we have been able to help through the Human Relations Board. Basically, we haven't found much cooperation with the chain of command. The Marine Corps is by and large a pretty repressive organization and they figure that the methods used 194 years ago are suitable today. It is simply not the case, and I think that the Human Relations Board can actually turn the Marine Corps, insofar as any military organization is able to do this, into an organization for human beings. As contrary and paradoxical as this might seem, it is possible.

Q: You don't train recruits, do you?

A: No, I don't see recruits. I see people fresh out of training. My mission is primarily to provide these men with proficiency in their general military subjects and tactics, to enable them to do their job.

Q: You did go through boot camp?

A: Oh, yes. I'll never forget it.

Q: Was there a prayer for war or about killing in boot camp?

A: There are Marine prayers which, you know, I would say in effect that they urge you to kill. All through boot camp you are instilled continually, you run around chanting "kill, kill"—things like this.

Q: In boot camp?

A: In boot camp, and actually at the time you are too afraid to do anything or say anything different. Myself, I went through it and was pretty enthused with the whole thing, not knowing any better. And normally everyone who goes through Marine Corps boot camp, if he isn't broken by the first week, he won't be. So naturally they've got ideal subjects. If the Marine Corps is able to send their people over right after boot camp and ITR, they have the most ideal material in the world. They have the most efficient killing machine there is. There is no doubt of it at all. You are systematically humiliated and molded into what they want, and if you try to right it you will be beaten. That's all there is to it. You can't win at that level. It's only after you get out you learn a little bit that you can affect it at all. Even now, it's very slow trying to change anything. Do you know why they almost never use Marines for riot duty?

Q: Why not?

A: They are afraid that Marines would get out of control. We are never sent to places like Los Angeles or Detroit. I fully suspect that after all that training if Marines participated in patrolling a large riot area among American civilians they would manage to kill a few. The desire to kill becomes almost a reaction, an impulse. They treat you like an unthinking animal and they want you to act like one also. Basically Marine policy is to refrain from sending out riot patrols unless a Marine base is threatened. In Hawaii there was an anti-war demonstration near our base and we set up machine guns and other automatic weapons but we were not sent out on patrol missions.

▪ Steven Lambrose

Q: What is your name?

A: Steven Lambrose.

Q: Where are you from, Steven?

A: Long Beach, California.

Q: What did you do before you entered the service?

A: Well, I worked part time driving a truck for Formica Factories and I went to Long Beach City College for a year and a half.

Q: What high school were you graduated from?

A: Long Beach Woodrow Wilson.

Q: You were drafted?

A: Yes.

Q: When was that?

A: That was in April of 1968.

Q: And what was your experience at the induction center?

A: Well, I guess it's a normal experience for everybody to go through up there. Running around in their shorts and having everybody yell at you. After we went through all this, they had a little room back in the rear of the building and as each man went through their physical, they had to file into this room. There was a civilian in there that said the Marines were authorized by President Johnson to draft so many men.

Q: That's what he said?

A: Yes. He told us that, and he had two Army PFCs sorting the files and separating all the men with any kind of police record and putting them into a separate box and putting the rest into another box. And when they came back into the room with the two boxes, they called off the men's names that had the police records and drafted them into the Marines. And then they took about one out of every five and put them into the Marines also.

Q: Were you selected for the Marine Corps?

A: Yes, I was the last one they picked.

Q: For the Marine Corps?

A: Yes, and when they got us all dressed again, they took us upstairs to give us the old swear-in, and I refused to take the oath. They told me that it is a federal offense to refuse the draft and all that, but I went and talked to a counselor. He asked me what my problem was and I told him that I just wouldn't go into the Marines. I was willing to go into the Army but not the Marines. So he got it switched so I could go on into the Army, and that's how I got good old Fort Ord. The start of my Army career.

Q: Where was that induction center?

A: I think it's on Olive Avenue in L.A., and it's quite a shoddy building. It's in quite a ragged section. It's like around the city center somewhere. On Olive Street. I believe so. It's really rundown.

Q: And did they ever explain why they took the men with the police records into the Marine Corps?

A: You weren't in a position to really ask questions, because like right from the very start, you know, it strikes fear into your heart, and you don't ask. You stand there in your shorts in the first place, which tends to complicate the position, with the guy standing up there with all his buttons and bows. They kind of had the guys buffaloed right at first.

Q: Did you presume that when they picked out the men with police records they were not going to go into the Marine Corps?

A: I couldn't really figure what they were doing with them.

Q: How did you know that they had police records?

A: I was talking to the PFC and I asked him why did they take —I think there was seven of them. They just came in and called their names and they left. They had been drafted into the Marines. Then we were just standing there afterwards, while I was waiting to go up and see the counselor, and I asked him who the first five were. He said they were drafted into the Marines for their police records.

Q: What were their records, do you know?

A: He said it was, you know, burglary, breaking and entering, things like this. And he just said that like "The Marines just kind of think these are people that have always had bad breaks." Of course, they think there is a psychological value in it, I imagine. Maybe you get rid of killers that way, I don't know. The Marines are killing

140

machines, that's all they are taught really. I guess that those kind of people are easier to convert.

Q: You haven't been to Vietnam?

A: No. I spent all my time here in the United States. I took my basic at Fort Ord and my advanced infantry training at Fort Dix, New Jersey, and then I went to Fort Campbell to be a drill corporal, but I was only a drill corporal for like about one month, and then I was transferred to a regular unit where I became a stockade guard for about three months. Then I was transferred on down here to Fort Hood, Texas, where I've spent most of my time. I'm still in the Army now.

Q: Where were you a stockade guard?

A: Fort Campbell, Kentucky.

Q: How were the prisoners treated?

A: There was quite a bit of harassment. The men that were put into the box got more than that. There was a lot of brutality, you know, beating up of the men there. I guess that's a known thing to all the stockades. They are put into the box, which is about six by six by six square, and they were put on a ration of—it wasn't bread and water, it was more than bread and water—but it was, you know, lettuce, bread, water and potatoes. No meat. It's a way of disciplining the men that are in the box. It caused acute diarrhea. It's used as a tool to discipline these men. It's used all over the stockade system.

Q: How many days were they left in the box?

A: Well, it depended on if the stockade CO liked them or not, really.

Q: If he didn't like them how long might a man remain in the box?

A: Well, there was a man in there that was quite political and they—I guess that is their favorite kind to get in a stockade. They harassed him into taking a swing at one of the NCOs when I left— he had been there ninety days.

Q: In the box ninety days?

A: Yes, in the box.

Q: Bread and water and lettuce, the whole time?

A: Right, and like they have shower privileges. They are supposed to get one shower a day. It's the only time they can leave the

141

box in the day, and they hadn't even granted him this. They took a pan of water and a wash rag in there to him.

Q: Was there a latrine in there?

A: They have a bucket in the corner and sometimes they let them leave the box and empty it themselves, but mostly they take it to the guard, and he empties it for them and brings it back.

Q: Are the prisoners in the box beaten?

A: Yes. Not all the time but often. One night they had a protest at the stockade, you know, against conditions there. They had what you might call a little riot and then the guys were badly beaten. They brought in the hoses. They made no attempt to like try to quiet them peaceably. They just brought in their hoses and sent them in with clubs to quiet them down. Like, all the mattresses were taken away from them and they had to sleep on the springs. So they couldn't tear the mattresses up, and the next day, kind of to retaliate against the prisoners, they had a shakedown inspection and, you know, like it was just beginning to get really cold, and it was sleeting and they brought all the prisoners in and had them strip completely down and lean against the wall and be searched and he kept them out there like about thirty minutes.

Q: Outside?

A: Yes, and then he finally let them get dressed and go inside.

THE WAR

■ Peter Norman Martinsen

Q: What is your name?

A: Peter Norman Martinsen.

Q: Where and when were you born?

A: I was born in San Francisco, November third of '44.

Q: What is your educational background?

A: I have a couple of years of college, or rather the equivalent in the Army Language School.

Q: How old were you when you joined?

A: I was nineteen when I enlisted. I joined in June of '63. I had just dropped out after going to school for a year. I went to Berkeley, University of California, and my grades weren't too good, and I didn't flunk out, but I dropped out—lack of interest—and I joined the Army. I actually volunteered for voluntary induction, but my father said, "You know you're an idiot to do that. If you take an extra year, you get a choice of what you're doing." So I took an extra year and they made me a cook.

Q: That wasn't your choice?

A: No, that wasn't my choice at all.

Q: What does your father do?

A: He's a civil engineer.

Q: How did you become a cook?

A: I enlisted under the assumption that I would get some kind of a choice, and I had the opportunity, but I didn't take the choice, because the Army sergeant said that since he knew that I was going to score high on the aptitude test, "Let the Army make the choice for you." I did very well on the aptitude test, especially the mathematics. I got them all right, and my I.Q. came out high. I got a 147 on that. One-sixty is maximum on the Army test. And a bunch of other tests came out high, and they made me a cook.

Q: Where were you trained?

A: I went to Fort Ord for my basic training and stayed over for cooks' school. Later I was assigned to Dugway Proving Grounds, Utah, where they gassed up all the sheep. It's the biggest Army post in square miles. Very few people, though. It's a nerve-gas, bacteria-warfare testing area. I was a cook there for the officers' club. It was really against the law to do this, but they assigned me anyway. Someone had to cook for the officers. It is supposed to be a voluntary job, but they couldn't get civilian cooks to do it. I took an extra year in the Army—it's called a Short Discharge and Re-enlistment —to get out of Dugway and try to get to Language School. So I was reassigned to a very nice post in San Francisco.

Q: How long had you re-enlisted for originally?

A: Three years. After a year you can take what is called a Short Discharge and Re-enlistment. The Army gets another year, and you get a choice of what you want to do. Well, I used it more intelligently this time. I got not only a decent post, but I got in Language School after haggling for a while. They transferred me to the Army Language School on the East Coast, which is in Washington, D.C., Anacostia Annex. I was there for six months, studying Italian. That was from January of '65 until July of '65, and from there I took a couple of weeks' leave. Then I was assigned to the Prisoner of War Interrogation School at the Army Intelligence Center. I remember it was on July 15th. The Army has its Intelligence School at Fort Holabird, in Baltimore, Maryland, and there they teach the intelligence skills. There are many of them, but they have four main courses. One is called Order of Battle, and it is for record-keeping. They teach you how to keep the files on what the enemy is doing.

144

Then the next one is called Imagery Interpretation, which is Aerial Photo Reconnaissance, and then there is Prisoner of War Interrogation, which is the course I was involved in, and then there is Counter-Intelligence training, which are the actual secret agents, the spooks, as we called them.

Q: You only went to the POW school?

A: I only went to POW school but it's actually called "IPW School." It's just that that's what the computer had me assigned for. I studied there for seven weeks, and it was just during the final week, not only were the Watts riots going on, but the President made a speech for escalation, and when they committed the First Marine Combat Unit there. I was reassigned to Fort Meade, Maryland, which was very close, about halfway between Washington and Baltimore, and there was an interrogation company there. We sat around and did nothing but rake leaves and occasionally translate a document for the CIA, and then the build-up really began. The 11th Armored Cavalry Regiment was stationed at Fort Meade but in stripped-down strength. They decided to beef it up and send it to Vietnam, so they reactivated two squadrons of it, reactivated the intelligence detachment, which was the 541st Military Intelligence Detachment. They needed eight enlisted interrogators and I was assigned as one of the enlisted interrogators. And so I was reassigned to the 11th Armored Cavalry Regiment, with the subsidiary detachment, and we went by boat to Vietnam.

Q: Before you get there, tell me about POW school.

A: The school is a lot of things. Some of them are classified. I was primarily oriented towards the Soviet, interrogation of a Soviet prisoner or Eastern European prisoner, Eastern bloc, because at that time Vietnam was not big, and there were only four hours in the curriculum devoted to Vietnamese-style interrogation. You had to judge the style of your interrogation by the literacy, the climate and so on of who you are going to interrogate. They teach you a number of skills and try to pump as much order of battle into you as possible, order of battle being how many tanks they have, what kind of tanks they are, and so on. Then they actually teach interrogation techniques, none of which are illegal, except for the use of stress and harassment. For instance, the big-brother technique. Now this is classified "confidential," which is an Army classification:

Confidential, Secret, and Top Secret. It's the lowest classification. Big brother comes into the room, sees the prisoner, picks him up and throws him against the wall, kicks him perhaps. Little brother comes in and he's obviously of a higher rank.

Q: He's nicer.

A: Nicer, much nicer. He berates the big man—who's a little bit slow and stupid—tells him to get out, and the prisoner, of course, out of gratitude, talks. The police use this all the time. But it's classified confidential. Why is it classified? Because it's against the rules of war, the Geneva Convention. It's against the law to treat a prisoner any differently than you would supposedly treat a civil prisoner in your own country. This is just one interrogation technique. There are other ones. For instance, if you have a wounded prisoner, we were told to see what happens if you deny him medical treatment until he offers to give you the information. Most wounds are painful. You have a prisoner who hasn't eaten for days, deny him food. Have a prisoner who is out in the hot sun, keep him there.

Q: Were any direct techniques of torture taught?

A: No, not in the curriculum. Now, after the courses, you say to the officer or the sergeant teaching the course, "Sarge, really, how do you interrogate under combat situations?" And they say, "Well, you take a field telephone and you attach it to the man's balls and you wire him up. Then you ring him up."

Q: Who said that?

A: A sergeant. I heard this from officers too. "You ring him up, he always answers." And isn't that illegal? "Yes, but it doesn't leave marks." He said the central rule in interrogation is unsaid officially. But it was always there. It's almost palpable in the air, "You do not leave marks." Do anything you want, but don't leave marks. And this was what was going on, and I talked to people later on who had gotten back from Vietnam, and they discussed the use of the Army field telephone for giving shocks, and this was a very common instrument. It was used very much, and the common term was called "wiring him" or phoning him up. And he even placed the wires any place you can place a wire. Ears, fingers, testicles, on any appendage.

Q: And then you got to Vietnam?

A: We got to Vietnam on a crummy leaky boat.

146

Q: From where?

A: From Oakland.

Q: Sailed when?

A: In August—I was trying to think whether we arrived in late August or early September—but anyway we arrived in Vung Tau. We left from Oakland, we went by plane from Fort Meade. Actually from Friendship Airport to Oakland and from there on the boat, the whole unit. One squadron plus the Intelligence Detachment went over and the other squadrons followed on different boats.

Q: What happened then?

A: Well, we had to stage and set up the regiment because we came over just ourselves with a minimal amount of supplies. Our tanks and so on were coming in later on, and then they arrived in Saigon and we went down and picked them up.

Q: What outfit did you arrive with?

A: I arrived with the 11th Armored Cavalry Regiment. And we staged in Long Binh, which later became the area for MACV. I should say USARV, U.S. Army in Vietnam, and we staged there, and then we moved out to an area south of Xuan Loc. This was the regiment. The supporting engineer battalions, the supporting medical company, our detachment, a security communication company, which did nothing but eavesdrop on the enemy so to speak and eavesdrop on us for communications security, and we set up, There wasn't too much going on because their main concern was setting up housekeeping and then moving out. We lost one of our men in an ambush. He was an imagery interpreter, Wallace Malone, and he was killed in an ambush. This was very strange for an intelligence man, especially a photointerpreter, to be killed, as they just don't do hazardous duty. And we were all very bitter about this, and we got our first group of detainees in and—

Q: What's a detainee?

A: A detainee is anybody who is captured. A detainee is a man, woman or child, anybody you happen to pick up. Then it's the prisoner interrogator's job to determine whether you have a prisoner or you have what they call a *Hoi Chanh*, which is a rallier, somebody that deserted from the other side. Whether you have an innocent civilian, or whether you have a civil defendant, which is somebody you determine has broken the civil laws of the country but not nec-

147

essarily a political type of thing, that is an NLF person. And of course the prisoner, an out-and-out North Vietnamese or Vietcong prisoner. Anyway, they detained a large group of people and they brought them in. This actually wasn't the first interrogation, but this was the first time I saw the very vicious use of force. Other times, I saw knives held to their throats, and people being beaten physically, and when I say people I mean men, women or children. Many times they'd bring in sixty or seventy people, men, women, children, women nursing babies, just everybody. Everybody they happened to think suspicious, because the unit was on edge. They had just moved in, and they didn't know what to expect. Anyway, so we got this group of people in—

Q: Do you remember when this was?

A: This was in October, late September or early October of 1966.

Q: And where was it?

A: This was in Long Khahn Province, the base camp at Long Giao, and we were interrogating these detainees. We were very bitter because Malone had been killed, and the war had actually been brought to us. Before, the war just didn't really affect us at all. We hadn't been mortared, we hadn't been shot at, we hadn't been sniped at. It was just a lot of mud and dysentery and a lot of malaria pills. We started interrogating these people, and I wasn't getting too far with the man. I had been beating him with my hands, on the face. I was convinced at the time that the guy was a Vietcong, he was of draft age, he was not in the Army, I was just convinced. I couldn't get anything out of him, and the lieutenant kept screaming at me to break the guy. That's the term in interrogation, you break him, the prisoner.

Q: Do you remember the name of the lieutenant?

A: Oh, yes, the name was Lieutenant Douglas Quinlan. A product of our fine Southern universities' ROTC program. Anyway Lieutenant Quinlan said, "Here, I'll take over," and he got out the field telephone, and he bared some insulation off the wires, and he wrapped them around the man's wrists, and the man still didn't talk, although he screamed.

Q: He cranked it?

A: He cranked the field telephone, right, and the shock that you get is just directly proportionate to how fast you turn it, because it's direct current. Then he applied wires to the man's genitals. I couldn't watch it, I left. I said you can't do that, you just can't do that, and I left. Well, he did it anyway, and the man still didn't break, and this was the first time I saw the rather strong use of the telephone. But this wasn't a big operation, just a lot of little what they call search and destroy, village sweeps. They ran constantly, involving eighty or one hundred people in our area. And then we sort of set up housekeeping and we did a lot of village sweeps and they would detain many, many people. These people would be men, women and children. We would determine if we were still suspicious about a man, and working in very close harmony with the National Police there, which are kind of—well, they are actually a military force, but they call themselves the national police. Anybody that we determined to be a civil defendant we turned over to these authorities. And then he or she would go to jail. Now a civil defendant can be anybody that has broken the curfew, that doesn't have his ID card with him. Many Vietnamese didn't carry their ID cards because it was a valuable possession. They wanted to keep it at home where it was safe. And so when we determined that we had somebody detained and that something wasn't right about the detainee, and yet we couldn't really call him a civil defendant because he hadn't really broken any law that we could determine, we would just take him up to the province capital of Xuan Loc and drop him off at the National Police Station, where he would be arrested for loitering and that was it. These people just weren't heard from again.

Q: Do you know what happened to them?

A: No, I don't, but I know this happened many, many, many times, I mean, in well over a hundred cases. In many instances, these people had been taken from their homes thirty or forty kilometers away and brought into the camp and later were just dropped in town, the town being Xuan Loc, nowhere near their town, and this isn't in an area where you can just hitch a ride. Anyway, we did many of these interrogations with force and beatings, and electrical torture was used, rather extensively, perhaps in some fifty or sixty percent of the cases. We captured one man with a weapon—he was a Vietcong and he was wounded—but we refused him medical care until he talked.

Q: How was he wounded?

A: He was wounded in the leg and in the shoulder. Well, the bleeding had stopped, because he had been there a day, and he was found hiding in the brush the next day. And we tried unsuccessfully by withholding food and withholding medical care to get any kind of information, and since he was the first definite Vietcong that we knew that we had captured. This was in October 1966 and the regimental commander was very anxious to get whatever kind of tactical information he could get, and he couldn't get any, and this was very frustrating to him and very frustrating to us. I was one of the interrogators. We tried every technique we could think of from beatings to withholding food, withholding medical treatment, withholding water, electrical torture, the whole works, and nothing worked. The man just wouldn't talk, that's all there was to it, and—

Q: How long had he been tortured?

A: Uh, we had him in our hands about two days, I believe.

Q: What kind of electrical torture?

A: With the field telephone again. Then came Operation Attleboro. It was the first of the major Westmoreland-initiated search-and-destroy operations where large, large numbers—they finally built up their forces—where large, large numbers of forces were taken out and rambled across the countryside. It was in November of 1966. It commenced when a company of the 196th Light Infantry Brigade got ambushed in War Zone C, which was near the Cambodian border. They evidently really put them through the meat-grinder, and the American commander was inexperienced, the commander of the brigade, and he kept putting in company after company instead of committing a large force. So he lost a whole battalion, and then they called in the 25th Infantry Division to help out and they lost a whole battalion. So then they called in a brigade of the First Infantry, and that is what eventually won the battle for them. We were involved. The way that our unit was involved was we had one squadron, the First Squadron involved with the First Division, on Route 13, which runs up through Loch Ninh, from Saigon, and we were running road security but we didn't have any prisoners at all, but anyway, that's the first big operation. Back to base camp for refitting and refurbishing and when you have armored vehicles, as they have, they had to be constantly maintained and it takes a long time. After they go through an operation like that, they put new tracks and overhaul the engines, transmissions and so on. So come January, Operation Cedar Falls starts. Cedar Falls was designed to clear out the so-called Iron Triangle, which was an NLF-controlled area. It was a contested area—that is, the government could go in there during the daytime, but the NLF ruled it at night. They used part of our regiment to seal off one side, and then they used another part of the regiment to push through and push whoever happened to be in there up against the blocking force of the 25th Infantry Division and having the First Infantry Division on the north close things up. This was when the first tremendous air bombardment started. Then they just started clearing everybody out, and when I say everybody, there were four thousand to five thousand inhabitants which were put through a screening process. These people couldn't carry anything through but the clothes on their back. And whatever animals they could bring. There was livestock running around free, their homes and possessions were bulldozed flat.

Q: Many different villages?

A: Many different villages. Big villages, the village of Ben Suc. There was a village of Ben Suc, Provincial Route 14, I believe, I was in Ben Suc when they did it. Ben Suc, the people were taken out and put on flat-bed trucks. They were brought in, and I received the end product of the flat-bed trucks in a detention camp. They had oxen, chickens, anything they could take with them. They had their personal possessions they could carry and that was it. The rest were left in the houses, which were bulldozed flat. The people, every house had a tunnel underneath, every house has a tunnel in Vietnam. This tunnel is not because they like to dig tunnels, it's because it's the only way to live safely due to bombardments, and these tunnels were filled. Undoubtedly people were in them. I don't know that for a fact, that people were in them, but many relatives told me that they had left people behind who were afraid to come out, and they were bulldozed flat. The tunnels were filled.

Q: Would that have killed the people in the tunnels?

A: It must have. You have never seen such complete destruction. There's jungle on either side, and an old disused rubber plantation on the north, which belonged to the Michelin people, and on the south is all jungle, it's scrub-brush jungle that would take you an hour to walk a mile. It's very rough jungle. The people don't go into it. Bordering that, is the area where Ben Suc is, and Ben Suc is right on the Saigon River. Ben Suc and Rach Kien and several other villages. I could point them out on a map. I still have it in my memory, because I worked from a map constantly and I could just point it out right on the map which villages were bulldozed. These villages were just bulldozed flat. Next step—anybody who didn't surrender was shot on sight. Our unit was under operational control of the 173rd Airborne Brigade, and our command post was set up in Ben Cat, which is on Route 13, about thirty kilometers north of Saigon, I believe. And we were set up in a graveyard overlooking the town, and this was where the interrogations were taking place. There was an officer in charge of me, but he didn't do anything but drink beer, so I did the screening of most of these people. The only time a newsman came around was when a correspondent from Reuters came out and I told him to get the hell out of the camp. I mean—this wasn't covered, it was covered later on—I saw pictures in *Life* magazine of the people in Phu Loi, after they had been taken out of there, living in just incredible squalor, in another "detaining camp," they called it. A concentration camp is what it was. But out of all these people, they were mainly females. Their husbands were not with them. "Where's your husband?" "He's in the Army." "Where's your husband?" "He's in Saigon." "Where's your husband?" "The American planes killed him." "Where's your husband?" Almost none would admit, even the visibly pregnant ones, that their husbands were alive, and these were the people who were fighting on the other side. These were people still in the jungle. So anyway, the military, the men of draftable age, unless we actually discovered them with a weapon or something, I turned immediately over to the Vietnamese authorities. I actually was in charge of inducting Vietnamese civilians into the Vietnamese Army. Thirty or forty times this happened. The main source of detainees, for interrogation purposes, came from the actual combat level. A lot of people were fighting, which was further down south in the Triangle, this is where the torture really was. And it really was incredible on this operation.

Q: You saw this?

A: I saw this. I unfortunately participated in this. Interrogation takes place in a tent, and it is closed and you don't want people bopping in and disturbing your interrogation. This is just from a practical point of view, so unless you actually stick your head in you don't see what's going on. But you can tell the sound of fists hitting flesh. Anyway, this prisoner admitted that he was a captain. He admitted that he was also a military historian for this particular NLF area, this military region, he however would not tell me a thing. I wasn't getting anything. They were very anxious for tactical information—it's called hot poop—and they wanted it now. They kept saying, "Get it now." O.K., I couldn't get it, so Special 6 Martin Pearce, who was the enlisted interrogation section leader, and Charles Crocker, who was another interrogation officer—

Q: What was your rank at this time?

A: I was a Specialist 5. Specialist 6 Pearce was just a step above. And they started interrogating him. I had gone out to eat lunch and I came back and found Lieutenant Crocker was putting bamboo splinters under the man's fingernails.

Q: Where was the man?

A: The man was in the tent sitting down, tied to a chair. We have these metal folding chairs, part of the interrogation equipment. He was tied to a chair, and he had one hand tied to the table with a field-telephone wire—there's thousands of miles of it, everyone uses it for every kind of thing. They tied his hand flat and were inserting bamboo splinters under his fingernails. At the same time that this was occurring, Specialist Pearce had field-telephone wires wrapped around the man's ears and was torturing him that way. The man didn't talk. This didn't do him any good at all. When you get such high-ranking officials, command is immediately notified. Prisoners are passed through the hierarchy and they go from regiment to brigade headquarters, from brigade to division, from division to corps headquarters, from corps down to Saigon if the prisoner's importance warrants it. And this particular one did and they wanted him to go to First Infantry Division headquarters right away for interrogation, and so he was moved out. Shortly thereafter, Lieutenant Crocker was criticized by the detachment commander for putting the bamboo splinters under his fingernails, because it left marks and there's blood and obvious swelling. Lieutenant Crocker was not criticized for having electrical field-phone wires around the man's ears. He was involved the next day with torturing a sixteen-year-old girl, with putting electrical field-phone wires around her ears.

Q: Did you see that?

A: I saw it. I mean it just goes on and on. There was one man who was so severely tortured electrically that he actually went into a form of shock. Then everyone was afraid. They didn't know what to do. And finally a man came in—I can't remember his name because he wasn't an interrogator, he was technically an imagery interpreter. The commander more or less used him as a bodyguard because he was an old hand. He was a Ukrainian, I believe. He spoke God knows how many Slavic languages. Anyway, this man tried to bring him out of shock by placing lighted matches against the man's eyelids, which didn't do any good. This was at night. I watched this, then he was taken back to the prisoner compound. About two nights later, a man died. One of the captains was interrogating this man who'd admitted to being a Vietcong village chief. He was not getting too far, but he was just about to break when he keeled over and died. The captain at the time was just wiring him up, which is the term for using the field telephone. Now the man was dead. I did not see him die, but I saw his body, and I heard the captain tell what happened. We were sitting around drinking beer and this was at night time, and the captain came over and had a beer and said, "Yeah, he was just about ready to break when he keeled over and died." And I said, "How are you going to explain this to our detachment commander?" and he just shrugged his shoulders and walked off. And they came and picked up the body, "they" being the medical staff from the brigade surgeon of the 173rd Airborne. Then I later heard that his death was due to heart failure. Undoubtedly it was. The man probably had a weak heart. The man was tortured to death clearly and simply.

There was another bad case I was involved in, to a degree, and then later on a lieutenant took over. A North Vietnamese Army captain, self-admitted, a very important man to be captured, was brought in, and they were very anxious to get information from him.

Q: He admitted to being a captain?

A: He admitted he was North Vietnamese Army. And I started out by being very nice, talking about this particular village sweep and the great preponderance of women and no men, but we screened

154

all the women. Didn't determine anything of value really, we just wasted everybody's sleep, and then they discovered a man hiding in the drainage ditch. He was hiding there with his weapon. We knew he was actually a Vietcong, and there was just no doubt. I started to interrogate him. I said, "Look, we've got the goods on you, you know, you had just better come clean, or else it's all over." And he started to get a little scared, but he didn't show it too much, and it turned out he was fairly high-ranking, he was the head of what they called people's education. He was a political man, and he was on the wrong side of the river for some odd reason. Evidently, he had been talking with some other leaders. My interpreter picked up a mallet, what they use for cracking nuts, walnuts, and started beating the man on the shoulder blade, and he just kept tapping and tapping on the shoulder blades and his knees until finally blood started to flow and then the areas swelled up incredibly and the man finally started to talk a little bit but not too much and that's when he told what he was. Then I said, "Fuck it, tell him the hell with it, we are going to shoot him." I got a shovel—all the armored personnel carriers have shovels, and I grabbed a shovel off one—and I said, "Here, have him dig his grave." So he dug, and as he dug, the interpreter was hitting him with the mallet, and he looked up at me and I had an M-79 grenade launcher, which is a forty-mm (about and inch and two thirds) and looks like a cannon when you're looking at one from the wrong end. He was looking at that, and I told him he was going to die in Vietnamese, and he was digging his grave right there and he wasn't yet dead but he was going to die soon. He completely broke down and I didn't kill the man. The interrogation officers were watching it, but I knew that if it had become necessary to kill that man, nothing would have happened to me. I just knew it, and I don't know, I use the term necessary but if *I* had deemed it necessary at the time I could have killed him and nothing would have happened to me. I had complete power over the prisoner. You can do anything you want. You're told not to leave marks, and you can always say he was trying to escape. We performed about fifty or sixty formal interrogations and in just about every one force was used and this was on women too.

Q: Fifty or sixty in what period of time?

A: This was in about eight days, nine days.

Q: In this operation?

A: Yes, and these include women. A particular point including women. There was a long tunnel that literally stretches for miles—ten miles long is what it was called in Vietnamese—in the Iron Triangle, and its existence was rumored for a long time and everyone was looking for this tunnel, and they finally found it. Our forces went down this tunnel and they saw some people hiding. They chased them to this tunnel and tear-gassed the tunnel and people finally came out the other end of the tunnel; I think it was twenty-four hours of chasing them through this tunnel. And they were very, very severely gassed. The prisoner stated that one person had died of the gas but that could not be proved. However, there were four girls, four nurses, and one man who was crippled. As I recall he had a wooden leg. He was the guard of these girls, and they were brought in, and the girls were in extremely bad shape. They were all coughing and wheezing and they were suffering and they hadn't eaten for days. We just said that we weren't going to feed them till they talked. The girls were in very bad shape but at the same time the prisoner compound was not segregated as to sex as the Geneva Convention calls for. The girls were brought in and one girl was in particularly bad shape. I called the surgeon in and said, "This girl is very ill, give her something," and so he gave her a shot of what I think was adrenalin and a couple of hours later after interrogating one of the girls I went back. I wasn't using force with these girls although I was withholding food and water and medical care except for this one girl. The one girl's breathing had gotten worse and you could hear her lungs just gurgling. I had pneumonia four times when I was in the service and I knew just exactly what it was and you could hear it from this girl. I told the doctor again who was a lieutenant colonel that "This girl has pneumonia; I know because I had it before myself." The doctor told me that I ought to stop practicing medicine and he gave her another shot and assured me that she would get better. Well, she lapsed into a coma, her fever was just incredible, and they took her about ten kilometers up the road to Lai Khe to a hospital where I'm told she died. Now can you say she was gassed to death? I don't know. You can say that proper medical care was definitely not given. All this time she was lying on the damp ground, she was not in a bed.

Q: Have you ever seen any women tortured?

A: Yes. I saw a girl with electrical wires around her ears. She was tied to a tent post. Tents are about eight feet tall, and she was tied to a tent post and the wires were placed around her ears, and the wires were placed on her fingers. Another girl about eighteen or nineteen, the wires were being touched to her nipples. We had four tents and four interrogations going constantly and if you weren't interrogating you were typing interrogation reports or trying to get drunk to forget it. And it was not a thing where you sat around and watched too much, but you'd often stick your head into a tent to get one interrogation report or another. It was just a horror palace which went on constantly all the time.

Q: Four tents continually operating?

A: If the prisoner load warranted it, and the prisoner load on this operation did.

Q: How many interrogators?

A: Myself, Specialist Pearce, there was Larry Camp, and two interrogation officers and four interrogation men and then a couple of people who were just floating around who were actually support people, such as the guy who was the major's bodyguard and driver and Jack-of-all-trades. But this was not a steady flow and it fluctuated so that the 172nd MI Detachment was interrogating also. They were using the same techniques. I witnessed it, although we didn't work with them often, but this is the thing, it goes on constantly. At Cedar Falls I saw more use of electrical torture and not necessarily beating. Beatings were a mark of sophistication that we later acquired. Beating a person with the open hand will not leave marks at all on the face, and you can beat a person almost senseless without leaving any obvious reddening of the skin. That was Cedar Falls. When we got back to Vietnam the monsoon season was coming to an end, roads were starting to dry out and it became very dusty. It actually ended in November, but the roads dried out late January or early February and they started having more and more operations involving the armored vehicles. All the time we didn't spend in actual interrogation we spent in building fortifications, filling sand bags. I tried to find as many excuses to go into Xuan Loc to get laid and get drunk as much as possible and just stay drunk as much as possible. Our unit of thirty-two men used to consume eighty-eight cases of beer a week. The reasons why I say it was eighty-eight is because there were eighty-eight cases of beer on a pallet, and that's the way they shipped the beer. We used to drink a pallet a week. Sometimes in particularly heavy circumstances we'd drink a pallet in three days and that includes the men who didn't drink. Most of the other interrogators drank very heavily. The questioning was not done while people were drunk, although they could have been drinking, they were not necessarily drunk. It wasn't done out of a drunken rage or drunken stupidity, it was very coldly calculated. The next operation was Junction City. It was a big operation and we were not too much involved in it. It was right near the Cambodian border, near an area of constant NLF interdiction, because it's right next to War Zone C. It's an area where the government has publicly stated that it's wiped out the Ninth VC Division five or six consecutive times till it finally got so embarrassed that it finally didn't claim to wipe it out anymore. We had a fire-support base, we were running convoy support. The only detainees I had were eight rubber workers. A captain who was charging around in his tank said, "I got bored and brought the fuckers in 'cause they didn't have ID cards." He literally strapped them to the back of his tank and charged off down the road and dropped them off with me. The reason why he picked them up is because they didn't have their ID cards, but it's very common for the Vietnamese to not have their ID cards. We learned that after a while. At first we thought it was the most heinous crime in the world, not carrying your ID card. Back we went, further down Route 13, and set out the final phases of Operation Junction City. We all got laid and drunk and stayed drunk as much as possible. Then we emerged directly into Operation Manhattan, which was another big operation with a lot of interrogations. This combined operation went on for fifty days. And here our troops were gathering lots and lots of people and bringing them in. These people were NLF. A lot of them were whores who came out to serve our troops. It was an amazing operation; the whores were there before the rear elements were there because the whores were with the rear element. The whores and the beer vendors. Amazing thing; it's almost like having a rooting section. We interrogated many, many people. The monsoon was just about ready to start, and we knew it would be about the last big operation before the wet season started. Later on Westmoreland de-emphasized search and destroy. In those efforts, everything is destroyed. The whole area is completely combed, flattened and burned, ground into the dust as nothing but a tank will do. We got many prisoners. Electrical torture wasn't used too much, as the major had put out the word to cool it a little bit.

Q: Why?

A: We had received word from Westmoreland earlier that "It has come to my attention that prisoners are not receiving rights due to them under the Geneva Convention, according to article" etc., etc. "This must immediately stop." The major just read it off to us. And the next week he was rapping a prisoner on the head with his M-79 grenade launcher.

Q: You saw that?

A: Yes.

Q: What operation was this one?

A: Operation Cedar Falls. And this was the closest I came to getting shot, that's why I remember so distinctly. I was unloading cases of beer from the jeep—we had just made a beer run—and I had three cases in my arms when I heard this pop, pop, pop, and it sounded like exploding C-ration cans. A lot of us didn't eat all the C-rations. We used to throw them in the fire and then they exploded, especially the peanut-butter cans. I heard this pop, and I heard this other voice say "duck" and I turned around and there was this madman running around with a carbine in his hand and shoved it right in my stomach, pulled the trigger and it didn't go off. Fortunately it jammed, and I ran like hell, dove in a hole. He ran in the other direction. He later got gunned down, and I never saw a man more thoroughly dead than he was.

Q: Who was he?

A: He was a Vietcong platoon leader. In a moment of carelessness an interpreter had left his carbine laying around and the guy just casually picked up the carbine and started popping away.

Q: Did he shoot anybody?

A: He shot an interpreter in the big toe. The guy got a Purple Heart and I think he got an award for valor. He was reading a dirty Vietnamese book at the time. The major ran after the prisoner and I ran after him, but by the time I got my gun the man was already

159

shot. I had been carrying a pistol, but I had taken it off because I carried it in a shoulder holster and it kind of chafed my armpit. And the commander was running down yelling, "Kill the sonofabitch, kill that mother-fucker," and he had his grenade launcher, which he liked to carry as a sort of swagger stick even though he never shot the damn thing. He came back and the prisoner's alleged assistant was on our side of the compound. And first of all he walked up and kicked him in the mouth, and he yelled, "If you try that, you sonofabitch, I'll kill you." And the prisoner was hog-tied. I mean his hands and his feet bound together. Then he proceeded to hit him on the head as hard as he could with the stock of the M-79 grenade launcher. After kicking him several times, he finally walked off screaming obscenities. "I'll kill you, you mother-fucker, I'll kill you, you sonofabitch."

Q: This was the officer who had just given a lecture on the rights of prisoners?

A: Right. When we went to Vietnam, just before we left the U. S., we had a major who wasn't in any way involved in the detachment. He was a West Pointer and he needed a certain amount of command experience to reach his next rank. They put him in the detachment because it was an easy way to get his command experience. He had all staff jobs and then he was in the detachment for two months in the United States and then three weeks in Vietnam. Then he got his promotion to lieutenant colonel, which is what he needed the time for in the first place. The rank was too high for this detachment. The post only called for a major, so he was transferred out about the same time we finished our staging and moved into Xuan Loc. He was not involved in any type of interrogation whatsoever and that's when the new commander came in. I might add he was a man who had been in the OSS in World War II in the same area in South East Asia, or at least he said he had been. He had been in a hell of a long time. He had a very low rank for a man of his age. To get back to Manhattan, I can't really say why they stopped the use of electrical torture. We had lots of prisoners in Manhattan. The prisoners were beaten physically with the hands, extreme beatings. I remember one time when a guy walked up and said, "Boy, that was a rough interrogation, my hands were getting tired from hitting him in the mouth so much." And this is the thing that goes on and on. A fellow was found hiding in an irrigation ditch. He admitted that he was NLF. He said he had left his weapon behind. It was my job to interrogate him. We got into a helicopter and went down to find the weapon. We dropped right off into elephant grass about three feet high. It was a risky area to be in, and I didn't especially care to be there. We walked out to the Saigon River and he said it was right near the bank, and he was sort of hunting around, and then he finally broke into tears and he said, "I lied. I actually didn't have the weapon." He was actually expanding on his own importance. He was only an ammo bearer. And when my interpreter came he was going to kill him on the spot. But he just proceeded to mash in his face with his carbine. I told him to stop but not soon enough. We loaded him back in the helicopter and left. He broke his nose. I mean it was obvious by the way the nose was lying on the side of his face that it was broken. Later we had an interrogation report that the enemy was bringing B-40 rockets. B-40 rockets are not the kind they used to bomb Saigon but rather anti-armor rockets. They penetrate steel. It will penetrate seven inches of cold steel, the very depth of tanks, so we were very concerned. We knew it wasn't a new weapon, but we didn't want any of those particular ones around. We thought that they were stockpiled for an assault on us, and so we charged out to the village, and evidently they had just rolled right into the village and surprised them, loading these things and stockpiling them. Right below the village was an entirely NLF area, and this was an area that was four miles from the Fourth Division, the Third Brigade headquarters. You can really see the influence this pacification had on the area. Anyway they went in and the Vietnamese were so surprised that they started dropping everything and ran for their weapons. They just got cut down. One prisoner was brought in and I think he had a hand grenade explode at his feet. It blew one foot almost completely off and maimed his leg. The other leg was very badly cut, a terrible wound. He was brought in and everyone immediately knew that he was a VC. He admitted it. I'm not proud to say it, but I was involved in interrogating him. He was in extreme pain, no morphine, no stitches, no nothing, no water till he talked. The doctor, the regimental surgeon, said, "O.K." This went on for about three hours. The man was begging for water and moaning with pain.

161

The medical evacuation helicopter took him back to the Third Brigade of the Fourth headquarters. He was just out of our hands then, but he didn't get any medical treatment at all, aside from a tourniquet to stop the bleeding. The armored cavalry would surround a village in the middle of the night and wait until morning and roust everybody up and march them down the center of the village, sort people out, and keep the ones we wanted to interrogate. The sortings are called screenings, and if there is someone that you would like to interrogate, you might do a tactical field interrogation on them right there. Then if you think you might have something, you might want to take him back. You don't want to do this too often because you have to make an interrogation report every time you bring one into camp and have to log it in and all that, so I had to type the damn thing. So I wanted to stay away from that as much as possible. Toward the end of my tour in Vietnam, I counted 652 formal interrogations.

Q: You alone?

A: No, as a total detachment. Of these, I think I counted my name next to sixty-five or seventy. These are formal reports that went out. There were three hundred or four hundred semiformal interrogations and well over a thousand screenings. Anyway, back to the village sweep. They sealed off the village and all the women and children came out. They all lined up. It was as if they all wanted us to believe in divine conception. There were about thirty men, all of them old, and literally hundreds of pregnant females, or women who had just recently borne children because they had babies nursing. We asked our interpreters, "Where are the men?" "Well, they're out in the fields." And we said, "How come they are not in the Army?" "They are in the Army, but it's not in our Army." Every interrogation had a Vietnamese interpreter, because none of us were fluent enough to handle it. We tried to learn as much Vietnamese as possible because you couldn't trust the interpreters.

Q: Was there much abuse of women?

A: No. I was involved in an interrogation once where there was a Chinese girl, which was rare. This was back at the base camp, I think, and was between operation Cedar Falls and Junction City. This girl was brought in and they said she had been pointed out by villagers as being in the Vietcong cadre, and she was a very vocal girl, spoke Cantonese, Chinese and Vietnamese. The only reason why I know this is because we had an interpreter who was half Chinese, so he spoke it to her. Every time she would lapse into one language, we would use this interpreter, you know, to show her that she wasn't fooling us and that we could tell what she was saying. I beat her up—she was about fifteen or sixteen, not any older. She might have been fourteen. I beat her very severely, and this didn't stop her, just made her angry. Another person beat her, the interpreter beat her, and finally the other person said, all right, take off your clothes, and she looked at us as if to say "Fuck you, I'll take off my clothes." She starting unbuttoning her blouse and I said, "No, stop," and I walked out of the tent.

There generally was no sexual abuse. We used it as a threat, but it didn't work. The beatings, it's surprising how you would beat a man for an effect, slap him in the face to get his attention, and slap him again to get his attention. Then you got a little bit angrier. Again and again and again, and pretty soon you are slapping him out of anger, and pretty soon without even realizing what you're doing, and it degenerates into a mindless animal thing that is hard to describe. It's hard to think that you are that way, that an individual is that way, and that this can happen to him but it does happen. This not only happened with me but with the eight other interrogation men. I'll tell you how big the unit was. To give you the idea, there were thirty-two men in the unit.

Q: In the interrogation unit?

A: No, in the intelligence detachment.

Q: What was the name of the intelligence detachment?

A: 541st Military Intelligence Detachment.

Q: And that was comprised of these thirty-two men?

A: Yes. There is no 542nd, and I don't know of a 540th either. It's just the way things happened to get named in the Army. Anyway, there were eight interrogation enlisted men. There is supposed to be one Specialist 6—he's the section leader, enlisted; four Specialist 5s—they are called Senior Interrogators, which is what I was doing; four Specialist 4s, which are called Junior Interrogators. Then there was one captain, who was the senior interrogation officer, and the section commander, and then three officers below him. This was what the organization called for. But we were always short one lieutenant, and we were always short a couple of enlisted men, and we were always overranked on the enlisted men. We always had a couple of more Specialist 6s and Specialist 5s than we had Specialist 4s. It was a very rank-heavy outfit. In this intelligence detachment as in others there was the CI, the Counter-Intelligence, and then the imagery interpretation and the order of battle. It was a small microcosm of the intelligence school. One, the order of battle, is the record-keeping unit, and the other three are supposedly intelligence-generating. And in this unit all the interrogators, and some people who weren't interrogators but wanted to try their hand at it, had used force, torture, harassment at one time or another. Most of them constantly and consistently. As to the 172nd MI detachment, which we worked with on Cedar Falls, I witnessed interrogation using electrical torture, and the same with the First Military Intelligence Detachment, which is the intelligence detachment of the so-called big Red I. The First Infantry Division. Also, there was the Fourth MI detachment of the Fourth Infantry Division. I didn't do any interrogation work directly with them, but they showed me an apparatus for placing the electrodes for the field telephone on a person's back, by his collarbone, where evidently there is a sensitive nerve system, and this is evidently where they like to place them for maximum effect.

Q: Were you ever court-martialed or given an Article 15?

A: No, no. My record is spotless in the Army. I got the good-conduct medal, and I got the Army commendation medal and the usual Vietnamese garbage which they give you. The Vietnamese government gives you one and the American gives you another for being in Vietnam. The Vietnamese service medal is the one the Vietnamese government gives, and the Vietnam campaign medal is the one we give.

Q: The National Service medal?

A: Everybody gets that who's been in six months' active duty or longer. In other words, you are guaranteed a row of medals if you go to Vietnam. It's kind of window dressing to get and keep the troops happy.

Q: You got the commendation medal?

A: Yes, I got the commendation medal.

Q: Signed by the Secretary of the Army?

A: Yes. I got the Army commendation medal in the mail, after I left there. I was discharged from active service on June 23, 1967. I left Vietnam on the twenty-second and flew directly back to Oakland and was discharged.

Q: During that entire period, from the nineteenth of August 1966 until the seventeenth of June 1967, were you involved in interrogating prisoners?

A: Well, no, because the nineteenth of August was when supposedly we were in Vietnam, but we weren't. You're counted as being in Vietnam the minute you board the boat and it leaves the dock, and I think the boat trip took eighteen days, so I think that finally put us in Vietnam around September sixth or seventh. During my entire stay in Vietnam, aside from the normal maintenance of the area, it was my job to interrogate prisoners.

Q: And during that whole period, you were torturing prisoners?

A: The use of force, yes. Electrical tortures and beatings. There is a volume called the Law of Land Warfare, I think its FM-100-51, and it's an abridged version of the Geneva Convention, having to do with the handling of prisoners and the treatment of civilians and so on. I haven't read it cover to cover, but I've read a good deal of it. I could cite you chapter and verse which was departed from significantly. I mean, not departed from but just directly opposite of what happened in Vietnam. Sexes not being segregated, people being fed improperly in comparison with the troops, not being allowed mail, no proper sanitary facilities, no medical treatment, inadequate this and inadequate that. I mean, it's just that every single one of these is a breach, and I think the Geneva Convention classified these acts as war crimes. This is the convention that we signed in 1948.

Q: And you got medals for your service in Vietnam?

A: Yes.

Q: Do you have them?

A: Yes, I guess I do. Medals for performance in the best tradition of the United States Army. Oh, I was a professional. They are all pros. There's no doubt about it, when the Army sets out to do something well, whether it's torturing or killing or whatever, it does it well and does it efficiently.

Q: When you got back, did you talk with your family about it?

165

A: Not too much. My older brother and I discussed it and he said, "Don't rock the boat," and it took me a couple of months just to recover from Vietnam. A psychological thing, you know. I was healthy as a horse, but just to recover psychologically. I went back to school in Berkeley, and all the while I was looking for some way to say it. You just don't walk into a newspaper office and say here I am, and I've got a story for you. So I went to Berkeley, and I got in touch with somebody, actually it was an anti-war group there, who was slanted towards reaching the servicemen, which was unusual at the time. In 1967, no groups were servicemen-oriented— they all thought servicemen were dogs. Most of my friends were still back in the service, and I wanted to, you know, to just help them open their minds a little bit. I went around for about four or five months, trying to speak in various places and trying to get on TV shows and trying to pass the word. Nothing happened. I got ignored. The FBI came and visited my mother and made some very unveiled threats about what would happen to me if I didn't shut up. Anyway, I gradually got disenchanted because everybody was either calling me a liar or a fool or both. And a lot of my relatives said, "Commie. Pinko." Just being a conservative American puts a monopoly on truth.

Q: What were your political views when you went in?

A: I guess you could consider the fact that I was for the Vietnam war and I thought it was a pretty clear case of an outside aggression. After being there in the country, speaking the language as little as I did, but still speaking it. Just talking to people—Christ, I talked to many thousands of people, literally thousands of people, all over the Third Corps zone, and they just don't want us there, except for the people who are taking money from us.

Q: How do your parents react to your statements?

A: They don't want to believe it. "Perhaps the boy next door. Not my son. I know how I raised my son, by God, and he can't do that. John next door maybe, but not mine." So I stood up and said it, and I'll say it again too, and it's getting frustrating. It's been frustrating for a long time, because nobody wants to listen. I don't want to go to jail for anything, and I've had my fill of newspapers and TV talk shows. I want to accomplish something, but nothing can be accomplished when the American public remains as they

166

are, blissfully ill-informed. But anyway, back to politics. Politics, my politics have, well, after you see what's happening in Vietnam and experience what's been happening in Vietnam and you look around you at what's happening in the United States too, and you tend to realize that Vietnam is not just a single sick thing, in an otherwise fairly healthy society. It's just a symptom of the sickness of the society itself. My Lai occurred, and I came to the conclusion and a couple of other people came to the same conclusion that the American consciousness was ready to be able to accept the fact that Americans are not all good people, that it doesn't take a Nazi necessarily to kill six million Jews. Anybody when placed in the war contacts, with the dehumanization, the brutalization, especially the frustrations of being in the war where it is obvious that you are hated by the people you are supposed to help, is going to turn into a monster. Literally monsters, in many, many ways, and we thought that this would be the time, that the Americans could realize this. No, so I went to New York, to ABC. ABC shot off a good 1,500 feet of film and talked to me for an hour. They wouldn't put it on the air. Their explanation was that it was very hot, they had to have their legal staff examine it, and so we said, we shouldn't have messed around with ABC anyway, they are a pretty ragtag outfit. We phoned up CBS and they said, "Sure, we're interested," and they came around, and we wasted a couple of hours of their time, some more hundreds of feet of film. I phoned them that afternoon, and they said, "Well, it's real hot," and we said, "That's why we gave it to you," and they said, "It's a little too hot to put on right now." The frustration was just amazing. We didn't even bother going to NBC.

Q: How do you view your own role in Vietnam?

A: I should have, by all that I have been taught, I should have said no. At the very first opportunity, I should have said no and gone to jail, but I didn't. Then again, neither did anybody else, but I can't use that to justify myself. I cannot. I would just as soon forget Vietnam, forget that it ever happened in my life, but if more people are going to be saved from going through what we went through, and what the people went through at My Lai, especially the victims. If this can be stopped, if one person can be saved, it's worth saying, it's worth saying again, again and again.

167

▪ James D. Henry

Q: What is your name?

A: James D. Henry.

Q: When were you born?

A: April 4, 1947. Riverside, California.

Q: How old were you when you went to the service?

A: I was nineteen.

Q: What had you done until then?

A: I graduated from high school and worked at Sonoma State Hospital with retarded children. After that I was drafted. I refused induction once and was threatened by the FBI and all that, but nothing ever came of it. Finally, I accepted induction when they gave me my 1-A-O status—conscientious-objector status. It wasn't religious, it was moral.

Q: When were you drafted?

A: March 8, 1967.

Q: By the Army?

A: Right.

Q: And where did you take basic?

A: In Fort Polk, Louisiana.

Q: AIT?

A: Fort Sam Houston, Texas.

Q: And when did you finish AIT?

A: August '67.

Q: Where were you assigned from there?

A: Straight to Vietnam. Twelve days later.

Q: How did you go?

A: By plane. We flew over there, made it in twenty-four hours.

Q: Landed where?

A: At Cam Rahn Bay.

Q: What outfit were you with in Vietnam?

A: First 35th Infantry, part of the Fourth Infantry Division.

Q: And you were there one year?

A: Yes, I was a medic at the time.

Q: Attached to the same outfit the whole time?

A: Yes.

Q: Were you involved in any fire fights?

A: Yes, a number. All fire fights are different. The first one was in the pouring rain, and we really didn't know what was going on, at least I didn't. That was my first one.

Q: When was that?

A: October 8, 1968.

Q: Where was it?

A: It took place about twenty-five miles west of Chu Lai, in the mountains. During a typhoon.

Q: Did you receive any citations?

A: I was given a Bronze Star, with a V and the other regalia that goes along with all that. And a combat medical badge, which they give you for being a medic in the field. You don't really have to do anything for it.

Q: Did you ever see any mistreatment of prisoners?

A: Sure.

Q: What was the first instance, do you recall?

A: First prisoner I saw mistreated?

Q: Or civilian?

A: The first one was a twelve-year-old boy who was executed in my first fire fight. Some of the men brought him down from some hootches that were on a hill and we were standing next to a river in the pouring rain. The lieutenant was sitting on a rock, and they brought him down and the lieutenant said, "Who wants to kill him?" and two guys said they did. One guy kicked the kid in the stomach, and then a medic friend of mind took him around the rock and shot him in the back. I guess he shot him about eighteen times.

Q: You saw that?

A: I didn't see the shooting. It was behind the rock.

Q: You heard it?

A: I heard it. The body was tossed in the river.

Q: Why did the lieutenant want the child killed?

A: I haven't any idea. The kid wasn't doing anything. He just lived there.

169

Q: Any other instances of brutality or murder that you can think of?

A: Yes, there were many. One time we captured an old man about fifty, I don't know if we really captured him. All of a sudden they had him.

Q: Where was this?

A: It was in the same place, about three miles from there. It was the next day. They picked up this old man, and he had been following us, and we were taking him with us supposedly to send him in a helicopter, and we had to go up this fairly large hill. He had been beat up a little bit, and supposedly he had a heart attack on the way up the hill. Now, whether he had a heart attack or not, I don't know because he was behind me.

Q: You didn't see him die?

A: Well, I saw him dead. I didn't see him die. Two guys threw him off the hill, into a bunch of rocks, and we left his body there.

Q: Why was he with the outfit in the first place?

A: They picked him up for questioning, you know, and then when he died, couldn't question him any more, so they threw him off the hill. Another time, I was walking through some bamboo, about three days later, and the second platoon had this old man in a cave. All I heard over the radio was that they were going to test-fire some weapons, and so I thought they were test-firing weapons. There was a lot of firing and I walked through the bamboo and there was this old man, sitting in the cave dead, and they were using him for target practice, and they were still shooting him. He was dead.

Q: You saw them shooting the body.

A: Yes.

Q: Why did they do that?

A: I don't know why. There was another occurrence in February 1968. There had been a fire fight the day before and we lost a lot of men; we lost eight men. We found this man in a hole. He was of military age and in a spider hole. It's a little hole that one man can get into, it's camouflaged, and a couple of guys pulled him out and started asking him if he was VC or if he knew where the VC were. We all figured that he had something to do with the fight before, because the civilians there weren't friendly at all. We'd

170

found signs saying "First 35th go home" and "stop driving your tanks through our fields" and things like that. They pulled him out and then somebody got an idea. I started walking away because I thought we were going to move on, and then two guys held him down to the ground and this APC—it's like a tank, an armored personnel carrier—ran over him, and he did a lot of yelling and stuff. He writhed around because the first time it ran over him it didn't kill him, so they backed up over him again and killed him. And then we moved on.

Q: Was there any indication that he was with the VC?

A: No.

Q: He had no weapon, no uniform?

A: Nothing.

Q: And he made no admissions, of course.

A: Well, he couldn't speak English.

Q: And no one there could speak Vietnamese?

A: No.

Q: Did you ever see mistreatment of women?

A: I was aware of it, but I never witnessed any. I didn't like it, and the platoon I was with most of the time didn't like it, so it usually went on behind our backs, but I know a lot of women were raped. The first platoon raped five women one night on ambush. They raped them and then killed them. I know they did it.

Q: How do you know?

A: Well, because they told me.

Q: Approximately how many GIs were involved?

A: Ten.

Q: Do you know where it was or when it was?

A: Yeah, it was west of Chu Lai, about twenty miles west of Chu Lai, in that same general area.

Q: When was that?

A: That was in late October. They were setting up an ambush, to get some North Vietnamese carrying supplies and weapons, and these five women walked into their ambush, and there weren't any men with them. So they raped them and then they killed them. That's about all I know about that. It's all hearsay anyway.

Q: Did you witness any other mistreatment of civilians?

A: Yeah, well, I saw nineteen women and children killed. I guess you could call that mistreating them. It was a small massacre.

Q: Where was it, when was it, and what was it about?

A: February 9, 1968. We—it was the same day the guy was run over by the APC. About one half hour after that. We walked into this little village, a hamlet, and we were going to take a break, so we all sat down, and then the Third Platoon lieutenant called up the captain and told the captain that he had nineteen civilians rounded up, which was the normal procedure, to round them up and see what they had on them.

Q: Do you know the captain's name?

A: Captain Boswell.

Q: Do you know his first name?

A: I think it was Robert. I might say he was an excellent captain. Anyway, they were rounded up and then Lieutenant Moll asked what was to be done with them, and Captain Boswell just asked him if he remembered the order that had come down from higher that morning, and the order was to kill anything that moves, sort of general. I guess you could take it how you want it, and so I was a little startled as was everyone—

Q: Did you hear this conversation?

A: Oh, sure.

Q: Where were you?

A: I was sitting in a brick hootch. There was a radio operator next to me, so I could hear it over the horn.

Q: Do you know the name of this village?

A: No, I don't. No, we didn't know any names, we just, you know, we didn't use names, we just went in them and went out.

Q: What did the lieutenant say?

A: He just Rogered out, "Roger and out."

Q: This was a radio discussion, was it?

A: Yes.

Q: How did you know it was Captain Boswell?

A: Well, because I was watching and I know his voice. Besides that he used his call signal. And you know, they always use their call signal.

Q: Who else was in the brick hootch?

A: Oh, about five or six guys—most of them were from the first platoon. And anyway, the lieutenant set out and I was beginning to get a little upset and I started walking over to **Captain Boswell**, who wasn't too far away from me, and as I was walking over there two guys brought this young girl out of the hootch. She was naked, so I assumed she had been raped, and they threw her on the ground. While this was going on, Captain Boswell kept trying to call back Lieutenant Moll. I think he wanted to change the order, he didn't order him to do it, but I think he thought that Lieutenant Moll would, and I am assuming that he was trying to change the order.

Q: How far was Moll from Boswell?

A: About fifty meters.

Q: He was radioing for him?

A: Yes, Well, you don't want to yell, you might get shot.

Q: And you were going out to find Boswell at this point?

A: I could see him, he wasn't very far from me, and I was just walking over to him, and they brought this girl out, and they threw her on the ground and then about five guys opened up and that was the end of the nineteen women and children. And the girl.

Q: There were eighteen people plus this girl there?

A: Well, I didn't count the bodies. They said nineteen over the radio and I could see a whole bunch of them squatting around, so I presume the number was correct.

Q: You saw them fire on them?

A: Oh, yeah, everybody did.

Q: How many people were firing?

A: Four or five.

Q: Do you know their ranks?

A: Oh, they were all privates and Lieutenant Moll. And then after they were shot, everybody was just sort of dazed and stood around and then we moved on, and nobody talked too much after that.

Q: What kind of weapons did they use?

A: M-16s.

Q: What physical effect did this have on the victims?

A: Well, there was a lot of flesh and blood, chunks of flesh flying. The M-16 is a high-velocity weapon. Makes flesh fly even at medium range. At close range, it's pretty damaging. Nobody said much.

Q: What happened to the bodies? Did they bury them?

173

A: No, we just left them there. One of the APCs, they were on a small rise, and one of the APCs pulled up on the rise, I guess to see if they really shot them, and they pulled off real quick. The guys looked down and looked kind of sick, so they pulled off and the lieutenant of the APCs was pretty disgusted. I mean he was furious.

Q: Who was that?

A: I can't remember his name. I think it was the first time he had ever been in the field. And I don't think he had ever seen anybody killed before, especially seen civilians killed. That upset him quite a bit. That upset a lot of people.

Q: Were the civilians all women?

A: Women and children, and there might have been some old men there. I don't know. I think there were some old men in there, too.

Q: Did you ever see anything else like that in Vietnam?

A: Nothing that massive. I never saw anything that massive. There was a lot of killing. No, I never saw anything that massive before, and that was sort of the topper.

Q: Did you ever see the prisoners interrogated?

A: No, I never did. Oh, a couple of times the guys did some pretty raunchy things to prisoners. They tied a rope around his neck and then tied a pig to him. Also, they tied a rope around a prisoner's neck and dragged him around and beat him up quite a bit. Until the captain stopped it.

Q: Was that Captain Boswell?

A: Yes, Captain Boswell. He was a good captain. He was pretty gung-ho when he first came over and he was all for the war, and he sort of became disappointed after February 9, when we got in a great big fire fight. And after that, he just wanted to protect the company against higher. He didn't like higher at all because they sent us on some absurd missions. He considered them to be absurd and so did I. He just tried to keep us out of trouble after that. Like one time, they sent us off this hill to go down and find some NVA. Well, we went down the hill and killed one NVA in a tree, and then turned around and went back up the hill because Captain Boswell didn't want us to get in a trap like A company had gotten into a couple of days before. They had gone off the hill and the colonel kept telling them to push on down, and they killed three or four NVA on the way down, and the colonel kept telling them to go on farther, and go on farther, and see what they could get. Finally, they ended up almost getting completely wiped out. They got in a trap in bunkers, and the colonel wanted us to go down farther too, and Captain Boswell wouldn't do it. He was pretty disappointed by that time, and he was just out to protect his men. A lot of people blamed him for a lot of the guys that got killed, but it really wasn't fair of them to blame him.

Q: About how many civilians would you say you saw needlessly killed?

A: I would estimate about forty, including the nineteen. Well, there's no reason to ever kill civilians. All civilians killed—they didn't need to be killed. I mean, there wasn't any point in killing any of them. They hadn't anything to do with the war. Because they are killed by both sides, they are killed by the Vietcong, they are killed by the North Vietnamese, they are killed by the Americans, they are killed by the South Vietnamese. They are the ones that are having the trouble. They are the ones that can't get away.

Q: Did you ever protest, after you got out of Vietnam, about what you had seen?

A: There were a lot of guys that were going to report the massacre. Lieutenant Masterson was going to file a report because he was furious. He was a platoon leader—the Fourth Platoon—and he was in an absolute rage when we got back to my location. He was furious.

Q: He wasn't an eyewitness, then?

A: No, he heard it over the radio and knew that it had happened and he was going to report it. The lieutenant of the APCs was going to report it. I was going to write the San Francisco *Chronicle* about it, right then I was going to. In fact I started the letter that night. But the next day we got into a huge fire fight and it was sort of just lost in the war, and it was sort of just put out of everyone's memory, everybody that didn't like it, and nothing ever became of that that I know of. Supposedly, the lieutenant of the APCs reported it. That's what I heard. Now whether he did or not, I don't really know. And if he did, nothing ever came of it. When I got home, I ran right to Don Duncan on my second week of leave. I was down here in September 1968.

175

Q: Did you know Duncan?

A: No, I had just read about him, and I went to find a friend of mine first, Bill Royce—he is a parole officer at San Quentin— and he advised me to see Duncan. And so I went to City Lights and asked where I could find him and searched around and finally I went to *Ramparts* and we met up there. I told him the story and he began to write it up and tried to publish it in *Ramparts,* and this went on for a couple of months while I was in Texas, and ultimately *Ramparts* wouldn't publish it because they were afraid.

Q: Were you interviewed by Duncan for *Ramparts?*

A: Yes, at that time he was working for *Ramparts*. And he wrote the story for *Ramparts*. But I guess they were afraid, I don't know, they were afraid of something.

Q: When did you get out of Vietnam?

A: August 31, 1968.

Q: August 31st. So it was in September that you were talking to Duncan?

A: Yes, on my second week of leave, I drove up to Seattle to see my brother first, and then on the way back I tried to get ahold of Duncan.

Q: At that time, no one else had said anything about this, had they?

A: No, never. It was the first real major massacre that had come out, and, well, it never did come out until now. You know, it's been over a year and a half now.

Q: What did you do after *Ramparts* declined?

A: Well, in the meantime, I was talking to a lawyer, Davis Bragg, in Texas.

Q: He's in Killeen, Texas?

A: Right. And he told me to get some political backing, or some official support before trying to do it, while I was in the Army.

Q: You were still in the Army?

A: Yes, at that time I was stationed at Fort Hood.

Q: How did you hear about Bragg?

A: Don told me about him. Don told me to go to see him. And so I tried that. First, I wrote to a congressman. This congressman, I thought, had the reputation of being a real liberal. He wrote back that he was sorry but that since I didn't live in his district, it really didn't concern him, and he couldn't do anything about it because I wasn't one of his constituents. And the reason I wrote this guy in the first place was because Ed Reinecke was my Congressman and I really didn't care to tell Reinecke anything. I don't want to call him a moron, but I didn't exactly agree with his politics. He's now Reagan's Lieutenant Governor. Finally, I ended up writing Reinecke, and he wrote back and said that he would surely look into the matter and he was very concerned, and that was the end of it. He probably didn't look beyond the second page of the letter I wrote him.

Q: You gave him all the details which you've related to me?

A: Yes, all that we discussed. I didn't give him any names, I said nineteen women and children were executed, and I saw them and that I wanted to do something about it. And he gave me the old Congressional put-on, I guess. All the letters were registered. He gave up his seat to run for Lieutenant Governor. Goldwater has his seat now. Barry Goldwater, Jr.

Q: You received one response that said he was looking into it and was that the end of it?

A: That was the end of it.

Q: Did you do anything else?

A: Yes. I went to a lawyer, at Fort Hood, an Army lawyer, and asked him, you know. And I asked him if this was in confidence, you know, between a lawyer and a client. And he said certainly, so I told him about the massacre. I didn't really trust him. I wanted to see what he was going to do. I told him that I wanted to publish a story about it, and he said don't do it while you are in the Army, because they can get you.

Q: How can they get you? Did he say?

A: They can get you on anything. They can get you on Article 15, a million times, for blinking one eye, for not doing anything and you're on 15, and at that time my record was spotless, so I said okay. The next thing I know, he comes back into the room and he said I had an appointment with the CID. I went down and saw the CID and he harassed me quite a bit, telling me that he would get to the bottom of it, and he would find out what I was trying to pull on him or what I was trying to pull off on the Army.

Q: Did you get the impression that he was trying to find out the facts?

177

A: Well, I got the impression that he was trying to get my ass. To silence me.

Q: What rank was he?

A: You don't know about CID. They wear civilian clothes. They are not civilians though. They are sly little people. I got the impression that he was after me.

Q: Did anyone in your outfit ever collect portions of a body as a souvenir?

A: Ears?

Q: For example.

A: Yes. There were quite a few guys with ears stuck in their headbands. They usually didn't keep them very long because they rotted. Some guys put them in jars with chloroform.

Q: How common was it, in general?

A: It disgusted most guys. A friend of mine in A company, which was our sister company, said one time that when A company goes into a friendly village, if it's not VC when they go into it, it's VC when they leave. They do so much damage. A company was sort of notorious for sex acts that they could force the Vietnamese women to perform.

Q: Are you talking about rapes?

A: Rape, and just making them do these—do weird, perform weird sex things. I never heard of our company doing it. They raped a lot of women, but I never heard of them making them perform various things. The main point of the whole thing is that the guys that kill the civilians are responsible, but the military is ultimately responsible for not training them differently.

Q: Why do they kill civilians and mistreat others?

A: I don't know, psychologists don't, psychiatrists don't.

Q: What do you think?

A: Hate.

Q: Was it after a fire fight when guys were injured that the massacre took place?

A: Yes, but that's still no excuse.

Q: No, of course, there is no excuse, but I am asking for the reason.

A: That's no excuse for anybody. Racism is most of it—that is what I attribute most of it to. Just pure, simple racism. Because the

178

Vietnamese aren't the enemies, they are gooks and they are not white, they are gooks—anybody can outrank them, even a private. They are little and they are supposedly backward, and yet they can do a lot of things I can't do. Most of it is just racism. You are over there and a lot of people are getting killed, and you don't know why, and you are supposedly supporting these people, and you see the ARVNs, the Vietnamese infantry, they go around dragging their rifles on the ground, and you just don't like dying for them. And so the hate goes out, the hate goes out against them all, it doesn't matter who they are. I attribute most of it to racism, but you can't blame racism for all of it. Most of it is the Army and a lack of training, because some of the killings are led by officers. Or are done with the permission of officers. And there is just no training about how civilians should be treated, and plus the men don't—they all of a sudden find themselves with the power of life and death in their hands, and they have never had this power before, and they have never had any power before. I mean, they just get out of high school and all of a sudden they have all this power, and it does something to them. Plus I don't think they have anything in the way of real moral strength by the time they get over here. Some do, quite a few do, the older ones do, but most of the average guys you know, they haven't considered what they are doing, they haven't considered why they are going to die, they haven't considered even why they are there. They just go. It's the thing to do. They were told to go and they go.

Q: What are you doing now?
A: I'm going to school.
Q: Where?
A: Valley Junior College.
Q: What are you studying?
A: I am majoring in political science and history.
Q: What do you intend to do?
A: Teach, ultimately, hopefully.
Q: Where?
A: I don't know where, a junior college somewhere.
Q: Political science?
A: Right now it is political science.
Q: You're how old?

A: Almost twenty-three. I'll be twenty-three April 4th. I'm twenty-two now. I was nineteen when I was drafted. I've been out almost a year now. I am still in the Army.

Q: You didn't get your discharge?

A: It's one fear I have of this, of speaking out. I may be reactivated. I was separated, but I am in the active reserves until 1973. So any time they could come and say, "All right, Buddy, get your uniform."

Q: Why are you in the reserves?

A: That's when you're drafted, you're drafted for six years. Not two. Everybody thinks it's two. It's not two, it's six. I have an honorable separation, but I'm not discharged yet, you see. I'm out of the Army but I'm still in technically, on paper, somewhere, they still have me in the Army.

Q: When did you get the separation?

A: March 8, 1969. That was a nice day.

Q: Do you have any Article 15 in the Army?

A: No, I never had anything. I never had a reprimand, never had anything. I had a spotless record, I never did anything.

Q: What was your rank when you left Vietnam?

A: Spec 5. That's equivalent to buck sergeant.

Q: And that was your rank when you were separated?

A: Right, that is my temporary rank, supposedly still.

Q: Have you told your parents about what you saw in Vietnam?

A: Oh, I told my mother everything. I wrote my mother letters telling her. I never told her exactly what happened because I was afraid the letter might get lost or something might happen to it. I never told my father anything until just the other day.

Q: What does your father do?

A: He's an assistant superintendent of Santa Fe, at Barstow. He's an electrical genius or something. His wife, my stepmother, is a teacher in San Bernardino. My father was a little upset because he thought I was—how did he put it?—he said he didn't want me doing anything wrong, anything detrimental to the country. He's sort of the Old Guard, and I told him that I wasn't doing anything wrong, and I told him, "Right is right and wrong is wrong, and everybody knows the difference between the two, and you can't rationalize wrong, and you can't rationalize it or justify it. And you can't hide it." After that little bit, he said, "Well, all right."

Q: How about your mother?

A: Oh, well, she's been for my disclosing the facts.

Q: What does your mother do?

A: She's just a housewife. She raised me and my brother. She's very much against the war. When I was in Vietnam, she sent me all the clippings that were going on and all the protests and everything, and I would have hated, if I had gotten killed, I would have hated to be the person to come out and tell her.

Q: What did you get the Bronze Star for? Do you have a copy of the citation?

A: Yes, I do. I don't have it with me. I have it somewhere.

Q: Know what it says?

A: A lot of crud.

Q: Such as?

A: Oh, saving lives, staying up all night with the wounded and you know. I don't know if I really deserve it. There were other people that did more, you know. The only thing with medals is that some people get seen and some people don't. Some people get them for not doing anything and some people don't get them for doing anything heroic. Medals are a farce. Our colonel got an Air Medal, which is a pretty impressive medal. He got an Air Medal for flying over a fire fight. Well, we were in it. He was so high up you could hardly see the helicopter. Of course, the colonels put themselves in for them. Officers get them for just being there, you know. They give them to each other.

▪ Billy Conway

Q: What is your name?

A: Billy Conway, RA 576129534.

Q: When did you enlist?

A: February of 1968.

Q: When did you arrive in Vietnam?

A: May 1968. I went through basic at Fort Ord and AIT at Fort Ord, then direct to Vietnam by plane after a fourteen-day leave. I landed at Long Binh.

Q: What outfit were you with?

A: The First Cavalry Division. Second of the Twelfth.

Q: When did you leave Vietnam?

A: I was wounded in the legs by shrapnel in an operation in the Central Highlands during November 1968. I was sent to Okinawa, to Camp Kue Hospital. When I was released from the hospital in January, they stationed me on Okinawa. They wouldn't let me come home. They said because I didn't pull a full tour in Vietnam I would pull the rest of it there.

Q: Did you see much action before you were wounded?

A: In the seven months I was in action a good five and a half months. Fire fights, ambushes and sniper fire.

Q: Did you ever see any prisoners or enemy wounded mistreated?

A: I saw many prisoners mistreated. They would catch a prisoner and knock them around with fists, weapons, or kick them. Lifers mainly were the worst offenders. During the end of October, just before I was wounded, we were at a town about 135 or 140 miles from the Cambodian border. The town was Don Tang. My squad was sent into a tunnel about eighteen miles outside of this little village. There were nine of us in the squad. Eight of us were sent down into the tunnel. When we got down there we found nine wounded NVA soldiers, North Vietnamese Army, and three NVA nurses. Seven of the guys took the prisoners out of traction, took the prisoners who were in casts out of their beds. Then they threw them right over into a corner. Then they grabbed the three nurses. The nurses were between eighteen and twenty-six I would guess. They began to hit them and stripped their clothes off. When the girls fell down, they would grab them by their breasts and pick them up that way and then hit them again and knock them down again. First they took one girl. Two guys held their weapons on two of the girls so that they couldn't move. The other five guys took the other girl and threw her on a mat. Two pinned her arms back and two held her legs apart. The other guy then raped her. After he finished, then another guy raped her. The girl screamed. The guys hit her and told her to shut up. The girl kept saying, "*Chieu Hoi*," meaning that they just wanted to surrender. Each of the five raped the girl. Then the other two raped her while two of the others held weapons on the two other girls. Then the same thing happened with the other girls. Each girl was raped many times. They were screaming and crying the whole time. When they finished raping them three of the GIs took hand flares and shoved them in the girls' vaginas. The girls were unconscious at that point. No one had to hold them down any longer. The girls were bleeding from their mouths, noses, face and vaginas. Then they struck the exterior portion of the flares and they exploded inside the girls. Their stomachs started bloating up and then they exploded. The stomachs exploded and their intestines were just hanging out of their bodies.

Q: What happened then?

A: They called another squad into the tunnel and they took the male prisoners out. The bodies of the girls were left there. The tunnel was then blown up. You know, sealed.

Q: What was the higest ranking non-com in the tunnel when the girls were raped?

A: A sergeant, E-5.

Q: Was this ever reported to anyone?

A: I tried to tell my platoon sergeant about it, but he didn't want to hear about it. I had nightmares about it. When I was home on leave much later my wife used to wake me up because I was screaming in my sleep.

Q: Were you awarded any citations in Vietnam?

183

A: The Purple Heart, Bronze Star for bravery and the regular Vietnam ribbons.

Q: What was the Bronze Star for?

A: A friend of mine had his leg blown off with an AK 47. He was way out in front. I went out and brought him back. I'd do it for any brother. The Army thinks that you have to get a bullshit medal for it.

Q: How do you feel about our presence in Vietnam?

A: It's a waste of human lives. It distorts the GIs' feelings and changes them. My main ambition is just to get out of the Army and live a sane life. I want to be a printer. I was nineteen when I enlisted. I wanted to get a high-school diploma and I wanted to get training that I couldn't afford to get any other way. I got some training all right. But not what I wanted. I have a wife, a child and another on the way. I just want to live with them and live a normal life.

Q: Where were you born?

A: In Philadelphia. I was raised in Los Angeles. I attended San Fernando High School.

Q: Where are you stationed now?

A: At Fort Lewis, Washington.

▪ Barry White

Q: What is your name?

A: My name is Barry White.

Q: Where are you from, Barry?

A: I am from Danville, Virginia.

Q: When did you enter the Army?

A: October of '68.

Q: What had you done before then?

184

A: I had been a college student and worked as a medical technologist prior to coming into the military.

Q: Where did you attend high school?

A: In Boston, Massachusetts.

Q: What college did you go to?

A: I went to the University of Virginia for my undergraduate degree and then I studied for my master's in medical technology.

Q: How old were you when you entered the service?

A: When I entered the service I was twenty-two.

Q: Where did you take basic?

A: I took basic at Fort Bragg, North Carolina. Also AIT there.

Q: When did you get to Vietnam?

A: I got to Vietnam in January of 1969.

Q: And when did you leave?

A: I left there in July of '69, after I was wounded. I stayed in the hospital there. I was wounded in June and I stayed in the hospital there until July and then I went to Japan. Then I went to Hawaii and then here.

Q: How long have you been at Fort Hood?

A: I have only been at Fort Hood now for about two months.

Q: And how much more time do you have left?

A: I've got thirty-seven days.

Q: You know the exact number.

A: I certainly do.

Q: What did you do in Vietnam?

A: I worked as a medical technologist in a laboratory, 44th Medical Brigade in Long Xuyen.

Q: And what were your duties?

A: My main duties were working in the immunohematology department, or blood banking. As the major function in any laboratory in Vietnam is to see that there is blood. The blood there is used for massive transfusions for wounded patients and it is also supposedly to be used for, well, any wounded people that come in whether they be Vietnamese or American GI.

Q: Did you have a chance to observe the use of blood for Vietnamese and for GIs?

A: Yes, I did.

Q: And what were your observations?

A: I found that there was a great prejudice against the Vietnamese people as far as the use of blood. If it came down to a situation whether if there were a young child there who was dying, he was hemorrhaging and a GI who was hemorrhaging, of course the GI received the blood. Also there were cases that it was not a decision between whether a GI received the blood but just the fact that it was a Vietnamese individual. The majority of the medical staff in the military is against the war in Vietnam. They feel it is not our war and we really have no purpose there. Actually, I think that this rubs off into their work and they take it against the Vietnamese people because they feel that they are lazy, that they don't care that we are there. Generally, this was the attitude I would see from the villages I worked with. They didn't want us there.

Q: Were there Vietnamese who actually died in the hospital because they were not properly treated?

A: Right. There was a case of one child that I can remember. It was a young Vietnamese girl who was brought in comatosed. No injury, she was brought in by her mother and it was diagnosed that she was a leukemia patient and, of course, the immediate thing that is usually done with leukemia patients is that they receive blood transfusions. They even take it on as massive therapy. It was the decision by her doctor there in the hospital.

Q: American doctor?

A: Right. That she not receive transfusions, that it would be hopeless and that we didn't have enough blood as it was. This was his actual decision from talking with the pathologist that I worked for. They both came to the decision, I should have said, that actually it would be useless to transfuse. Having a mother who is a doctor, I have been brought up with the attitude that there is always hope, and I don't like this. I don't think it's good medical ethics.

Q: How old was the girl?

A: I believe she was around eleven years old.

Q: What happened to her?

A: She died.

Q: Did many children die in the hospital because of refusals of the staff to treat them?

A: I can't say a lot died because of refusal of treatment, but a number of them did.

186

Q: Did you receive any citations while you were there?

A: I received the Purple Heart and I received the Vietnam Medal.

Q: How did you get wounded?

A: We were out around the perimeter of our base camp when some mortar rounds came in.

Q: If you had a year left and you got orders to go back to Vietnam, would you go?

A: No.

Q: What would you do?

A: For not going I would be court-martialed, and I would rather be in the stockade than go there and aid the war effort.

▪ Joseph Grant

Q: What is your name?

A: Joseph Grant.

Q: When did you enter the Army?

A: Nineteen sixty-three.

Q: Where was that?

A: I was drafted in Chicago and sent to Fort Knox, Kentucky.

Q: You took your basic training in Fort Knox?

A: Yes.

Q: And where did you go from there?

A: Fort Polk, Louisiana?

Q: Was that for AIT?

A: Yes.

Q: And after that where did you go?

A: Well, I went to Germany. I was with the 24th Division and then I was transferred to the Second of the 21st.

Q: And when did you get to Vietnam?

A: I was at Vietnam in July of '67.

Q: For how long?

A: One year.

Q: When did you re-enlist?

A: I re-enlisted in '65—November.

Q: For how long?

A: Four years.

Q: Did you re-enlist in 1969?

A: No, I didn't. I was discharged.

Q: Had you planned to make the Army your career at one point?

A: Yes I had.

Q: What changed your mind?

A: Well, it was a lot of things. Discrimination. Rank, for one thing. And what I saw in Vietnam.

Q: What was the highest rank you ever obtained?

A: I was staff sergeant.

Q: You were discharged as a staff sergeant.

A: Right.

Q: And what rank did you have when you were in Vietnam?

A: Buck sergeant.

Q: What were your duties in Vietnam?

A: Well, I was squad leader for about seven months, then I left and went to S and T Battalion.

Q: What's S and T?

A: Supply and Transportation.

Q: The first seven months you were a squad leader?

A: Right. First Battalion. Eighteenth Infantry. First Infantry Division.

Q: And where was that stationed?

A: Dzi Anh Base Camp. Lai Kae and Quin Loi.

Q: Were you on any search-and-destroy missions?

A: Right.

Q: You have taken pictures of some operations, is that right?

A: Right.

Q: Would you describe a specific search-and-destroy mission?

A: Well, this was back in March, and we were at the waterpoint. They had the Fifth Battalion of Vietnamese soldiers down there then; they were clearing this village out and searching, and so the next morning we were to go in and it had been shelled. They used artillery and napalm. We had to wait about six hours to move in there. We moved in and searched a lot of the huts and stuff, and I ran across a lot of these bodies. It wasn't the result of small arms. It was artillery. They had started firing that morning 'cause we could hear from where we were at. We saw the jets coming in. They made about two strikes, I think. Two strikes that lasted about an hour and a half. Then they hit with artillery for about a good three or four, maybe five hours. We went in searching after we got the word.

Q: And when you arrived in the village you saw bodies?

A: Right.

Q: How many bodies?

A: I'd say it was about seventy-five. Everything—men, women, children.

Q: Everyone was dead by the time you got there?

A: Just about. There were a few still around. Suspects.

Q: And what happened to them?

A: They took them down to the camp and the Vietnamese interrogated them.

Q: Did you see any interrogation of the prisoners?

A: No, I didn't. Every once in a while you might find a suspect and they make him talk.

Q: How do they make him talk?

A: They take bamboo to them, bamboo splinters. Or tie them down and they take a dong, a coin about the size of a nickel, and heat it and stick it in their fingertips.

Q: What other methods did you see them employ?

A: They tie them up and put a snake tie on them and bend their head to their foot and bring it back backwards and keep on sticking a knife in.

Q: Do they cut them with it?

A: They stick them.

Q: In deep?

A: About an inch.

Q: How many people did you see interrogated in this fashion?

A: I saw quite a few.

Q: Did you see any other methods employed?

A: Every now and then they would get them in helicopters and throw them out. They would say the prisoners jumped out. One time I saw a Vietnamese. I don't know if he was a suspect or what. He had a chain around him and was dangling out of the helicopter.

Q: What part of his body was the chain on?

A: This was around his foot.

Q: And he was hanging out of the helicopter?

A: Right.

Q: When was that?

A: During or around about September 1967.

Q: How high above you was it?

A: Three hundred meters.

Q: And how far was the man hanging from the helicopter?

A: Oh, I'd say about ten or fifteen feet out. From the ground that was the way it looked.

Q: How did you get the pictures that you took in Vietnam developed?

A: Through the Koreans. The only way you can get the pictures developed in South Vietnam, stuff like naked women, is in Hawaii, but they won't develop any war material for you. The Koreans, they got the White Horse Battalion. They got the equipment there.

Q: They did their own developing?

A: Right.

Q: They developed and printed the pictures right there in Vietnam and gave it back to you?

A: Right. They charge about five dollars for it though.

Q: For a roll?

A: Right.

Q: Did you ever see villagers interrogated by GIs?

A: There was a lot of times when we know there were some in there and maybe we'd stop a couple of these mamas, just tell by the way they looked they were trying to hide something. So we'd ask them questions and get the interpreter and if they came out with something like "we don't know" we'd slap them around.

Q: Who slapped them?

A: GIs.

Q: Did they use rifles?

A: Sometimes. Rifles, their hands, or steel butts.

Q: Was this the general procedure if you went into a village?

A: Yes.

Q: Were some of them badly beaten?

A: Yes. I seen one woman hit in the head with a rifle butt. She was just about unconscious. She was bleeding badly.

Q: And she was being asked what?

A: Location of the air-lift supplies. We knew they had supplies in there. When we asked Mama-san, "Where's the VC?" and she said, "We don't know," and when she said it she was shaking, and she kept looking back and we knew something was going on. So the guy hit her in the head with a rifle. And I see a GI I knew, and he's like he's gonna cut her or something. He had his knife out like he was sticking it in her back, and the CO pushed her down.

Q: Did you ever witness anything like the massacre at Song My?

A: Not that big. I saw a smaller one at Vu Dop. Anything that looked like a Vietnamese was shot. The First Cav was on the other side, about fifteen minutes from us. They went into the village. We stayed out on the perimeter.

Q: What did they go in with? What kind of weapons?

A: They went in with choppers. They landed with choppers.

Q: What side of the village did they come in on?

A: From the south. They had 16s, 50s and 60s, and they had deuces, and they had helicopter support.

Q: What's a deuce?

A: That's a mortar. They were shooting in from the south and then when people came running out they came out toward the east. Everyone was running with their hands up.

Q: They were running towards you with their hands up?

A: Right.

Q: And what kind of weapons did your squad have?

A: Machine guns and 16s, etc.

Q: How many people came running into your unit?

A: About seventy-five.

Q: What were they?

A: Vietnamese civilians.

Q: What happened to them?

A: They were shot, killed.

Q: Men, women and children?

191

A: Right. Mostly women. About fifteen men, about fifty or seventy women.

Q: When was this?

A: I had just gone on R and R. About December right before Christmas, if I'm not mistaken.

Q: Just before Christmas of 1967?

A: Right.

Q: What happened to the village?

A: It was destroyed.

Q: How did you destroy it?

A: Burn it down.

Q: With what?

A: Gasoline, lighters, anything. Matches.

Q: What happened to the bodies?

A: They dug a hole and put the bodies in. Then put lime in there, for the bones, I think. Then poured on gasoline and burned the bodies.

Q: How was such a big hole dug?

A: Well, the First Engineers were on base camp with us. They were called in. They brought a bulldozer with them. That's how the hole was dug for the bodies.

Q: How could they get a bulldozer through the jungle from the base camp?

A: It was brought in by a helicopter. A Chinook. They can pick up bulldozers.

Q: Who sent the bulldozer? Who gave orders for it to be sent?

A: It had to come from the battalion executive officer or higher.

Q: The bulldozer was brought in specifically to dig the hole?

A: Right.

Q: How long did you stay in the area?

A: We stayed all day. Then we were lifted out.

Q: By helicopter?

A: Right.

Q: How many villages did you see similar things done to?

A: Two others.

Q: Did any of your buddies collect parts of the enemy's body?

A: Yes, but they made us stop that one time. The guys would cut the ears off the Vietnamese, dry them out and string them around their neck, wear them that way on a string, like a chain. They were, you know, souvenirs or something. Half the guys go crazy. Just take a dead body and run a knife through it or keep on shooting it or something.

Q: You've seen that?

A: Yes.

Q: How often did that happen?

A: A lot of times. A guy loses a buddy, he gets hit or something, he's mad, so he takes it out on a dead body.

Q: Did you ever see a prisoner killed?

A: Yes. There was this man, he wasn't even a prisoner, but he was horsing around. An MP says to him, "Dee dee."

Q: What does that mean?

A: It means take off. He didn't, so the MP shot him. Killed him. The guy was about fifty-five, maybe sixty. That happened in 1967. I had been in the country only two months. It was just outside our base camp.

Q: Why did he shoot him?

A: Just for the hell of it. You can do anything there.

Q: Did you ever get orders to take no prisoners?

A: Yes. Often. On search-and-destroy missions. They told us to kill anything that moves. Men, women, children, animals. The order was if you do take a prisoner he is your baby. You must feed him from your own rations. So we killed everyone.

Q: What happened when you came across a wounded soldier?

A: You mean Cong or NVA?

Q: Yes.

A: Dust him off. Shoot him.

Q: How often did you see that?

A: Quite a few times. One time there was this woman—mama-san. She was wounded in the side of her head and she was crying and hollering for help. We just kept on searching the hootches, found watches and things there. She was hollering, so this sergeant says, "Shut up this old bitch." And the guys went over and shot her. She was Vietcong though. She had a weapon.

Q: Was gas ever used by American forces in Vietnam?

A: Yes, but not too often. It was CS and we had this machine that pumped it into a tunnel complex. Sometimes the Cong was down there, sometimes people from the village, hiding if they knew we were coming. We'd put the gas down there. Later on, we just sealed up the tunnel with grenades.

Q: What happened to the people?

A: They would be killed. Couldn't get out.

Q: Was any special effort made to protect the Vietnamese children from the war?

A: You can't. They're part of the war. The first week in the country you get schooling. It takes seven days. We had eight or nine instructors. They had classes—this is the First Division—on everything. Booby traps, patrolling, communications, small arms, map reading. Everything. And we had classes about how the kids might have explosives or weapons hidden on them. That they might try to get near us and kill us. They could be walking charges.

Q: What were you told to do about that?

A: Well, by the time the course was finished you were pretty much suspicious about kids coming up to you. You were supposed to wave them off and, if they kept coming, to shoot them. Sometimes the guys would just shoot them.

Q: Did you ever see that happen?

A: Yes.

Q: More than once?

A: Yes. Maybe at least four times.

Q: Did the four children have charges or weapons on them?

A: No, not in those cases.

Q: How old are you now?

A: Twenty-nine. I was twenty-two when I entered the Army.

Q: You have an honorable discharge?

A: Yes.

Q: Were you ever court-martialed in your years in the Army?

A: Never. I have a clean record.

Q: Did you receive any medals or citations?

A: Yes. I have five of them and our outfit got a Presidential Citation.

▪ Pete Schuler

Q: What is your name?

A: Pete Schuler.

Q: You are stationed at Fort Hood now?

A: That is correct.

Q: When did you enter the Army?

A: August '67.

Q: And where are you from, Pete?

A: Originally I am from Chicago.

Q: What schools did you attend?

A: I attended the University of New Mexico, and then I went to Berkeley for two semesters, discontinuously rather. I went back for the spring semester and then I knocked off summer and came back in the fall semester. Then I worked for a while and then I came into the Army. I was sent to Fort Bragg, North Carolina, for basic training and from there I went to Fort Huachuca, Arizona, for AIT.

Q: When was that?

A: That was from November '67 to January '68. Then from there I went over to Vietnam.

Q: When did you go to Vietnam?

A: January of '68.

Q: Where did you land in Vietnam?

A: Long Binh base. At the main placement center at Long Binh. From there I went to Camp Eagle, which is just above Hue, 101st MI unit.

Q: Airborne that is?

A: Right—101st Airborne.

Q: That was Military Intelligence?

A: Right. Military Intelligence, the S-2 section. I was there about four months before I was transferred to Saigon I went to the 519th MI Battalion and I was assigned to work at CDEC, the Captured Document Exploitation Center. I was at CDEC from approximately May '68 up until I believe it was May or June '69, and then

I was transferred to the immediate neighboring compound, which was sixty, which is the combined intelligence center, Vietnam. Then I returned here the nineteenth of October.

Q: And what are you doing now here? What have you been doing since October?

A: I reported at Fort Hood December first, and then I went to the 501st MI detachment working with the military intelligence unit of Fort Hood. I actually worked there for about three weeks until I was relieved of duty, and I have been just staying at the barracks doing nothing since then.

Q: Why were you relieved of duty?

A: The official reason was that my security clearance either wasn't validated or hadn't been validated.

Q: After two years in MI?

A: Right. They tell me that it's a standard procedure that everybody returning has to have their security clearance validated but like it takes a matter of a week or so to have it done and it's going on two months for me now.

Q: If that's the official reason, what's the real reason?

A: Well, they know of my political beliefs. I have spoken to several of the officers and they know that I frequent the Oleo Strut, and this is why, you know, I've been taken out of the intelligence division.

Q: What do you do now?

A: Well, up until today I have been just sitting around the barracks, sweeping up floors and taking the jeep down to the motor pool every once in a while to have it washed or change the oil or something similar to that.

Q: While you were in Vietnam, did you ever witness the interrogation of prisoners in the field?

A: While I was with the 101st, I witnessed the interrogation in five or six different periods of interrogation out in the field, interrogating maybe a total of ten or twelve prisoners. This was from the first of January up until approximately May of '68.

Q: And what was the method? Who was doing the interrogating?

A: The interrogation was carried out by both Americans and Vietnamese. On certain occasions Vietnamese translators would do the interrogating and American MIs would be taking the notes or use the information or asking the questions through the interpreter. Other times American linguists would be doing the interrogations themselves.

Q: What were the ranks of the Americans?

A: Usually the ones I witnessed were Spec 4s and Spec 5s, but it certainly wasn't uncommon for officers to interrogate also, lieutenants and captains.

Q: What were the methods used during these interrogations?

A: The methods depended upon the prisoner. If the prisoner was cooperative, well, then the methods were humane, I would say. If the prisoner wasn't cooperative, well, then any, almost any, type of interrogation would have taken place. I—I witnessed the use of —the well-known use, I suppose—of telephone cables and electrodes upon the prisoners.

Q: Placed where on the prisoners?

A: Placed on the prisoner's testicles, and if the prisoner became obstinate, well, then it would be merely a matter of turning the handles on the telephone machines themselves to charge electricity to the wires and to the prisoner's testicles and there was always a reaction of one kind or another.

Q: Is this a common technique?

A: Yes, I think so. I witnessed it myself and I have heard many people talk about it. My whole tour over there it was spoken of by people that, you know, talked to me about it in casual and standard-like terms.

Q: This was known by the officers?

A: Yes.

Q: What other methods were used?

A: Physical beatings were carried out quite frequently. More by the ARVNs, the South Vietnamese, than the Americans, but I did see Americans beat prisoners.

Q: How?

A: Well, with their fists and feet.

Q: Were the prisoners tied?

A: Yes, they were tied. Usually they'd be on their knees.

Q: Where would their hands be?

A: Their hands would be tied behind their backs, occasionally.

Sometimes their feet would be tied also but usually this wasn't so because they had to transport the prisoners from one point to another and they had to walk, so usually just their hands were tied behind their backs.

Q: Were they ever hit with weapons?

A: No, I never saw any hit with weapons, but I certainly saw a lot of them kicked with feet and knees, usually while they were already on the ground. They would be on their knees with their hands behind their back and usually they would be pushed forward and fall to their knees without the balance of their hands, and many times while they were being interrogated they were in a kneeling position to begin with, and it wasn't uncommon to—rather, I did see them beat them with hands and feet. I've been told this happens more frequently if a prisoner is captured after or during a fire fight or a particularly fierce fire fight where the Americans may have taken many casualties and then, well, the passions of the interrogators would come through and all kinds of methods of interrogation would result.

Q: What other methods did you see?

A: Dragged behind an APC or something like that.

Q: Have you ever heard of that being done?

A: I've heard of it being done. I never saw it.

Q: That's an Armed Personnel Carrier?

A: Yeah, that's correct. You know, to tie them behind an Armored Personnel Carrier and drag them until they feel like talking. I imagine some never talked.

Q: Did you ever hear of the use of helicopters?

A: I've heard of prisoners being interrogated on helicopters while the helicopters were in flight. If prisoners proved to be valueless, wouldn't speak, they were just pushed off.

Q: Who told you about that? Is that common knowledge in Vietnam?

A: I can't say if it's common knowledge or not. I've talked with some old interrogators, some lifers, I should say, who have been in Vietnam for five or six years, and they told me about doing this type of thing.

Q: They said they did it?

A: One did.

Q: Ever hear of the use of bamboo splinters?

A: Yes, I've heard of that being done by both sides, but I have never had anybody tell me that they did it themselves.

Q: Did you ever hear of anyone collecting ears from the dead enemy?

A: Yes, I've read of this being done. I've read of this in material which I was supposed to have been gathering for the interrogation center where different individuals wrote that they had personally collected ears from dead Vietcong and had carried them about with them until they began to smell too much, and they threw them away.

Q: Why would they write this in an official document or a document which would reach you officially?

A: This is kind of difficult to say because part of the things that I know that happen in Vietnam was classified by the Army. You know, this was supposed to have been confidential material, that they would write these things home in letters, and for one reason or another they never got the letters mailed or the letters fell into our hands. The only way that we got those letters was that they were captured by the Vietcong and NVA, and then we in turn captured the material back. These were written in, you know, personal letters to be sent home, and they wrote about collecting ears and carrying them around and having collections of them in their hootches.

Q: Did you ever visit a major interrogation center where there were large numbers of Vietnamese?

A: Right.

Q: When and where?

A: Aside from the two intelligence centers that I have already mentioned, there was a third center in Cho Lon, about a mile north, northeast, I believe, of the main Cho Lon PX. It was a large compound, walled on four sides with barbed wire. Beyond the wall with no way of distinguishing just what the compound was. But the compound was a large—it was the main interrogation center in Vietnam. All the important prisoners captured in the Delta and the Highlands, and in the Northern Provinces, Quang Tri and Quang Nam Provinces, were shipped to this interrogation center in Saigon under armed guard. Usually, American MPs or American infantrymen sent on special duty, but the interrogation center was controlled and run by the Vietnamese, although they did have contingents of Americans, Koreans and possibly Thais working there. I am not sure about the Thais, but I do know it had Americans and Koreans and Australians also. While I was in Saigon, most of the time I was in Saigon, I lived with perhaps twenty or thirty American personnel who worked at the interrogation center, and I was inside the center itself five or six times and from what I know it appeared to be in good shape. But the cells that he—this individual spoke Vietnamese —told me that Vietnamese guards who worked there told him that most of the cells in which the prisoners were kept were really in atrocious conditions and not unlike many of the worst prison conditions that you read about today. But the important thing about this interrogation center to me was that in a period immediately following the first Tet offensive from I guess it was late January up until late February and early March and then the May offenses, the period immediately following these offenses, a total of very close to or perhaps more than two thousand prisoners were executed within this interrogation center. Presumably as a reprisal or as a tactic to perhaps save face for the losses that they had sustained during the Tet offensive.

Q: What's the source for the figures?

A: The original source was from a staff sergeant who worked at the center for nearly two and a half years. He was staff sergeant at the time. I believe he's out of the service now.

Q: Do you remember his name?

A: Paul Guard. He told this to me. I believe it was last summer.

Q: In Vietnam?

A: Right. He said this was in a period I guess of from four to six months that these prisoners were executed.

Q: Did he say how they were executed?

A: No, he didn't. He didn't say how, but it is common knowledge though—I mean throughout at least Saigon and the personnel that are aware of this location—that many VC and NVA prisoners are executed systematically.

Q: In the center?

A: Within the center, yes.

Q: And the center is run by the South Vietnamese?

A: The South Vietnamese, right.

Q: Did some of the prisoners find their way there because they were captured by Americans?

A: Yes, very much so. Particularly, as I said before, if they were believed to be important prisoners, but most prisoners that are captured within Gia Dinh Province, the province in which Saigon is. Most of the prisoners captured within Gia Dinh Province immediately surrounding Saigon are usually brought to this interrogation center. They have other centers throughout Vietnam not as large and I don't think as many different allied units work there as they do in Saigon. But since the important prisoners are brought to Saigon and interrogated, they are interrogated not only by the South Vietnamese and American fighting forces but at least their interrogations benefit civilian police forces also. I know the Vietnamese National Police have access to all the interrogations, the interrogation reports, and possibly even are there for the interrogations. And also such groups as the Phoenix group, which operates out of Saigon.

Q: What's the Phoenix group?

A: I'm kind of hazy on this myself, but to the best of my understanding it seems to be an offshoot of possibly the CIA working within Saigon to interrogate, put their fingers on important political prisoners within Vietnam. They have used a variety of means to determine just who is a politically important prisoner. From what I've read they have been, by at least some definitions, successful in rounding up a lot of prisoners.

Q: Did you ever get information from your work which was different from what the press reports?

A: I think the main thing I found out through my work with captured documents and working with interrogation reports was that in the very early part of '68, during the Khe Sanh siege, in which the Marines were cut off by land from supplies and reinforcements, was that I believe it was reported to and by the press that the Seventh Air Force was mainly responsible in keeping the siege from being successful by repeated air strikes day and night, both with B-52s and, I believe, well, the usual rocket attacks that the Air Force centered around the base itself. But from the reports it was reported that there were perhaps as many as twenty or thirty thousand North Vietnamese troops waiting in reserve to come up and reinforce the troops that were already laying siege to Khe Sanh. But the Vietnamese had to give up the operation entirely because of a bubonic-plague epidemic that broke amongst the troops. Because of the air strikes they couldn't go out and collect the bodies and the bodies lay out there in the fields for a number of weeks and the rats began to feed on them and as a result the bubonic-plague epidemic broke out and they had to evacuate the area entirely. So, in effect, indirectly the Air Force was responsible for saving the Marines but directly the bubonic-plague epidemic saved them. At least, it was responsible for the Vietnamese calling off the siege on the base.

Q: How do you know that?

A: Well, from captured documents and interrogation reports.

Q: You were there on October 15th, the first Moratorium day?

A: Right.

Q: What did you see?

A: On October 15th during the Moratorium I saw many of the field-unit troops in Saigon wearing black armbands and I heard a lot of troops, soldiers, express the desire to wear them and I heard a lot of denials, you know, saying that they couldn't wear them, but the troops that were in Saigon, at least on their own, detached from their units for at least a short period of time, were wearing the armbands.

Q: How many did you see?

A: I think I saw anywhere from seventy to one hundred just in the course of that one day.

Q: Are the black GIs organized in Saigon?

A: There is a restaurant called the Soul Kitchen in Saigon. The Soul Kitchen is located on a small alley just off of Chu Min Ky Street, not more than—it's not even a quarter of a mile outside the main gate to the air base. This kitchen was set up by a black civilian who was formerly in the American service. But he came back and was working as a civilian in Vietnam and then rented or bought this restaurant in this alley and set it up designed to cater mainly to black GIs. They sell soul food, barbecued ribs and chickens and chitlins and greens and cornbread and this type of thing. In the many times I have been in there I have met and talked with dozens of black GIs from virtually all over Vietnam. Troops that came into

202

Saigon on a three- or five-day pass, from all over, really. It appears that most every black GI in Nam knows about the kitchen and many of them, at least when they go to Saigon, make it a point to go there. At least many of them have a chance to talk with each other and discuss their feelings about the war while they are there. It's become an important vehicle for black GIs within Nam right now.

Q: Have you been in there?

A: Yes, many times.

Q: What is the feeling that is expressed there about the war?

A: The predominant feeling is that it's one of exploitation of the blacks mostly, I think. They realize that they're in the field in a larger majority than what they exist as back home, and I think they realize, at least they have the feeling, that they pull more hazardous duties than most of their white counterparts—not all of them but most.

I met Miss Phung, I believe it was, in February '68. It was not quite a month after I had gotten into Vietnam. This was still while I was at Long Binh, and then after I returned to Saigon I met her again and during the course of my tour of duty over there, which was nearly two years, I saw her off and on. Sometimes for long periods of time and she would remain in Saigon and then occasionally she would go up north for one reason. At first she had claimed to see her mother and then stay with her family for a while and then she would come back to Saigon. She was black. I guess she was the only black Vietnamese that I knew while I was there. She was, although I saw maybe, saw a total of perhaps seven or eight black Vietnamese, but she was the only one I got to know. I believe her father was a Senegalese with the French Army. Her mother was Vietnamese. Her mother was—I believe her mother was living in Pleiku while I knew her. Kai Phung was about seventeen or eighteen years old. She was, at least while she was in Saigon, she was a part-time prostitute. For all I know I think the money went for subsistence since she didn't have anything that I knew of. No clothes or decent place to live, really. So her money usually went for food. I suspected for a long time she didn't really tell me until I had known her almost for or even longer than a year that she was actively working for the Gia Dinh VC, Vietcong, and many times when she'd go north she would be acting as a liaison agent carrying messages to different units. She didn't work all the time. She'd make a trip or two and then she'd knock off for a month or a couple of months. After I found this out, like I say I had known her for about a year and she introduced me to, oh, four, five others of her friends who were also working for the Vietcong as either liaison agents or some other capacity. They were young and they weren't important capacities but they had been working for quite some time, I understand. I wasn't popular with her friends and I was only trusted by her, I suppose because I had known her for such a long time or at least on a rather steady basis. She had personal problems we used to discuss because she did speak fairly good English although I don't think she had more than a couple of years of schooling. One thing, at least during the latter part of '68, through her and her friends I did come to realize that Saigon had been tremendously infiltrated by Vietcong. The government for quite some time had been able to, had carried out a successful program of checking or identifying Vietcong through a simple process of having Vietnamese carry at all times identification cards, but by the end of at least the last quarter, perhaps even the last half of 1969, all Vietcong within the province made it a point to have identification cards, and it was virtually impossible for the government now to identify them except for perhaps old, main-line Vietcong who had been working for many, many years and who had become important and were thereby readily identified by the government.

Q: How much time do you have left here?

A: With an early out for school I have four months.

Q: What do you intend to do for the next four months?

A: For the next four months I intend to go to school in the evenings and during the day at a junior college across the road from the Fort. With the duties I have now I certainly have the time, and I have administrative permission to attend classes during the day as my military duties are pretty much nonexistent.

Q: What are you going to be studying?

A: I've got four courses. I signed up for a course in journalism, personality adjustment in psychology and then I've got an introductory course to philosophy and contemporary problems course in sociology.

Q: After you get out of the Army, what do you expect to do?

A: I would like to return to school for at least a short time, either to Berkeley or to the University of New Mexico. If I get an early out —that is, if I get out of the Army in late May or early June—I'll be obliged to go to school up until the date of my normal ETS, which would be August 25, 1970. The Army releases men up to ninety days early with the provision they go to school full time.

Q: What does ETS stand for?

A: Expiration time in service.

Q: After you get your degree, what do you plan?

A: I would like to be able to do some writing. I've become deeply interested in Vietnam and would like to go back there under—as a civilian, of course—and do some writing and a great deal of research into the social-political-military problems and situations in Vietnam. I've met a great deal of people over there who could help me do that writing and I know my way around and believe I could still have access to many information sources over there.

Q: What do you feel about the war?

A: Before I went to Vietnam, my feelings were highly ambivalent. After I got to Vietnam my feelings were strengthened against the war, and I think that I began to become even more disillusioned with Americans over there for even more reasons than I had before I went.

Q: What reasons?

A: Primarily in that I never saw any indication by the people at large that they were willing to be ruled by Saigon. I saw no indications that Saigon could or ever had effectively ruled the people. So many people were disenfranchised from any governmental partaking except the landowners and landlords. While the Americans' attitude in general towards a minority race of people, their feelings of self-righteousness in almost everything they undertook, these are Americans I am talking about. I don't know, I was just turned off by the whole situation, everything I came in contact with completely. I never felt once that we were doing the right thing and going the right way or going about it in the right manner. I deeply believe I think the United States made one of its biggest, you know, political tragedies in the States when they refused to give Ho aid during the later Forties when he actively sought it from the Americans.

Q: May I ask you a personal question? I know how difficult the position was for you, but how do you feel about having been there, being against the war and yet, in effect, supporting the effort by your presence and your work?

A: Right. Really, at the time it was like being in a constant state of schizophrenia—I mean having to do one thing and live one way, and yet really entirely believe another way—believe so strongly about it that there really was—I never met anybody over there in my entire tour that felt anywhere close to what I felt. There were many people who opposed the war, but opposed it either for self-centered reasons or on the basis that the Vietnamese just couldn't ever handle or understand a democratic or capitalistic society. In other words, that they were, you know, inferior people and we were wasting our time by even trying to help them. My feelings, I guess were—I was bitter the whole time, having to be there, and for having to do what I had to do even though our main mission and our goal was to attempt to save American lives. There wasn't any attempt in particular to save the Vietnamese, Koreans or Australians or Thai lives, but just—we were, you know, our purpose in collecting these documents was to trace movements of units and weapons and supplies and individuals, so that at least the Americans could plan their own actions more effectively and many times avoid the military traps, ambushes or bad campaigns.

Q: If you were given orders to go back now, would you go?

A: No, I don't think I would. You know, I think it would have been much more desirable, morally desirable, say, to desert. I don't think I could go again. I know I couldn't go again. Certainly not to Vietnam.

Q: What is your rank?

A: Specialist 5.

Q: Were you Spec 5 in Vietnam?

A: Yes, I was.

▪ Bill Hatton (*continued*)

Q: You've been to Vietnam?

A: Right. I just came back about four months ago.

Q: When were you there?

A: I was there from September 1968 to December 1969.

Q: What did you see?

A: I saw My Lais. A lot of small ones and a lot of individual brutality. I wouldn't say they were on the same scale; they were not large-scale massacres that I saw. I can remember an incident of a kid. He was about eight or nine years old. He was shot when we were on the MP guard. It was in daylight and there was no apparent reason. It didn't happen to be Marine shooting. A Navy SP down there shot the kid, thought he was endangering the area. Ridiculous things like that. They wouldn't let us, you know, fraternize with the Vietnamese. Actually, I found Vietnamese to be pretty friendly people, pretty heavy. I knew a Vietnamese family in Cam Loa near Con Chin, and they were probably some of the finest people I know. But by and large on the part of the Marines, I would say that it seemed to be the unconscious mission of the Marine Corps to make the Vietnamese people hate us, and of course they succeed quite well. Vietnamese people, in my opinion, hardly are concerned whether we win or not. You hardly saw any young Vietnamese between the age of, say, fourteen to fifty who was in the village. They were mostly in the mountains with the VC and the NVA and this I think is pretty indicative of the situation over there.

▪ Gary Gianninoto

Q: What is your name?

A: Gary Gianninoto.

Q: When did you enter the Navy?

A: I went into the service in November of 1966. I had a choice between either the draft or enlisting. It wasn't really a choice but at the time I thought it would be better to enlist than to be drafted. I would have had more of a choice for school or something like this.

Q: How old were you then?

A: I was nineteen.

Q: What had you done before entering the Navy?

A: I had graduated from high school and came out and worked with my father landscaping. I joined the Navy for four years.

Q: Where did you take your boot camp?

A: In Great Lakes in Illinois, and I went to basic training there and went to hospital corps school there. I had asked them at the time when I made my choice as to whether or not I would serve any time with the Marine Corps and they said, "No." So I then said, "O.K." In my ignorant way I said O.K., I will be a hospital corpsman, and so I went into that after fourteen weeks of training. They sent me to field medical service school in North Carolina to train for five weeks with the Marine Corps for field duty where I would become a field technician in the Medical Corps. After those five weeks I was sent to Portsmouth Naval Hospital, where I served about two or three months and then I received my orders to report to Hawaii, which I thought was a break at the time. When I got to Hawaii they said, "We are going to go on a pleasure cruise. We are going to run around to Okinawa, Philippines and Taiwan." The Tet offensive was in full swing. We got out in the Pacific and they announced to us that we weren't going to the Philippines after all—we were going to Vietnam. So we arrived in Da Nang after twelve days, in Da Nang harbor.

Q: What rank did you reach?

A: E-3.

Q: You were by then attached to the Marine Corps?

A: I was attached to the Marine Corps. See because when you go in to become a hospital corpsman in the Navy, you can be assigned to the Marines. The Marine Corps only trains men to kill. They don't train any doctors, dentists or anything like that. They take them from the Navy, and you do a twelve months' tour.

Q: You were there for a year?

A: I was there for ten months. I was there from February '68 until December '68.

Q: What did you see?

A: Well, we got to Da Nang and we stayed there for about a month. The entire three battalions were totally unprepared for any combat duty, but it was on an emergency basis that they took us. So when we got there, they decided to let us practice war for a month. We just ran little mock patrols, set up mock ambushes and things like this just to get an idea. Meanwhile, they were beefing up the battalion with more men as they could get them, because a lot of men had been lost because they were only, you know, seventeen years old and they couldn't go into combat zones, so they had to leave them off in the Philippines. We went there more or less like a skeleton battalion, and they had to build it up. And the first month was—well, it was without anything really, and then we moved up to Hue on our operational task force, and a part of I don't know how many battalions were involved. The entire division was involved, First Division, and we got off to Hue. My company was employed on an island as a security force for a Navy fuel depot, which was very lucky for us because we had hootches to sleep in. The other three companies in the battalion were all out in the boondocks sleeping in the water and the mud, like leeches. The operations that we did go on I had a chance to witness a lot of things that were, you know, really quite unbelievable—I mean for individuals just like myself to, you know, commit cold-blooded murder for no apparent reason at all. I had a friend of mine—I say a friend because I thought he was a friend, but he was just so dehumanized. I mean one day he just picked up a rifle on a patrol, it was in midday and he just picked up this rifle and said, "See that farmer"—he was an expert rifleman, he was a sniper at one time—and he just shot him with his M-14.

Q: The farmer?

A: Right. Just shot him dead.

Q: When was that and where was it?

A: I believe it was just a little bit north of Hue and it was in April '68, the middle of April. The man was brought up; he said it was an accident. These are the Marines, and they brought him up. He went and saw the battalion commander. He was fined forty dollars and he was reduced one pay grade.

Q: For shooting the man?

A: Right, for shooting and killing him. We had to attend the funeral. We stayed and attended the funeral. The family was given three hundred piastres, which I believe is about thirty dollars, by the battalion commander and a case of C-rations to sort of smooth things over, and then we sat there through the funeral, and we just moved on.

Q: Who reported him?

A: It was reported because he did it right there. He was the rear security for a platoon which consisted of about forty men, and they had just stopped. Everyone knew he did it. He had been to Vietnam once before and they found he was unfit to serve any longer. They had sent him back to the States, but here he was right back again six or seven months later. So that was the first one. Then there was a case of seven men from another company in my battalion.

Q: What battalion?

A: This was First Battalion, 27th Regiment. They had taken some suspects, NVA suspects. We had just gone through an operation that was—we lost a lot of people, and these men were, you know, mad and disgusted. They took the five suspects, and first they hung them, then they stabbed them, and then they shot them and threw them in this river right outside of the village.

There were cases where we would go on sweeps, operational sweeps, which is like a search and destroy. That's what the Marine Corps called it—a sweep—and we'd go through villages, burning down hootches, trampling the crops, killing the livestock, then throwing grenades in the family bunkers. The people were terrorized by the Marines. I mean they terrorized them to death, and the people were scared. They didn't know when to come out of their bunkers. Some jerk would yell in there, you know, come out, come out. The

210

people wouldn't come out, so he just rolled a grenade in there and that would be it. It'd be sealed off and everybody would just forget about it and just keep moving on.

Q: Did you see much of this?

A: All the time. The burning down of the hootches, the whole thing.

Q: Which villages?

A: The villages all outside of Hue. The several operations that we went on, we'd go out for five, seven days, two weeks or something like this, and it was the same every time. The same type of attitude, just like I said. There were people who raped. You know that was a little more risky. They didn't want to pull that, although I did know a couple of people who did. But the burning and the tearing open of the rice, huge bags of rice, and just scattering it all over, and the killing of the livestock and the trampling, stomping of the crops.

Q: It was continual?

A: All the time, really. All the time. It's no exaggeration. It was just something that was accepted. That's the way they did it. They were taking out their disgust. They were misdirecting their hatred, really.

There was good reason for hatred. Our own officers sent tanks over our own wounded. I mean, the brass would kill our own people, as well as kill the others. Misdirected artillery, tanks moving in to destroy a bunker and it would run over our own wounded without any regard for whether or not they were laying there, and it really got to the point of the ridiculous all the time. Things like this were always happening.

Q: Did you see the mutilation of bodies?

A: Mutilation—we would take prisoners. They were suspects until they were confirmed. I don't know who confirmed it. I guess when they went through the interrogation, then it was confirmed. But anyone who didn't have an identification card might as well have been a Vietcong. I mean, it didn't matter whether he was seventy years old or seven years old, and they would be taken prisoner. I think they picked the most sadistic men out of the platoon to watch these people, because they tied their hands behind their back. They're very tiny people anyway, and these guys would be huge

211

Marines, and they'd tie their hands behind their back, bind their feet just enough so that they could walk, and they would taunt them, harass them, burn them with cigarettes, make them drink bottles of tabasco sauce. Kick them in the groin. One day when I stayed back with an operations sweep of the island that we were on for the Navy and prisoners were coming back after hand grenades had been thrown at them and they had fragments of grenade. You know, just thrown far enough away so they just catch a little bit. Then another guy came in who was poisoned. They made him eat one of the heating tabs used to cook the C-rations. Several of the Marines had got him and forced his mouth open and pushed it down his throat, and they made him eat it.

Q: What happened?

A: He was poisoned, and they had to send him to the hospital outside of Hue. I saw all these things because I stayed back. They had taken a lot of people that day and really brutalized them, kicked them, stomped them.

Q: When was that?

A: This was early May.

Q: Around where?

A: Right outside of Hue. There was always things like this, but it was really, you know, the officers, the captain, the CO, whoever it was that yelled back, you know, "Stop burning the villages down," but you know it didn't really do too much good because these men, that's the way they felt, you know. They didn't know.

Q: Did anybody cut off ears as trophies?

A: No, by the time we got there, there had already been a big thing about that and they had been tightening up on it. They didn't want any ears anyway. I mean they used to brag about their confirmed kills. Especially the snipers. Sometimes we'd be a blocking force for another battalion who would be sweeping a village and forcing the people out, and the people would run. If it looks like they have a rifle or weapon, you kill them. You're sitting there and they may be fifteen hundred feet away to two thousand feet away and it's hard to tell, so they'd just take shots at them, things like that. It would be like a rifle range. The Marines would sit there and yell, "Well, I think he's got one. Yeah, I think so too," and bang you know. "Oh I missed him." Bang. But there were several good shots, and they rarely ever missed. It was no big thing because we'd just pick up and move away from there anyway. And they'd shoot the water buffalo and pigs and it was really very morbid, the whole thing. This is the attitude that a lot of them took. They were pushed around day after day and they just didn't know what to do, so they took it out on the Vietnamese. Because they're told that these people are inferior, they're backward, they're, you know, Oriental. They run through the whole thing and they just take it out on the Vietnamese, which is wrong. They rob them, terrorize them. I was with my squad and they stood in a hootch with two old ladies and two little children, two little girls, and they stayed there all night long and just tormented them. There was really no sense in it, you know. They had their flashlights and things like this and they would pull them out of bed and, you know, and then an old woman would get back in bed and someone would pull one of the little girls out of bed, and they would point the rifles at them and put them in their face, and, you know, put the rifle in their ear and things like this and, you know, pinch them, smack them. One of the little children might cry out and one of the Marines would smack her a couple of times in the face, slap her.

Q: You saw this?

A: Right. I mean it got to the point that after four months I just told them that they could have their war really, and I just refused any further part in the whole thing, and consequently I was sentenced to four months in hard labor. I served the four months and I came back out, and I just wanted to get out and get away from the whole thing. I wasn't political at all then, and I just wanted to get away from the whole thing.

Q: Did your values change?

A: Right. While we were in the brig, that brought a little bit to my mind because I saw how these men got together and just ousted, you know, the entire custodial staff there and in three days just threw them out and burned down the cell block. It just showed the solidarity of the men when they really want to, and they're really being kicked and pushed into the dirt.

Q: Did you have any unusual experiences as a medic for the Marines?

A: Yes. A lot of guys shot themselves just to get out of Nam.

Rather than just refusing like I did to fight, for fear of ten years in the brig and a dishonorable discharge, they just shot themselves. They would be out on a sweep and fire a few rounds behind us to make it seem like a fire fight. It was a false fire fight. Then they'd shoot themselves and pretend they were wounded by the enemy. And I had eleven men in my platoon alone that did this, and everybody—the officers knew about it but they were having so much trouble at this time just trying to keep themselves together that they couldn't worry about something like that. They couldn't prove it anyway. They didn't even have the time to try 'cause we were losing men every day constantly.

Q: How do you know that they shot themselves?

A: They'd come to me and ask me where in their body would be the best, you know, best place to inflict a wound so that they wouldn't damage themselves permanently but would be enough that they'd be removed from Vietnam, back to the States. They even asked for medication before wounding themselves. A couple of them I gave morphine beforehand, and some of them I gave morphine to take with them, and others I told them where I'd be, things like this. Because they were friends of mine. Rather than stuffing them in a bag, or seeing them piled up five or six high on a tank, you know, riding away dead after laying around for three or four days in a rice paddy, I'd much rather see them go back with a flesh wound. That's the way I felt about it. After I refused, I had every enlisted man in the company behind me.

- Robert Gordon*

Q: What is your name?
A: Robert Gordon.
Q: Where are you from?
A: Solana Beach, California. It's a small town in San Diego County.

Q: When did you enter the Army?

A: May 25, 1966.

Q: What had you done before that?

A: I went to school for a while and worked odd jobs before I got out of high school.

Q: Did you graduate from high school?

A: Yes.

Q: Where?

A: In North San Diego County.

Q: When you went into the Army where did you go?

A: I went to basic training in Fort Worth, Texas, because at the time they had a meningitis scare at Ford Ord, California. Then I made the horrible mistake of volunteering to go Airborne, but they channeled me into Infantry training, which I took at Fort Gordon, Georgia. From there I got waivered from Airborne training and sent to Vietnam as a light-weapons infantryman. At the time I had been in the Army about five months and I was already on my way to Vietnam.

Q: When did you arrive there?

A: Around October 31, 1966.

Q: And where did you go?

A: I was sent about two days in Long Binh replacement station and then I was shipped to Tay Ninh, at War Zone C, to the 196th Light Infantry Brigade.

Q: How long were you there?

A: I was in Vietnam three months as a grunt, which is, you know, regular ground-pounder, an infantryman.

Q: Did you see action there?

A: Yes. It was one of the big turning points of the war at the time. It was Operation Attleboro. We spent some time up there on the Black Virgin Mountain. There was supposed to be the Fifth North Vietnamese Division or something like that which is supposed to be one of their biggest fighting forces in the south.

Q: So you saw a lot of action?

A: My first three months were very active.

Q: After that where did you go?

A: I was transferred to the 25th Infantry Division at Cu Chi, which is about twenty-seven miles north of Saigon, which is also in war zone. At that time the 196th Light Infantry was under the jurisdiction of the 25th Division. Later it became an independent unit and from there it became part of the Americal Division, which is what everybody's heard about recently. Because of the incident, you know, which made the headlines.

Q: And then after Cu Chi where did you go?

A: I spent about eight months there.

Q: In the time that you were in Vietnam, did you ever see prisoners questioned?

A: Being in a light-infantry unit you know you're in a position where you're usually the ones that have to decide when a guy needs to be questioned whether you send him back to the G-2 units to be interrogated. I saw the interpreters question the North Vietnamese captives right on the spot before they were sent back to the higher echelons.

Q: These were Vietnamese interpreters?

A: Yes.

Q: How did they question them?

A: They didn't pull no punches about it. Kind of talk to them in a Vietnamese language and if they can't get any cooperation out of them they just slap around a little bit, you know. The usual things like you see on TV.

Q: Like what?

A: You know, like punching a guy in the stomach and slapping him around and knocking him on the ground.

Q: Were the prisoners tied?

A: Yes. You always kept them tied. Behind their back or else you kept them in a squatting position and kept a blindfold on them.

Q: Did they beat them?

A: Sometimes they did and sometimes they didn't. It depends on who the interpreter was, you know.

Q: Did you ever see them hit with a rifle butt?

A: Not too many by interpreters. I saw a lot of the people on the search-and-destroy mission beat the suspected Vietcong and push old ladies around and stuff.

Q: Americans?

A: Yes. I didn't see too many South Vietnamese actually beating any of the North Vietnamese because every time we ran into the

216

South Vietnamese they were usually laying on their hammocks doing nothing much of anything really, and they always had jobs like in the Saigon area.

Q: Did you ever see the interrogation of women prisoners?

A: One time really, you know, that I can really recall quite clearly was when I was pulling a bunker guard at the Cu Chi base camp and in War Zone C, which is the base camp for the 25th Infantry Division. It's one of the biggest base camps, I think, in Vietnam. We were right outside one of our bunker lines. They were interrogating a group of suspected Vietnamese. They had them outside. They were in a circle of South Vietnamese soldiers around them. A couple of guys tied them to a post and slapped them around a little bit. When they came to interrogating a woman they took this one woman's blouse off, you know—

Q: How old was she?

A: She looked to be maybe in her early twenties, you know. It's hard to judge the age of Vietnamese but she looked to be in her early twenties, and they took her blouse off and started pushing her around and laughing at her for a while.

Q: What do you mean, pushing her around?

A: They had her in a circle and they were pushing her from one end of the circle to the other and she looked kind of not too happy about it. Frightened. And the thing that really made me sick to my stomach was that they had kind of a belt that had wires on it. It fit around the woman's breasts and they snapped it together at the back like a brassiere. Well, it's not as wide but it just went across, you know, like the nipples, and they had a wire attached to it which went to the belt itself. It appeared to be very painful when they put the wires on the poles of a car battery.

Q: Did she scream?

A: Yes. After a while she just passed out, you know, from the pain, I guess. After they cut the thing off it left a whole burnt line clear across her chest and her back. They were burnt by electricity. The wire wasn't very heavy-gauge wire. They did this to several of the women, and one of the women, they made her take her pants off and had a wire between her legs, in her vagina. They put the poles on the ends of the wire on the back of the battery pole. The woman didn't even have a chance to say anything because she went into so much pain. I don't think the interrogators really cared if they got anything out of them anyway. They seemed to be toying with them.

Q: How many women were tortured this way?

A: Three different women got that belt thing around their breasts and one woman had the wire run through her vagina.

Q: Were there American soldiers participating?

A: No, at this particular incident. There were a couple of our sergeants, American soldiers, they weren't directly involved with the interrogation. They were supposed to be pulling guard duty on the bunker line and they were over there just kind of offering a few suggestions. They seemed to be enjoying it. They were over there laughing with the South Vietnamese soldiers who were conducting the interrogation. And this was out in the open compound. It wasn't done in a building or anything. People watching were mostly South Vietnamese soldiers.

Q: When was this?

A: During February 1967.

Q: Did you ever hear about the prisoners being taken up in helicopters?

A: The Australian pilot told me that in his company they used to tie a rope around Vietcongs' ankles and drag them across the treetops when they wouldn't talk. I hear a lot of them bragging about how they would have three Vietcongs in a helicopter and push a couple off to make the other one talk.

Q: Did you ever hear Americans talk like that?

A: I heard a lot talk about that. A lot of career soldiers, life prisoners, we call them, boasting about it, and about doing things like that. Knocking the shit out of suspected Vietcong. We were out on an operation, search and destroy. It didn't start as a search and destroy. We were just out there to chop down rubber trees and knock down trees in the forest. Around homes, you know, where we thought they might hide some tunnel rations or stuff like that. A couple of guys decided to go in and get some girls. They'd proposition the girl and if she didn't want to sell her body they'd just take it anyway.

Q: Were others mistreated also?

A: It was really common, pushing around old men and old

ladies, especially on the search-and-destroy missions when we were far away from base camp. We weren't near any large cities. They just took it for granted everyone was a Vietcong, so they always, you know, slapped the shit out of old ladies and pushed 'em around.

Q: Ever kill them?

A: No. Most of the killing that was done, that I saw, it was wounded prisoners that weren't really that wounded. Instead of calling a medic they usually just shoot them and leave them there, dump them in a rice paddy or something.

Q: How often did you see that?

A: I had the misfortune of, you know, doing it twice myself, which I'm not too proud of now. When I was in Vietnam I was a political know-nothing. I didn't really know what was going on behind the Vietnam war. That seems to be the biggest problem over there now. People really don't know what's going on, and they're just over there because somebody told them that the Communists are going to come all over and take over all our families and stuff like that.

Q: You're against the war now?

A: I'm strongly against the war, and I'd like to see the U. S. pull out. I made this decision because I really dug into the history of South Vietnam.

Q: Since you've been back in the United States?

A: Yes, since. I mean I've gone back one thousand years. Learned a lot of the revolutions that's gone on over there like the Trung Sisters, I think it was, who led the first revolt against the Chinese.

Q: How did you kill those two people?

A: I was in an ambush one time and we had gotten into a fire fight and I came across a moaning sound, you know. I asked the guy behind me to come up. "Come on up and let's check out the trail. I hear some noise over there." We had just blown a claymore mine and we saw two people coming down the trail through the starlight scope, which is a night seeing device. I passed the word back that there was a wounded Vietnamese in the trail. And the CO passed the word back up, "Kill him but don't make any noise."

Q: Who was the CO?

A: It was Captain O'Malley. At the time he was company commander. We had gone through about three different company commanders I don't know why but anyway he passed us the word, you know, to have him killed without making any noise. His radio operator had radioed back and said that we had contact now with a wounded Vietnamese in the trail. I passed the word back that he wasn't wounded too bad. The company was set up about one thousand meters way. We just had an ambush going outside the perimeter, so here I am in front of the formation with an M-16 with a plastic handle; they didn't issue us bayonets in our company. So how you supposed to kill a Vietcong with a plastic weapon that doesn't weigh more than a few pounds?

Q: What did you do?

A: Well, I hit him in the head a couple of times with the rifle butt. It didn't seem to be doing any good. He just kept on moaning, so this guy behind me who was considerably bigger than me had an M-14 and that has a steel plate on the end. He used the M-14 but it didn't do much good either. So finally I just said let's not make the guy suffer any more, so I took my friend's pistol—he had a nine-millimeter German Luger—and I just shot him in the head.

Q: Where had he been wounded?

A: He got some shot wounds in the chest which weren't very deep. He might have had one sucking chest wound but I didn't really have a chance to check him out; it was dark. He was carrying no weapons. I mean he had a pistol belt on and he had some medical supplies, I believe, but he didn't have a weapon. The other guy got away. Evidently if he did have a weapon, the other guy took it with him. At the time I saw him he didn't have a weapon at all. Similar incidences of this happened several other times.

Q: Did you see many prisoners killed? Wounded prisoners?

A: In the last six months I was there I imagine I saw maybe five or six, maybe more. You know that was a long time ago. I've been back over two years. Mostly I try to forget most of it and what happened over there. Oh, there was one time when we were on an ambush and we were outside a fairly large village. It was some ten miles north of the north gate of the Cu Chi base camp and we were on an ambush site, and the curfew was over at five o'clock in the morning at that place. The farmers would get on their oxcarts and go out to the fields five or six o'clock in the morning. Anyway, about five minutes before the curfew time was over, our ambush leader radioed us back to the CO and said there was movement coming down the trail. It was about five minutes before and the CO told the patrol leader to use his own discretion. There was an old man that came up on a bicycle. He didn't look like a peasant type person, so the patrol leader opened fire on him and as soon as he opened fire everybody fired on him and started shooting at the old man. Then his bicycle fell over and he had a white bag on it, and it turned out that he was a doctor that travels from village to village that helped the people.

Q: Was he killed?

A: He was killed. So the patrol leader just took the doctor's identification and burned it and threw the body in a ditch. That was the last I ever heard of it, and they never gave a mention of it again.

Q: Did you ever participate in burning down a village?

A: We were in a lot of villages that we burned down. We knocked them down and moved people to other villages that weren't supposed to be Vietcong-supported.

Q: Were any of the people hurt in any of these efforts?

A: Oh, there was a few people hurt, like a few incidents, where a South Vietnamese soldier didn't want his father's house knocked down, so he pulled a pin out of a grenade and stood in front of the house. We were knocking the houses down with our APCs and tanks.

Q: What is an APC?

A: Armored Personnel Carrier.

Q: What is that?

A: It's like a small tank. It's a little square box type of thing. His CO officer came over and took the grenade away from him and threw it in the well and beat the shit out of that South Vietnamese soldier who was, I guess, an enlisted man. Beat him with a rifle— he had an M-1 carbine—and he just gave the Americans the order to knock the house down even if the people didn't get out. The old man, the soldier's father, was hurt pretty bad. One of the cross beams from the house hit him in the head. He had a big gash on his head, but the old woman and the kids didn't get hurt too bad. Those houses are pretty flimsy, and even if they fall on you, they don't do much damage.

221

Q: How much more time do you have in the Army?

A: I have a year and a half. I spent a total of about five years and four months in the Army. I had a court-martial from Vietnam.

Q: What was the court-martial for?

A: Last year, I think it was in August, I came down on levy for the second involuntary tour to Vietnam and I wasn't too happy about it because I had already been there once before.

Q: Why didn't you want to go to Vietnam the second time?

A: Because by that time I had already become a little more politically oriented and I had finally made a decision that the people of North Vietnam weren't my enemies. I came down on levy and I started clearing post.

Q: What does that mean?

A: They were doing the paperwork in finance, personnel and other departments. I waited till I cleared everything and I got all my bags packed and then I said, "I'll catch you later, but I'm not going to Vietnam." So I went home and took all my records with me and I stayed home for three months. When I came back, I was pending court-martial, so that canceled my Vietnam levy. They hold your orders to Vietnam because you have pending judicial action.

Q: You were court-martialed for AWOL?

A: For AWOL, which was a lot easier to cope with than just refusing to go to Vietnam altogether and being charged with refusal to obey a direct order.

Q: How old are you now?

A: Twenty-three.

Q: What do you plan to do when you get out of the Army?

A: I plan to become active in the anti-war movement. Probably join the local chapters of Vietnam veterans against the war in my own home town.

Q: Did you kill many North Vietnamese or National Liberation Front soldiers during the war?

A: I was credited with eight by body count. It was a big thing then, but I'm not too happy about it now.

Q: How do you feel about it now?

A: Well, it's kind of really hard to explain because I was brought up in a really religious family.

Q: How do you feel about the war now?

A: I hate to see American soldiers dying over there. Still, I think that's a product of our government. In spite of the American soldier dying over there, and a lot of them have been my friends, I support the National Liberation Front.

■ Allan Wright

Q: What is your name?

A: Allan Wright.

Q: How old are you, Allan?

A: Twenty years old.

Q: Where were you born?

A: In Baltimore, Maryland.

Q: When did you enter the Army?

A: Oh, I entered the Army in February of 1967, in Baltimore, Maryland.

Q: Where did you take your basic?

A: I took my basic at Fort Bragg, North Carolina.

Q: Why did you go in the Army? Did you enlist or were you drafted?

A: I enlisted at the age of seventeen, figuring on getting out when I was twenty and learning everything I could about the Army in about three years.

Q: Had you finished high school?

A: No, I hadn't. I went through the ninth grade and then I quit when I was in the ninth grade.

Q: What high school was that?

A: That was Roland Park Junior High School.

Q: What does your family do?

A: My father's a machinist and he works in a factory and my mother works at a restaurant.

223

Q: And where did you take AIT?

A: I took my AIT at Fort Jackson, South Carolina. After AIT I had orders for Vietnam, and I went and took my thirty days' leave at home, in Baltimore. Then from there I went to California. Four days after being in Oakland I was shipped to Vietnam, by plane. I landed in August of '67 and I was there for a year.

Q: Did you see any combat?

A: Yes, I did. I was in a line troop.

Q: What was your company?

A: I was in the Fourth Division. First of the Eighth. And then my last three months I was with Alpha Company, Second of the 16th in the First Division, down south.

Q: In August of '68 where did you go?

A: In August of '68 I returned to the States, and I caught a plane and came home on leave. After leave I went to Fort Hood, Texas, where I am at the present.

Q: How long have you been here?

A: I have been here for sixteen months at Fort Hood.

Q: When are you due to get out?

A: I am due to get out next month, around the twenty-fifth.

Q: In your year in Vietnam, did you ever see prisoners interrogated?

A: Yes, I did in the First Division.

Q: Where was that?

A: That was down around the Dzi Anh area outside the Dzi Anh base camp.

Q: And who did the interrogation?

A: There were MPs and Vietnamese interpreters.

Q: And about when was this interrogation?

A: This was in late April 1968.

Q: How was the questioning done?

A: They would start by asking the prisoners questions pertaining to troop movements and things of this nature. After so many questions that the Vietnamese wouldn't answer them, due to lack of knowledge about it or due to just withholding information, they would bring rough treatment into it.

Q: What was the rough treatment?

A: Well, there was a couple different rough treatments they

224

used. There was beating them around. The prisoner would be encircled by the MPs or by the interrogator and he would be beat around the circle.

Q: Was the prisoner tied in any way?

A: His hands were.

Q: Where? In front or behind his back?

A: Behind him.

Q: And how was he beaten?

A: Physically. It was a physical beating by hands. By the hands of the MPs and the interrogator.

Q: And then what?

A: And then there was the old torture of sticking the bamboo splinters up the fingernails.

Q: Did you see this?

A: I've seen it done, yes.

Q: How does that work?

A: One person holds the hand behind his back and the other person holds the prisoner's hands while he is on his knees, to keep him from moving around so much. They put the splinter under his fingernails, the hand that is in front of him.

Q: And what kind of reaction does this bring?

A: Pain. They scream very much. And they will try to move, but the idea, the other idea of having the arm behind his back is every time they try to move they apply pressure on the arm behind the prisoner's back and it tends to keep him still.

Q: Who was doing this?

A: The interrogator and the MPs.

Q: The American MPs participating in this?

A: Yes, there were American MPs.

Q: How many different people did you see tortured in that fashion?

A: I would say just a few, because of the majority of the time we wouldn't be in the NDP, the night defensive perimeter it's called down south. Up north it would be the same thing as a fire base. We'd usually be on S and D, search-and-destroy patrol, or on an ambush patrol and we were not in the NDP. It was very rare that you would see an interrogation because they—it is usually done back in the rear of base camp.

225

Q: Did you ever hear of prisoners being thrown from helicopters?

A: As soon as I got over there I started hearing stories of that, about prisoners that were interrogated inside of a helicopter so many hundred feet up and, like I said, if he doesn't answer due to lack of knowledge, or you know, just withholding information, he would be forced outside of the helicopter to his death.

Q: Is that common knowledge among the front-line troops in Vietnam that that method is used?

A: Pretty well.

Q: Who told you about it?

A: Many different people. I heard it from people back in base camp and I heard it from troops out in the field that I have been with out in the field and a lot of old-timers. When I first got over there a lot of old-timers would tell me about it.

Q: Were you ever in an operation which burned a village?

A: Our unit was but I wasn't specifically with them at the time. I was on a detail back in NDP and our company went north to a village. They had three villages around our NDP and they went to the one north of us and evacuated all the people and burned the village.

Q: Why?

A: I never had any knowledge of why it was done. It was just the operation.

Q: Did you ever witness any mistreatment of any Vietnamese civilians?

A: I've seen them pushed around and shoved and literally thrown out of their houses or homes.

Q: Did you ever hear about Vietnamese girls being raped by GIs?

A: I heard of a lot of instances where there were sexual attacks, not that the Vietnamese girls could, you know, resist very much because a GI could be pretty nasty. After all he has got the weapon, not them.

Q: Is this common?

A: I've heard of a lot of times when you'll be going through villages. You have your troops spread so far out over the village that your commanders in one end of the village and some of the troops are back on the other end and anything is possible. Anything can happen. And what could she say, you know, she couldn't say nothing.

Q: Did you ever witness this?

A: No, I never saw any. But I've had people tell me about it.

Q: Did you ever hear about anyone in Vietnam that collected parts of the enemy body?

A: Yes, I heard a number of people who have taken bayonets and machetes and cut off fingers in order to get a ring off a body if the ring wouldn't come off—they would cut the finger off—and I've heard where bodies were mutilated literally by carving their unit patch on the body's chest or stomach.

Q: Which units did this?

A: The Big Red I was known for this.

Q: How about the 27th?

A: They've been known for it also.

Q: The First of the 27th?

A: First and 27th, yes. The emblems in the First Division are usually carved on the chest or on the stomach of the Vietnamese with a bayonet or something. There have been many times we've come across dead Vietnamese where we've found a First Infantry Division patch from the shoulder of the uniform stuffed between his teeth or in his mouth or carved into the person's body.

Q: Did you ever hear of anyone who collected ears?

A: I heard a lot about collecting ears up north when I was in the Fourth Division, but I never came in contact with someone who had it in his possession. There was one time in the First Division when a man came back the next morning after popping an ambush. They opened up on some Vietnamese who were in the area the night before and he had come back the next morning with a supplementary pack that you get out of C rations. He had a finger in it from a dead Vietnamese.

Q: What medals did you receive in Vietnam?

A: I received the Vietnamese campaign medal, the Vietnamese ribbon and the Purple Heart.

Q: When were you wounded?

A: I was wounded on May 22nd of 1968.

Q: Where, how were you wounded?

A: A Vietnamese claymore booby trap. They make them in a circular form which weighs about ten pounds.

Q: Where were you wounded?

A: I had shrapnel in my eye.

Q: How long were you out of action?

A: About three days.

Q: Just three days?

A: Just three days and then they sent me back out in the field.

Q: Could you see when you went back in the field?

A: Not very good.

Q: Do you get out next month?

A: Hopefully.

Q: Do you plan to re-enlist?

A: Not hardly.

Q: If you got orders now to go to Vietnam, would you go?

A: No.

Q: Why not?

A: I don't believe in what we are doing over there. I believe everything that we are doing over there is wrong. I believe that just being over there is wrong.

Q: Did you believe that in August of '67?

A: No, because I didn't have the knowledge that I have now about what is going on over there. The Vietnamese people don't want us there and all the troops don't want to be there.

▪ Robert H. Bower

Q: What is your name?

A: Robert H. Bower.

Q: How old are you?

A: Twenty.

Q: Where were you born?

A: Pittsburgh, Pennsylvania.

Q: Your family lives where now?

A: Coco Beach, Florida.

Q: What does your father do?

A: My father is an engineer for Bendix Corporation. Retired lieutenant colonel in the United States Air Force. He was in twenty years.

Q: Where did you go to high school?

A: In Florida. Then I took a journey around the States, to find out what it was all about, and ended up in Salem, Massachusetts, where I enlisted in the Army on December 21, 1966, to serve my country and God.

Q: Why did you enlist?

A: I got into a real patriotic attitude. I went into this real heavy God-and-country thing. And I thought that I should go to Vietnam and, you know, help the free world out.

Q: And did you go to Vietnam?

A: Yeah, right.

Q: First you went where?

A: I went to Fort Dix, New Jersey, for basic training and spent two months there and then I was sent to a—

Q: That was before there was a coffee house there?

A: That was much before those coffee houses. Then I went to Fort Knox, Kentucky, and took armored training as a tank crewman, in a tank. That was before there was a coffee house or a GI newspaper at Fort Knox. Then I volunteered to go to Vietnam and was sent to Vietnam in May of 1967.

Q: How did you go?

A: By plane and flew to Saigon. Went into Saigon and was assigned to Headquarters Company Fifth of the 60th Infantry attached to the Ninth Division. I stayed there for two months and was then transferred to the 11th Armored Cavalry Regiment, L Troop, Third Squadron, where I finished my tour, the next ten months.

Q: Did you get any decorations or medals?

A: Well, I was wounded twice and I had two Purple Hearts, and combat infantryman's badge, a Vietnam service medal, Vietnam campaign medal, National Defense medal.

Q: And when you went to Vietnam you were for the war?

A: Right, I was a hawk.

Q: And now you're not?

A: Now I'm not a hawk. I'm also not a dove. Yeah, I went through a lot of changes in Vietnam. There was a number of incidents, like when I first got to Vietnam they put me very uptight. One was the first time I was ever in combat, which was July 21, 1967, yeah, 1967. The convoy I was on was ambushed on Route 20 in Vietnam by the 273rd and the 272nd Vietcong regiment. After about a three-hour battle, the whole front of our outfit was wiped out except for two armored personnel carriers, one of which I was on. Well, after the whole battle was over, after the fire fight was over, we had bulldozers that bulldozed about 115, you know, North Vietnamese Vietcong dead into a pile. About an hour after they had started to dig a hole to bulldoze them all into, a lot of rear troops, like engineers and guys that would drive in trucks in the convoy that was way back, came up and started stabbing these dead Vietnamese that had been dead for about two or three hours. Started stabbing them, shooting off fingers and ears. I had seen a number of engineers from the 919th Engineer Battalion which was assigned to the 11th Cavalry take bayonets and just plunge them into the chests and, you know, fool around with, like stabbing them in the legs and things like that, you know, in the spirit of war, I guess, and it sort of got me uptight about that. Then about a month later our outfit had moved up to the Cambodian border up near Anh Loc, and we had captured a number of prisoners, which were tied up and bound with barbed wire.

Q: Where was the barbed wire?

A: Oh, it was down around their hands behind their backs, and around their arms, you know, around their shoulders.

Q: Cutting into them?

A: Yes.

Q: They were bleeding?

A: Well, there isn't a whole lot of blood. It was like, you know, punctures. They were bleeding, yes. And there was one who had been killed that was dragged around on the back of an armored personnel carrier from K Troop, which was our sister troop.

Q: Was he killed that way?

A: No, he was shot a couple of times in the chest and the abdomen.

Q: After he was a prisoner or before?

A: During the fight, but the body was dragged behind the vehicle through a village and then they turned around and dragged it back through the village. It was outside of Anh Loc.

Q: What happened to the prisoners?

A: They were kept in the middle of a confined area. There were about fifteen women and old men that were supposed to be suspects or sympathizers which were kept huddled up in a real small area all night. They weren't allowed to go to the bathroom or anything separately. They just had to shit right there. And they weren't fed, to my knowledge. I know one GI that took over a box of C-rations to this North Vietnamese sergeant who during the day had been wounded. He had been wounded in the chest, clear through, it was like all the way through his chest, You know, you could almost see through it. And in the leg, and his hand was maimed, and he came walking out, you know, surrendered. He was just like, you know, he was in shock, and somebody took some food over to him. He was the only one that I know ate, and I'm not sure what happened to him, whether he died or whether they got him some medical attention.

Q: How long did you see him after he surrendered?

A: It was about an hour, a good hour.

Q: Had he received any medical attention in that hour?

A: No, he hadn't. He had some old rags wrapped around his hand, but it wasn't anything done by our medics. You can tell, really. Wasn't anything sterile, that's for sure.

Q: Whatever happened to the prisoners, do you know?

A: The prisoners were kept bound up in the middle area all night until the next day. These were suspects now, suspects. They were taken by truck to some rear area. I'm not sure where. The prisoners were taken by some South Vietnamese special forces type. I don't recall, but they were like the equivalent to the American Green Berets and they were Vietnamese. No telling what happened to them. It was pretty quiet after that. Not much happened that really sticks in my mind until about January 28 of 1968. That was two days before the Tet offensive started, and we were back at the Cambodian border at Anh Loc again. The South Vietnamese capitalists, I guess you could call them, the ones that run all the prostitution rings and the dope rings, grass and opium, had moved up a whole bunch of girls and dope from Saigon, up to Anh Loc, because the Third Squadron of the 11th Cavalry had just gotten there about the fifteenth of January. We were supposed to be there for a couple of months, on an operation up there to stop infiltration routes from Cambodia. They had moved up a whole city like, prostitutes and tents and dope dealers, to deal with our squadron. Being near the end of the month, knowing pay day was coming up, you know, they had set up about the twenty-fifth or the twenty-sixth. GIs were coming out of like white superiority. They would beat up women after they had fucked them and then they would beat them up. Wouldn't pay them. We got to Saigon right in the middle of the Tet offensive, and there was like a whole shitload of looting going on from us.

Q: By GIs?

A: Yes, GIs. It was like the first time that our outfit had ever been deployed on foot. We had always been in our tanks. We left our vehicles and we had started doing patrols in the streets trying to clear out snipers, make a whole lot of positions that were pretty well held. And at this time, well, it was just like a freak town. You could do any of the shooting, you could throw grenades, anything, anywhere you wanted.

Q: In Saigon?

A: Yes. The area we leveled about twelve blocks just outside of Saigon.

Q: Why?

A: Well, suspected enemy. Now to my knowledge—and this was, well, like rumors that came out from, you know—well, nobody in our outfit in L Troop killed an enemy. We never saw one. We used tanks to demolish a church which was supposed to be a sniper in the steeple. There may have, there may not have been, but there were about a hundred civilians in the bottom of the church seeking refuge. I think that there were about thirty-eight wounded and a couple of killed. After we blew off the top of the steeple, after a couple of misses, it hit inside the church. There was a lot of looting, like breaking into shops, ripping off wrist watches,

232

rings, stuff like that, cartons of cigarettes. You know, things that the Vietnamese had, really a lot of trivial things. But you know, it was like a game. Here we were, God, you know, we could sort of rip off all the shit we wanted. And this went on for a couple of days. Right at the really peak of the Tet offensive in Saigon, like from February 1st to about February 7th. And I really, I really can't say that our troop killed one VC during the whole Tet offensive. We, I know we went in to Cho Lon race track where an outfit, an airborne outfit from the South Vietnamese, had been dropped. It was one of the first air drops that had happened in a long time, and like the Vietcong, they got them before they got the ground and it was just nothing but a bunch of bodies and parachutes. So they sent our outfit in to pick up the weapons and things from the South Vietnamese Army. To get what we could back from them, and when we got in there was nothing but a bunch of bodies. Everything had been stripped. But it was interesting to note that the bodies weren't mutilated by the Vietcong. Everything military was taken, you know, arms and ammunition. Then we were sent outside of Saigon about twenty miles to a place called Duc La, and we were on an operation there, a search-and-destroy operation. This went on from about the middle of February to the middle, the end of March. Where we were attached with the 51st Ranger ARVN Ranger Battalion. The South Vietnamese Ranger and 10th ARVN Cavalry were assigned to us. And we had a number of villages which were destroyed during this period. This was probably the period when I was there that I saw most destruction of civilian property. A lot of mutilation of dead Vietcong, a number of prisoners which were captured were killed.

Q: You saw that?

A: Yes.

Q: Could you describe a search-and-destroy mission?

A: Yes. March 16th or 17th of 1968. We had moved out of Duc La and moved to a small village outside of it. At this time there were like suspected Vietcong in the village. The village was being evacuated. Some people weren't moving. They wanted to stay. It had been their village, generations and generations, and they just weren't leaving their homes. Well, after about an hour's delay because of the evacuation, we were told that sniper fire was

233

coming from the village. I say we were told because we hadn't been receiving any, and that we were to move on. This was done in platoon level now. We had broken down our company and platoons had been lined up on different areas, and we would go, we went charging into the village firing away. A whole platoon of ten vehicles on this. I remember one side of the village where the tracers were catching the hootches and things on fire, and what didn't catch on fire was run over by APCs and tanks. By M-48 A-1 tanks. We destroyed the village, there was no ands, ifs or buts about that. As to civilian casualties, I saw a number. A few civilians were making a break from the villages. They were running from the tracks. They could see the village was getting squished, you know, smashed. Like one man, an old man on crutches who had a leg amputation and a little boy that had a couple of cows and two old ladies who could just barely walk, you know, they were really eighty or ninety years old. They were captured, and I remember they were thrown up against the track, like the police do here, against the squad-car type thing, you know, hands, feet spread apart. The old man kept falling over because they had taken his crutches away from him. He kept like falling over and they wouldn't let him sit down, and they would put him up against the track with his arms spread, trying to keep balance by one leg, you know, and then they would go through like looking for identification. Sergeant Smith was checking out IDs. He came back and said they were O.K. So after all this humiliation these people went through, especially this old man, they gave him back his crutches and let him go. They walked away. I don't know where they were going to. Their whole village had been destroyed. On March 18th, just a couple days after, we had moved out after we had destroyed that village. We had moved out and we had gotten ambushed. We had the 51st Ranger Battalion with us. They were sitting on the APCs. We had been ambushed from a hedge grove, an island in the middle of a rice paddy, with bushes and trees and maybe a few houses. Well, this was like about nine o'clock in the morning. And it was no bigger than, it was about half a length of a football field wide and about half a length long. It was like an island. You could just imagine it with trees, bushes and about three hootches, and like a lot of vegetables, little cornfield and beans, plants and things growing. Lot of vegetation. And we got this sniper fire. All the ARVNs jumped off the tracks and sort of laying down a base of fire. We moved back and sort of started firing over their heads, with our 50s and M-79s. This went on for about two hours. We tried to assault it. Now during this two-hour period they called in air strikes, jets. We're dropping 250-pound concussion bombs, napalm, strafing it with 20 millimeter, everything, for about an hour. So we tried to assault it. We go charging up. The 10th ARVN Cavs and Third Squadron of the 11th ARVN Cavs. The ARVNs would go charging up on foot, and they would get driven off. We couldn't get anyplace. We got knocked out all over the place. About noontime, we decided to take a break for lunch, so we called in air strikes again. And while we had lunch from twelve to one, they called in air strike after air strike and as soon as the air strikes would go, gunships would come in. About one-thirty, we just started to have another assault. We went charging up. Got repelled again. Never saw anybody there the whole time. It was just all this stuff was coming out of there, right.

Q: Automatic weapons?

A: Automatic weapons. They were launching rocket-propelled grenades that were falling over our tracks behind us and things and knocked out a couple of tracks. About three in the afternoon things were getting really bad. We were really demoralized. We had called in probably about $500,000 worth of air support. You have to keep remembering this was like fifty yards by fifty yards, and we had it surrounded from all sides, calling in artillery, air strikes, everything, and we couldn't get near it. About three o'clock they decided, O.K., this is it. We have to assault it, we have to override it. O.K. The Americans, you'll stay back and fire support from your vehicles. The ARVNs will charge it.

Q: Who made that decision?

A: Americans made it, of course. So about three-thirty or so we make this final assault. The ARVNs got up there and it was like really funny, because like this one ARVN he got in some shrapnel in his butt, he came wobbling back, you know, with this smile, you know, dig it?

Q: He was out of the war?

A: He's out. Other ARVNs were, like, they wouldn't move.

They would get up behind a little rice paddy and stop. And then the lieutenant—I remember the ARVN lieutenant had one of these Al Capone machine guns, Thompson 25 type things—was out there hitting them and kicking them, beating them on the backs with his gun, trying to get them to move forward, and they weren't going. They were holding up the whole assault. We were behind them moving slowly up in our armored vehicles, and they were laying on the ground, they weren't moving, so they told us, start firing right close to the ARVNs. So we started doing that. And the ARVNs got the point, and so they started moving again, slow, and like they were starting to fall, you know. They weren't hurt, they were just falling, like faking it. A medic would come over to them and see that they weren't hurt, and he would start kicking them, telling them to get moving. One of the ARVN officers would come over to them and start hitting them and pushing them forward and finally they got right up to the hedge grove. This was about four o'clock. Half an hour to go, about fifty feet. Got to the hedge grove, and they started routing out Vietcong. They weren't really capturing a whole lot, but they were killing them off. I remember one Vietcong came out of a bunker. His forehead was literally on fire from napalm. It was just like burning and searing and he was screaming and running out and they shot him down. They brought one prisoner back. They brought the prisoner from behind the A Cav, took him behind it and when the American adviser came over—he was a captain, I believe—came over and said something to the ARVN because earlier in the fire fight, one of the American advisers had been wounded. He had been shot in the stomach. They brought the Vietcong prisoner behind the track and after this American adviser had said something and left, they started like trying to talk to him. They asked him a couple of questions. He was pretty banged up, like he wasn't hearing too well or something, he was really kind of beat. Wasn't wounded physically that I could see, but, you know, but all that shit that had landed on him in the past six hours was enough to really wreck anybody's life for a while. They commenced to beat him with bamboo poles, split bamboo poles. Just beating on him until he would talk. He wasn't about to talk, and after about a half hour of really severe beating with these bamboo poles, with a bayonet. Bayonets really aren't too sharp either. It takes a little to cut with a bayonet. You can jab, but to cut with them is really kind of a hassle. They had cut a whole bunch of slices on his chest and they were still beating him. He finally died from the beatings and the cuts. He was slowly beaten to death.

Q: Did anyone in your outfit collect parts of bodies?

A: I knew a sergeant who had a finger in formaldehyde that he kept in base camp. He always told us that he got it off of a Vietnamese prostitute. He went back and cut off one of her fingers, just to teach her a lesson or something. Of course I also heard about a lot of guys who collected ears. I also heard about guys being pushed out of choppers. I heard a lot of that. I even talked to guys that had been on choppers, people had been pushed off. One was about a fourteen-year-old kid who they caught with an American M-16 and the discussion that went on in the chopper as it was flying was "Well, if he's a Commie at this age, he's going to be a Commie. There's no sense trying to rehabilitate him. He's not going to talk." He was like really scared from what this guy said, freaked out by these big Americans. And so what they did—choppers go about seventy, anywhere from seventy to about 120 miles per hour on low-level flying, about fifteen, twenty feet off the ground over a rice paddy. Pushed him out, and the impact killed him. I know a number of cases where like Vietnamese livestock was shot up by choppers. You know, they would see a water buffalo running or something, and automatically all this paranoia would flash that it was a Vietcong supply train, you know. One water buffalo in the middle of a rice paddy, walking around, you know. So they would swoop in a couple of times and get him scared, you know, and he would start running, and then they would come in and fire a rocket and blow him away.

Q: Did the ground troops participate in killing livestock too?

A: It was done a lot. Some of it was by accident but a lot of it was deliberate. Sergeant Smith, he used to always tell the story about the time he wiped out a whole pig family. A hog and a sow and a whole bunch of piglets were running and he wiped them out with an M-50-caliber machine gun.

Q: Did you ever get orders to take no prisoners in an operation?

A: No, I never got official orders.

Q: What was your rank then?

A: I was a Spec 4.

Q: Was there a black-market operation near where you were stationed?

A: There was a heavy black-market thing going on in Xuan Loc. They would sell guns and vehicles.

Q: Where did the Vietnamese get the guns from?

A: From GIs. There were not only guns sold but there were like trucks sold. It was fronted as a car wash and GIs would drive in and walk out. They would get anywhere from about eight hundred dollars a truck and four hundred dollars to five hundred dollars for a jeep.

Q: What kind of a truck would you get seven hundred dollars or eight hundred dollars for?

A: A two-and-a-half-ton truck, a one-fourth-ton truck. They would go into the car wash and get spray-painted and bumpers and engine numbers taken off. In a matter of two hours, all of this would happen. It would drive out and it would go to another part of the country.

Q: Who would it go to?

A: I don't know. I was told that it would go to South Vietnamese businessmen, people like that.

Q: Any of them go to the NLF?

A: I'm sure they did.

There were two 45-caliber pistols and two M-14's that came from an engineer battalion that I know of. We didn't use M-14s very much. They all went to the NLF. One was sold and the rest were given in exchange for a whole shitload of dope.

Q: Is it possible for a GI who has been in a line outfit in Vietnam for a year not to know that atrocities take place?

A: I don't believe it is possible. It's virtually impossible. I don't see how anybody who really could go through a month in a line company in Vietnam and at least not hear somebody's story about something. Because that's the whole thing in Vietnam. When a new guy comes into the company, a replacement for about the first three or four days, everybody's telling them about their great adventures or how our outfit did this. And just lays down the whole history of, you know, of your outfit and our platoon and your squad, and then you go on your own ego trip and rap out about how you killed so and so. I don't see how not even really echelon guys could go through a year and not hear about something like that. Maybe, like a lot of them really have nice jobs and stuff in Saigon and stuff. Anybody who has any kind of relation with a combat unit, I don't see how they could not hear about some type of atrocity.

Q: You know, many Americans don't believe that there are atrocities taking place.

A: You know, well, I find that hard to believe that the people wouldn't be hip to it. Because you have this rotation, you have five hundred thousand guys in Vietnam at this time, or close to it, who are constantly rotating, spent one year and come back, that's a lot of guys. I'm sure that seventy-five percent of them have stories that are probably much more dramatic than this one I have been rapping. They don't want to talk about it. They are really uptight for a number of reasons. They don't want to talk about it now that the My Lai story broke. It has scared many GIs about talking about anything they saw and certainly anything they did. Most of the guys that have come back have seen something of this nature, and it was like this guy said in the paper the other day, one of the guys that's with the My Lai thing. The reason that he didn't talk about it is that he just thought that everyone knew it. Everybody was hip to it. Guys now won't talk about it because they say to themselves, well, damn, it happened every day or just about. I thought everybody knew about it. Now the Army's coming out and busting us for war crime, which we may have committed, but who gave us the order to commit it?

I don't want to see Lieutenant Calley sent to the stockade. He might be gung-ho. He might be a lifer, but the problem is much more deep-rooted than that. It's not the Lieutenant Calleys that cause the massacres. The people who should go on trial for that are Nixon and Laird and Johnson. It's the people in power in our government that should be tried for these crimes, not the people that carry them out. It's like the war crimes in the Nuremberg trials. Who got punished for them? Eichmann never turned on the gas lever, he never let the trap door. He had somebody do it for him. What would have happened if they had tried to try all the henchmen and all the guards? This is what they are trying to do in the States today. Trying to try the henchmen. What happened in Nuremberg is that we tried them; what's happened here is that the war criminals are trying somebody else. Trying to lay it off on somebody else, the GI. The GI who is in almost all cases just following orders. I don't say it's an excuse, following orders. But should it be an excuse, a defense to give the damn orders?

THE RESPONSE

- James D. Nell (*continued*)

Q: When did you go to Vietnam?
A: April 1968.
Q: What rank did you have?
A: Corporal.
Q: What was your assignment?
A: I had several. I was a grunt for a while. And I was a squad leader later. I was in a lot of land-clearing operations.
Q: What was the relationship between the officers and the men in Vietnam?
A: It wasn't too good. Some lieutenants, they treated you like dirt. Some lieutenants were all right, but they all, they messed with the troopies too much. Drive guys to shooting themselves.
Q: Did you ever see that happen?
A: Yes, I have.
Q: Where was this?
A: I was on guard one night and a . . . a guy walked out of the back of his hootch with his M-16 and shot himself in the chest?
Q: Did he die?
A: He died two hours later. After they got him to the hospital.

Q: Did you ever see or hear of any of the men shooting officers?

A: Yes. I've seen it in the field.

Q: How did that happen?

A: Well, you're out in the field with a bunch of grunts for security and then sometimes they get on your nerves too much or mess with you too much. You just go and tell somebody about it, like a grunt, tell him. Grunt will put a price on his head, one hundred, two hundred dollars on his head. The first one that kills him got that much money.

Q: Where did the money come from?

A: From the troopies. Guys that pitch in and pay for it.

Q: How many enlisted men would contribute to the fund for killing the officer?

A: Generally everybody, almost. Just about the whole company.

Q: How many times have you seen this happen?

A: Five or six times.

Q: When would the officer be executed?

A: Out in the field. Next time he was out on a mission. Everybody would know it was going to happen. They would just wait until he was in the right position.

Q: After the officer was killed would the other officers know why he was killed?

A: I think they knew about it after it happened.

Q: Did this tend to bring about a change in attitude on the part of the surviving officers?

A: Oh, yes. They started using their heads right quick. They would stop messing with the troops.

Q: What outfit were you with?

A: The Ninth Engineers this last time.

Q: Where are you from?

A: From Ohio. Just twenty-six miles from Cleveland.

▪ Terry Kline

Q: What is your name?

A: Terry Kline.

Q: Where are you from, Terry?

A: Chicago.

Q: How old are you?

A: Twenty-three.

Q: Before you came here to Fort Gordon, what did you do?

A: Well, before I entered the Army I was attending college at Bowling Green University in Bowling Green, Ohio.

Q: How far did you get?

A: I am one year away from a degree. I have three years' credit.

Q: Were you drafted or did you enlist?

A: I dropped out of school to earn enough money to go back the next summer and I was drafted.

Q: Your three colleagues are now in the stockade. You are restricted to a very small area. Charges are pending against the four of you and the Army has announced that you will all be court-martialed.

A: Yes.

Q: What is the basis for the Army's reaction?

A: We signed a leaflet asking veterans of the war in Vietnam who are stationed at Fort Gordon to come forward and tell about their experiences in Vietnam. The leaflet said that Song My was not an isolated incident. None of the four of us have been to Vietnam, but we have talked with a lot of guys on this post who have been there. We don't think it's fair to stop the investigation with Lieutenant Calley or the men of his company or his superiors. Congress is investigating. The Army officers are investigating. We thought, and still think, that there should be a GI investigation. That's why we signed the leaflet and called ourselves the GI War Crimes Commission.

Q: When was this leaflet prepared?

A: The leaflet was prepared one week before charges were brought against us. The eleventh or twelfth of January.

Q: And was it circulated?

A: Yes, it was circulated in town and on post.

Q: How soon after it was circulated were you arrested?

A: The next day.

Q: Where were you when you were arrested?

A: I was in my company area and I was told to report to the CO in the orderly room. He told me I was placed on restriction in the company area for "alleged subversive activities" and that he would call me in later to tell me exactly what the charges were.

Q: Were you questioned by anyone subsequent to that charge?

A: I was called in to the CO, who told me that I was being investigated for these subversive activities and that afternoon I was called down to G-2, Fort Gordon Post Security, and I was asked approximately twenty-five or thirty questions from a mimeographed form concerning the GI War Crimes Commission. Then I was read the charges the following day.

Q: That was a mimeographed form about your leaflet?

A: Right.

Q: What were the questions?

A: The questions were: Who was behind the GI War Crimes Commission? Who was responsible for the post-office box? Whose telephone number was on the form? Did I know any of the other three people who allegedly had signed this letter? Was this my signature on the form? The next day the CO called me in and read me the charges and told me I was restricted to the company area again and outlined the area to which I was restricted.

Q: What are the charges?

A: I believe one is Article 134. I'm not exactly sure of the number of the article, but it has to do with uttering things that would undermine the loyalty of troops in the Army, and there is another charge which is a local post regulation against distribution of material on post without the consent of the commanding general.

Q: Did you distribute it on the post?

A: No, I didn't.

Q: What happened to the other three that signed the leaflet?

A: The other three were put in the stockade.

244

Q: There are a lot of veterans from the war here, aren't there?

A: Right, quite a few.

Q: Who are they and where are they?

A: Well, Fort Gordon is a big center for the signal school. A lot of people when they are through with their tour in Vietnam are sent back to Fort Gordon, especially to the signal school.

Q: They are most E-6s or E-5s?

A: Right. The company I am in is composed, I'd say the bulk of the company is E-5 and E-6.

Q: What is your company?

A: C-9 student brigade.

Q: C-9 student brigade of the Signal Corps?

A: Right. Signal school.

Q: And what have you been doing in school?

A: I've been an instructor. I took basic training at Fort Jackson, and I came here and went through the signal course for twelve weeks, and right when I got out of that course I started being an instructor at the signal school and I've been an instructor ever since. The day after this leaflet came out I was relieved of my duties as an instructor.

Q: What do you do now?

A: I just work in the barracks, just general barracks maintenance such as sweeping up, buffing the floors, fixing equipment in the building and things like that.

Q: Were you active in the GI newspaper that was published here?

A: I was actively engaged in the newspaper that was published, say, maybe six or seven months ago, but due to some members being shipped out and others being discharged, it fell apart.

Q: What was the paper?

A: It was called *Last Harass*.

Q: When was it published, do you recall?

A: We published four editions, one in October 1967 and December 1968 and March and then one last summer, in June or July.

Q: What happened to the GIs who were associated with it?

A: The person that started the whole thing, that really began the paper, was given an undesirable discharge, which was ten days before he was supposed to ETS out of the Army. And after he was given this undesirable discharge, they took two or three of the other people involved with the paper. A couple were sent to Vietnam and one was sent to Germany and a couple of us stayed here.

Q: That was the end of the paper?

A: Yes.

Q: In the leaflet, you indicate that Song My is not an isolated incident. What's your basis for reaching that conclusion?

A: I've personally had a lot of conversations with people in the barracks who have been to Vietnam and come back, and they just tell of just shooting people for spite and, you know, "A yellow gook isn't really a person. You just go around and shoot them." One guy was telling me that the latest thing, as you might call the fad when he came back, was just driving their trucks and jeeps down the road and seeing how many they could pick off. I'm sure there are all kinds of things that happened over there, that the press is trying to cover up and the Army is trying to cover up. At Fort Gordon all the usual stories circulated around.

Q: Like what?

A: The ones about cutting off ears and just shooting people indiscriminately for no reason.

Q: Have they talked about pushing prisoners out of helicopters?

A: I've heard that, too. I have heard the stories about just holding the guy out of the helicopter and they get to a certain target, just to drop him and things like this. Guys who did it just talk about it.

Q: Have GIs here who have been to Vietnam and talked with you about what they did discussed it with shame for what they have done or just matter-of-factly? Or have they bragged about it?

A: I haven't really met too many that would discuss it with shame. A couple of them may be bragging, but I would say most sort of matter-of-factly. You know, an everyday occurrence. They came along with the line about the conditions they were living in and if I was going over there, that would be the conditions I would be in and I would probably do the same thing.

Q: Do you believe that?

A: No. I don't think so. I wouldn't know until I went over there, but I doubt it. I can't see lining up women and children and just shooting them.

246

Q: Have you met people here who have seen this?

A: I've met people who have seen it. That said they'd seen it. That's what we wanted the commission for. To give them a chance to be heard. The reaction of the brass has been very sudden. The press hasn't said very much about the whole matter. There was, I think, one radio report about the arrests, and then nothing more except right here in Augusta. Evidently the Army doesn't want to let the GIs tell the truth about the war and the press doesn't seem too interested in telling the country.

Q: What do you think your action has accomplished?

A: I don't know. We can only do what we can do. I know that I won't go to Vietnam. I know that. I don't think that I would file for conscientious-objector status. I probably would just refuse to go and be sent to jail. But that's not enough to do. That's why we signed the leaflet.